France in Indochina

Colonial Encounters

Nicola Cooper

BERG

Oxford • New York

First published in 2001 by
Berg
Editorial offices:
150 Cowley Road, Oxford, OX4 1JJ, UK
838 Broadway, Third Floor, New York, NY 10003-4812, USA

Berg is an imprint of Oxford International Publishers Ltd.

Library of Congress Cataloging-in-Publication Data
A catalogue record for this book is available from the Library of Congress.

British Library Cataloguing-in-Publication Data
A catalogue record for this book is available from the British Library.

ISBN 1 85973 476 6 (Cloth)
      1 85973 481 2 (Paper)

Typeset by JS Typesetting, Wellingborough, Northants
Printed in the United Kingdom by Biddles Ltd, Guildford and King's Lynn

For my parents, Mike and Judy Cooper

Contents

Contents

List of Illustrations

—

Introduction

Why Indochina?

It is surprising that given the current scholarly interest in reassessing colonial attitudes, the renewed interest in francophone culture, and the prolific theorising which has occurred in post-colonial circles, that little attention has been paid to French Indochina. While France's North African territories have received and continue to receive much scholarly attention, and francophone Africa is emerging as a subject of intense academic activity, Indochina, though representing a considerable colonial investment for France, has rarely been the principal focus of academic studies.

Where commentators have addressed the question of France's relationship with the nation's largest colonial possession outside Africa, they have tended, for the most part, to focus exclusively on the Franco-Indochinese war (1945–54), and the period of decolonisation which it triggered. The period of French colonial rule in Indochina, which spanned some ninety years, tends to be relegated to the status of a prelude to the Franco-Indochinese war, occupying a chapter or two at the beginning of largely military narratives.

This book attempts to redress this imbalance by focusing principally upon French colonial discourses at the height of the French imperial encounter with Indochina: 1900–1939. It examines the ways in which imperial France viewed its role in Indochina, and the representations and perceptions of Indochina which were produced and disseminated in a variety of cultural media emanating from mainland France. Framed by political, ideological and historical developments and debates, each chapter develops a socio-cultural account of France's own understanding of its role in Indochina, and its relationship with the colony during this crucial period. This approach, which focuses clearly upon the discursive, socio-cultural dimension provides a re-evaluation of French Indochina and its legacy.

For the imperial nation, the newly-acquired colony will function as an empty space in which to create a new society: an empty space to be built upon, moulded, developed, populated, imagined and represented. The colony is in some senses a nowhere, and in Indochina's case this is reflected in the very name attached to the amalgamated territories of Vietnam, Cambodia and Laos. Indo-Chine, existing in an undesignated 'in-between' space, between India and China, occupies the liminal and unnamed zone of the hyphen, the gap.[1] As French colonial rule was consolidated in Indochina, the hyphenated name itself disappeared, as if to signal the assertion of a new society and identity. The nowhere was becoming a somewhere, and that somewhere was very definitely French: *l'Indochine française*.

L'Indochine française was a geographical, cultural, and political construction. The amassing of territory, its formal designation under the umbrella term of *l'Indochine française*, the Gallic affix marking the hybrid Franco-Asian identity of the regrouped areas, all testify to the concrete and purposeful construction, creation and maintenance of this colonised territory. Prior to French imperial intervention, the three regions, or *kỳ*, which made up Vietnam had been reunited after existing as separate and rival political societies for several centuries during the medieval period. The different status and administrative systems of Annam, Tonkin and Cochinchina applied by the conquering French were thus perceived as a divisive gesture, designed to reinstate regional hostilities. Centuries old rivalries between Vietnam and Cambodia were also overidden in the creation of the greater polity of *l'Indochine française*. (Figure 1)

L'Indochine française served also as an imagined elsewhere, an *ailleurs rêvé*. For the empty space of the colony often becomes in the imperial imagination a repository for unconscious desires and yearnings. Panivong Norindr suggests that 'Indochine' was 'an elaborate fiction, a modern phantasmatic assemblage invented during the heyday of French colonial hegemony in Southeast Asia'.[2] Similarly, Bernard Hue has noted: 'Que serait dans la littérature, l'image de l'Indochine, si elle n'était d'abord, et peut-être essentiellement, mensonge, c'est-à-dire fable, représentation mythique...'[3] Again, Alain Quella-Villéger, in his preface to a recent collection of 'Indochinese' literature, states that 'l'Indochine est un mythe...un rêve'.[4] So many discussions of Indochina seem to draw us into the realm of the fictional, the mythical, the intangible, the unconscious. Indochina was a discursive construction, a mythical, dreamed-for place, an exotic utopia. However, Indochina was also a very real lived experience, both for the sugjugated peoples and for the Europeans who settled in Indochina. This study will therefore attempt to straddle that precariously constituted, and perhaps artificially important, divide between 'history' on the one hand, and 'fiction' on the other. For the significance of Indochina to the mainland is not simply accessed through a reconstitution of a supposedly more authentic history of the Franco-Indochinese relationship, but also through the interrogation of the representations and stereotypes of that same relationship which arguably formed the most widely held image of France in Indochina.

Analysing the identity imposed upon a colonised territory by its imperial conqueror reveals as much about the imperial nation's sense of self, and its desires and needs, as it does about the colony. In examining the identity imperial France gradually carved out for Indochina, I will necessarily focus on France's own conception of the nation's imperial identity. The first part of this study, entitled

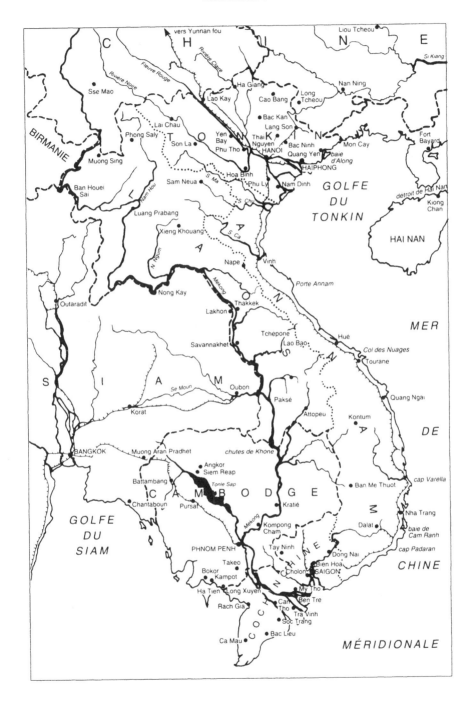

Figure 1. Map of Indochina

'Constructing Indochina' thus concentrates on imperial and colonial identities –
of France and Indochina respectively. It asks through what means these identities
were constructed and maintained, what discursive devices were implemented, and
what motifs emphasised in the construction of these identities. The first part of
this study is divided into five chapters: the first sets the scene through a discussion
of conquest and perceptions of France's interest in and intervention in Indochina.
The second and third sections discuss two of the principal tenets of French
colonialism: the concept of *mise en valeur* and the development of Indochina;
and the impact on identity of integrating Indochina into the framework of *la plus
grande France*. The fourth section draws together these cumulative features of
the developing Franco-Indochinese relationship in an analysis of the colonial
exhibition of 1931, as a means of gauging how Indochina was viewed by 'official'
France and how France viewed its role in Indochina. The final chapter sets against
these largely positive views of France's South-East Asian empire, an examination
of the critical voices which emerged in the 1930s in response to the indigenous
rebellion and colonial mismanagement in Indochina. The first part of this study is
thus interested in the establishment of colonial orthodoxies: in the creation of a
widely-accepted colonial order, in the propagation of an accepted version or vision
of Indochina, and of France's role as an imperial nation.

Alongside these orthodox representations and images of Indochina, there
nonetheless existed ideas and narratives which ran counter to France's idealised
model of its relationship with Indochina. The second part of the study, entitled,
'Disturbing the Colonial Order', examines these counter-narratives as a means of
unveiling latent discomfort or unease with empire; and to reveal certain doubts
and anxieties concerning France's role and status in Indochina. The first chapter
reviews the representations of Indochina in colonial fiction to reveal an often
dystopic view of colonial life and relations. The second focuses upon the conflicts
and tensions which emerged from gender issues, and their correlation with anxieties
over colonial authority and control. The final chapter of part two analyses a series
of concerns under the global term of boundary anxieties. These varied responses
to colonial rule and life in Indochina disclose numerous fears concerning the
integrity and stability of colonial identities.

The final part of the study, which reviews the decolonisation of Indochina and
its aftermath, questions the notion of end of empire. The first chapter examines
press representations of the French defeat at Dien Bien Phu, and suggests that at
this juncture, and even in defeat, belief in the French colonial doctrine remained
strong. The following two chapters assess more contemporary representations of
this lost South-East Asian Empire, and responses to Indochina from post-colonial
France. The second examines the way in which memories of the former colonial
relationship resurfaced in relation to Vietnamese migrants arriving in France; and
how those memories served to delineate the new post-colonial relationship between

French and Indochinese. The third and final chapter focuses on contemporary cinematic portrayals of colonial Indochina to demonstrate that many of the tenets of French colonialism, and many images of Indochina dating from the height of empire, still have currency today.

Terminologies

Because the principal focus of my work is metropolitan French attitudes towards, and representations of, these colonised areas of South-East Asia, I will be mirroring French usage of the period by using the term 'Indochina', *Indochine*, to signify Vietnam, Cambodia and Laos. This should not be viewed in any way as an acceptance or legitimation of the term *Indochine*, but rather should serve as a reminder that the geographical space imagined by imperial France, was in fact, an artificial construction. The successive terminologies used by imperial France to evoke these very separate and individual countries, *Union indochinoise*, and *Fédération indochinoise*, clearly played a significant role in ideologies of empire which successive French regimes sought to popularise during the period of consolidation.

Similarly, in order to avoid continual circumlocution, Indochina will often be referred to as a colony. Although only the region of Cochinchina was accorded the full status of a colony, Annam, Tonkin, Cambodia and Laos being placed under the protectorate of France, the way in which they functioned under a French Governor General amounted to full colonial rule.

Finally, it should be noted that for imperial France, Indochina mainly meant Vietnam, and that Cambodia and Laos tended to be eclipsed behind France's administrative focus on Vietnam. This led equally to a cultural focus which tended either to ignore the particularities of Cambodia and Laos, or to subsume their specific identities under the umbrella term *Indochine française*. It bears testimony to the success of the implantation of the notion of *Indochine française* that this umbrella term effectively effaced particularising discourses which may have otherwise distinguished more coherently between the component territories of Indochina.

Defining 'Colonial Discourse'

I will frequently refer to colonial discourse, or discourses, throughout the ensuing chapters. The idea of discourse derives from Foucault's notion of discursive practices. Foucault argued that discursive practices are characterised by the delimitation of a field of objects, the definition of a legitimate perspective for the agent of knowledge, and the fixing of norms for the elaboration of concepts and theories. Foucault's work has of course played a crucial part in the elaboration of tools with which to analyse the colonial situation, most notably in the work of Said[5] and Bhabha.[6] The objective of colonial discourse, according to Bhabha, is to construe the colonised as a population of degenerate types on the basis of racial origin, in order to justify conquest and to establish systems of administration and political control. Said uses Foucault to understand how the will to exercise dominant control in society and history has been disguised in the language of truth, rationality and knowledge.

However, colonial and postcolonial theorising has been undertaken largely by anglophone critics who, for the most part, have taken imperial Britain and the British Empire as their sources. This has tended to produce analytical tools which have been universally adopted. It is my contention that these are useful, but should be used with care in relation to French colonialism. They are not necessarily wholly adaptable to the analysis of French colonialism.

Secondly, although extremely useful, the notion of colonial discourse, as a singular and homogeneous construct, can constitute a universalising and essentialising gesture in itself. French colonialism was not necessarily dominated by a monolithic, overarching discourse – even if colonial France desired this, and attempted to construct one. What emerges from the study of French colonialism, is a series of colonising discourses, having in common certain features, but also shifting and adapting to specific historical situations, and to geographical locations. Within the nation's 'official' colonial discourse, that is to say, the orthodox colonial identity, doctrine, beliefs and practices which France constructed in relation to its overseas possessions, there nonetheless appear discrepancies and inconsistencies. France's 'official' colonial discourse is itself at times antithetical and paradoxical, consistent in some ways, yet in others radically incoherent. Additionally, there emerge a plethora of counter-narratives, or discourses which provide a counterpoint to the orthodoxy and authoritative power of official 'colonial discourse'. There thus exists a plurality or multiplicity of discourses surrounding French colonialism, and France in Indochina.

Finally, given that there has been little recent work on the colonial encounter between France and Indochina, I have often felt that I am merely scratching at the surface of a vast, untapped area of research. Indochina presents itself as a field ripe for academic colonisation. Aware of the ironies inherent in my project, and in my status as a critic of French colonialism, I am rather self-consciously mimicking imperial France in my own exploration of this virgin territory. Let me warily recall Said, who has pointed out the perils concealed in the discursive practice of academia, which like the discursive practice of colonialism, aims to produce knowledge about an unknown Other.

Notes

1. On the different spelling of Indochine/Indo-Chine, see Le Roux, P., 'Avec ou sans trait d'union, note sur le terme "l'Indo-Chine"', in *Cahiers des Sciences humaines*, vol. 32, 3, 1996.
2. Norindr, P., *Phantasmatic Indochina: French Colonial Ideology in Architecture, Film and Literature* (Durham: Duke University Press, 1996), p. 1.
3. Hué, B. (ed.), *Indochine: reflets littéraires* (Rennes: PUR, 1992), p. 21.
4. *Indochine: un rêve d'Asie* (Paris: Omnibus, 1995), preface.
5. See Said, E., *Orientalism* (London: Routledge, 1978); Said, E., *The World, the Text, and the Critic* (London: Vintage, 1991); Said, E., *Culture and Imperialism* (London: Chatto and Windus, 1993).
6. See Bhabha, H., 'Difference, Discrimination and the Discourse of Colonialism', in Barker, F. et al, *The Politics of Theory* (Colchester: Essex Conference of the Sociology of Literature, 1982), pp. 194–211; Bhabha, H. (ed.), *Nation and Narration* (London: Routledge, 1990); Bhabha, H., *The Location of Culture* (London: Routledge, 1994).

Part I
Constructing Indochina

–1–

Protection, Conquest or Pacification? Creating Histories of French Intervention in Indochina

Different political moods and changing international events throughout the period of French imperial interest and colonial rule in Cambodia, Vietnam and Laos, gave rise to shifting representations and interpretations of the conquest of Indochina. From a historiographical perspective, representations of the conquest of Indochina act as a barometer of colonial mood swings and of changing ideological foci. In the 1870s and 1880s when a vanquished France was looking inwards for national renewal, external events in Indochina were an irritation to the incumbent government and led ultimately to Jules 'le Tonkinois' Ferry's political demise. The spur of imperial rivalry with Great Britain encouraged the gradual acceptance of France's so-called imperial vocation, thus transforming the adventures of France's explorers, naval officers and soldiers in acquiring that Asian empire to rival British India into source of imperial pride. In a chastened post world war European climate, France, as many of its imperial counterparts, distanced itself from the acquisitive and violent origins of empire to concentrate instead on the humanitarian value of French colonialism.

These changing attitudes and events gave rise to different interpretations of the conquest of Indochina and of French involvement in South-East Asia. Different eras thus each established an appropriately plotted narrative of French intervention in Indochina. The justifications of a French presence in Indochina are revealing not only of France's sense of imperial identity, but also of the nation's sense of external international opinion. These narratives of conquest and pacification thus lay the founding stones of imperial identity, and also set the terms for the relationship between conqueror/coloniser and colonised. This first section will discuss the conquest in broadly historiographical terms, placing emphasis on the shifting and evolving French responses to its own imperial adventure in Indochina.

The various component parts of Indochina were annexed, appropriated, acquired and accrued by metropolitan France over a period of some thirty years, from approximately 1860-1890. As many historians of French imperialism have noted, French expansionism did not form part of a coherent policy. This observation is all the more true in the case of Indochina. The French acquisition of Indochina resulted more from a series of individual and autonomous acts on the part of explorers, merchants and traders, than from intervention from Paris. Indochina's political boundaries were formally delimited in 1887, when the French government created the *Union indochinoise*. French intervention in this corner of South-East Asia, however, predates this creation by several centuries. A combination of economic interest, imperial rivalry with Britain and the defence of French Catholic missionaries had led to sporadic forays into the area. Until the mid-nineteenth century it was the Catholic Church rather than the French nation which sought to implant itself in Vietnam, and to a lesser extent Cambodia and Laos. Jesuit missionaries, expelled from Japan, made their way into Tonkin in the 1620s. Alexandre de Rhodes[1] established the first French mission there in 1627. In the 1660s, the *Société des Missions étrangères* sent missionaries to Annam on the basis of Rhodes' reports; and in the 1670s, the Vatican sanctioned French missionary activities in the area.

The imbrication of religion and politics led to further French intervention in Indochina in the eighteenth century. Mgr. Pingneau de Béhaine, the Bishop of Adran, became involved in local politics when the Lay Son dynasty crushed the ruling Nguyens. The Bishop's support of the sole Nguyen survivor of this massacre led Pigneau de Béhaine to seek the sponsorship of Louis XVI. In return for French military and naval help, France was accorded full rights over the islands of Noi-nan and Poulo Condore. This entitled French subjects to the exclusive right to trade and to establish naval and commercial bases there. The French government renegued on its agreement, and Pigneau de Béhaine decided to take matters into his own hands, recruiting adventurers and sailors, and purchasing arms with funds obtained from traders based in the Indian Ocean. The Bishop's initiatives led to military intervention in 1789, which ensured the restoration of the Nguyen dynasty in 1799. The revolutionary period in France drew attention away from South-East Asia, and it was not until the accession of Minh Mang to the throne of Annam in 1825 that the French once more became involved in the area. Minh Mang's dislike of the interference of 'prêtres étrangers'[2] in his kingdom marked the beginning of an era of persecution of French priests in Indochina which continued until the end of his reign in 1840.

Until the mid-nineteenth century it was thus religious interests which governed French relations with the countries which were to become Indochina. However, when the British gained Hong Kong in 1842, French desires to establish a trading base in South-East Asia were renewed. The French annexation of areas within Indochina should be viewed within the context of the second Opium War (1856–60), for French interest and intervention in Indochina can be viewed in part as an attempt to contain British ambitions and territorial progress in South-East Asia. Indeed, comparison and competition with Great Britain was an abiding feature of French imperial rhetoric, and is particularly marked in relation to Indochina.

The Napoleonic era saw a more concerted approach to the establishment of a French presence in South-East Asia. Napoleon III had grand ideas about French prestige and economic development. He supported the missionary involvement in the area, sending the Montigny mission to the Far East in 1855 as a diplomatic move to reopen relations with the Court of Hué. Things came to a head over the persecution of priests under the reign of Tu Duc, who promulgated a new edict in 1855, which once more engendered the persecution of French missionaries. In response, France recommended that a protectorate be established over Cochinchina. Ostensibly a move intended to establish religious freedom, this intervention was not viewed as a conquest, as it was thought that the Cochinchinese were suffering under a tyrannical king and would welcome the French with open arms.

In 1857, a commission agreed that the protectorate was necessary and desirable; arguments concerning national prestige and international rivalry were uppermost in the debate. Thus in 1858, Admiral Rigault de Genouilly arrived in Tourane with 2,300 men. As Franchini notes,

> C'est dans ces conditions que s'engage le processus d'une conquête, sans plan véritable, avec des objectifs non précisés, adaptables aux circonstances et aux décisions des chefs militaires.[3]

Rigault de Genouilly met with many difficulties in Tourane and his troops soon fell prey to profound disillusionment. The Admiral himself felt reproachful towards the missionaries who had made assurances that Cochinchina was ripe for French intervention. Where were the thousands of indigenous Christians who were supposed to join the ranks of their liberators? The Cochinchinese did not appear to be a population impatient to shake off the yoke of a tyrant.

The Expeditionary Corps indeed met with tremendous resistance in Tourane. They lacked supplies, and Rigault de Genouilly's manpower was decimated through sickness. Neither was the Admiral making any headway in negotiations with the indigenous populations. Nevertheless, Rigault de Genouilly took Tourane in August 1858, but because he did not have sufficient forces to push on towards Hué, it was decided that the French Navy strike at Saigon, which was captured in February 1859.

Due principally to the continuing war with China, Rigault de Genouilly pulled out of Tourane, and the conquest of Indochina was later relaunched from Saigon under Admiral Charner, once the treaty of Peking had been signed with China in October 1860. His mission, under the direction of a new *Ministre de la Marine et des Colonies*, Chasseloup-Laubat,[4] was to gain as much territory as possible before proposing peace terms. If he met with indigenous resistance, Charner was to press on further to Mytho and Bienhoa.

Charner had established himself in Mytho when Admiral Bonard took over operations. Chasseloup-Laubat hoped to build upon this improvised conquest and to establish a sort of suzerainty which he hoped would allow for the establishment of free trade to be extended to Siam and Cambodia. Bonard duly seized Bienhoa, Baria and then the citadel of Vinhlong and the island of Poulo Condore.

Tu Duc, who was plagued with internal rebellions which were backed by the Chinese, now appeared ready to cooperate with the French invaders. In a treaty of 1862, France was accorded the provinces of Giadinh, Bienhoa and Mytho, and Poulo Condore. Vinhlong was to be placed under continued French occupation until pacification was accomplished. Three ports, including Tourane, were to be opened to French commerce. Religious freedom was to be established, and no part of the territory was to be ceded to a foreign power other than France. Admiral de la Grandière completed the pacification of the provinces acquired under the treaty of 1862. He annexed further territories of Vinhlong, Chaudoc and Hatien, thus completing the colony of Cochinchine. In August 1863, a further treaty was signed placing Cambodia under the protectorate of France.

During the Second Empire, French intervention in Indochina was motivated principally by competition with Britain for economic influence in the area. With very little territory in Asia, Indochina was France's only 'yellow badge', and the French foothold in Indochina allowed the penetration of the Chinese market via a path where the British were absent. A period of intense economic interest in Indochina began in the 1860s and 1870s. Many expeditions were undertaken, by renowned explorers such as Doudart de Lagrée and Garnier, to ascertain the navigability of routes in Indochina. Chasseloup-Laubat, also president of the *Société de géographie* demanded the exploration of the Mekong and plateaux in Laos and a study of relations with Yunnan (China). The aim of the mission was to draw up an inventory of the area's natural resources, to create new *courants commerciaux* which would open out onto central China, to explore unknown regions. It was the actions of these explorers and adventurers which led, ultimately, to the 'Tonkin' crisis of 1873. Garnier had accompanied Doudart de Lagrée in the exploration of the Mekong (1866–8), and was subsequently sent by Admiral Dupré (Governor of Cochinchina) in 1872 to oversee the free passage of Jean Dupuis, a French trader based in China, through the delta of the Red River (in spite of instructions from Paris to cease all action in Tonkin). Seizing the occasion to establish trade routes, Dupré also envisaged establishing a protectorate over Tonkin. As the Royal Court at Hué refused to negotiate with the French, Garnier decided to use force, and seized Hanoi and various strategic points throughout the delta in November 1873. (Figure 2)

In the ensuing war, in which pirate bands fought with the Indochinese against the French invasion, Garnier was killed. Then when mandarins rallied the local population against Christianity and 'ces Français d'intérieur', and several Christian villages were burned down, the situation seemed to have escalated beyond all control. Instructions from Paris were that Dupré withdraw.

Figure 2. Statue of Francis Garnier, Saigon

During these early, difficult and unstable years of the Third Republic, France was (understandably) reluctant to commit itself to backing rather intemperate adventures in Indochina. Admiral d'Hornoy, Ministre de la marine et des colonies, wrote to Dupré citing the heavy cost to the mainland, the unfavourable climate in Europe and internal political instability as his principal reasons for wishing to cease all action in Indochina:

> Je comprends tout ce qu'a de séduisant cette conquête du Tonkin, ce qui est, en réalité, l'absorption complète de l'Annam. Il est possible que, dans l'avenir, cela nous eût fait un royaume comme l'Inde Anglaise. Il est possible et même probable qu'avec vos propres moyens, vous puissiez vous emparer de Kecho. Mais prendre n'est rien. Organiser, garder et défendre, voilà le difficile, voilà ce qui coûte.[5]

Although a treaty was finally signed between France and Indochina, confirming the cession of Cochinchina to France and establishing trade routes, Tonkin was nonetheless evacuated, and opinion in Paris became hostile towards events in Indochina. Ideas of further conquest in Indochina gradually faded until the 1880s. Domestic events and crises at home had focused attention on the mainland and on Europe until the 1880s when metropolitan interest in colonisation was renewed. Indochina occupied a central role in the colonial debate between 1880 and 1885. More than any other area into which France sought to expand, Indochina embodied the colonial problematic which was under scrutiny during this period.

As early as 1872, Gambetta had anticipated the debate of the 1880s in observing that

Pour reprendre le rang qui lui appartient dans le monde, la France se doit de ne pas accepter le repliement sur elle-même.[6]

Indeed, the well-documented polemic which was to divide France's politicians was one which pitched colonial expansion against an inward-looking stagnation born of the 1870 defeat and a *revanchardiste* vision of France's status and prestige. The clash of these opposing views came to a crisis point over events in Tonkin, where Commandant Rivière had renewed the French assault on Hanoi. These actions led to Chinese military involvement, indeed to the threat of a full-blown Franco-Chinese war. Negotiations with Peking paving the way for a compromise (the partition of Tonkin between a Chinese zone of influence in the north, and a French one in the south of the region), foundered however, when Ferry's second ministry opted instead to set about the conquest of Tonkin in 1883.

Rivière's subsequent death allowed for war credits to be obtained from the Chamber and a new expedition to be sent to organise a Tonkin/Annam protectorate, which was eventually secured in 1884, amidst much vociferous opposition in the metropole. The second 'Tonkin crisis' erupted however in the wake of a surprise Chinese/Indochinese assault on the French fortress of Lang Son. Metropolitan opinion, unconvinced by Ferry's expansion in Tonkin and outraged at the possibility of suffering a 'Sedan colonial',[7] ousted Ferry on 30 March 1885.

In spite of Ferry's fall, and continuing opposition to colonialism particularly from the Radical Party, the protectorate treaty of 1884 between France and Indochina was ratified in June 1885. Indeed once the crisis of 1885 had passed, the majority of political opinion in the Chamber rallied to the colonial idea, and it was during this period that the French colonial ideal began to take shape. The prolific debate which raged in the French parliament effectively defined the nation's response to imperialism and expansion.

In the aftermath of *l'affaire tonkinoise*, Ferry's speech to the Chamber of 28 July 1885 drew a sense and logic from events in Indochina, and set the terms for a 'politique coloniale' specific to France. What had essentially amounted to the piecemeal acquisition of Indochina was represented as a veritable demonstration of imperial policy. Distinguishing between a 'politique qui consiste à aller au hasard'[8] and 'une entreprise coloniale (...) poursuivie à l'origine d'un plan concerté, d'un dessein arrêté à l'avance',[9] Ferry sought to provide his (mis)management of events in Indochina with an order and purpose, a weight and import which this brief historical overview has sought to dispute.

Similarly, Ferry constructed a conception of colonial expansion which sought to coincide and accord with Republicanism and humanitarianism, whilst simultaneously emphasising the renewal of French grandeur and prestige. Indeed, Ferry's vision was to exercise a tenacious hold over French ideas of colonialism for decades:

[la France] ne peut pas être seulement un pays libre; (...) elle doit aussi être un grand pays, exerçant sur les destinées de l'Europe toute l'influence qui lui appartient, (...) elle doit répandre cette influence sur le monde, et porter partout où elle le peut sa langue, ses moeurs, son drapeau, ses armes, son génie.[10]

French intervention in Indochina was thus born of religious evangelism and pursued through a combination of international imperial, and maritime rivalry. Often the result of action on the part of naval officers or largely autonomous explorers, with little if any direction from Paris, the French acquistion of the component territories of Indochina owed more to *la force des choses* and the escalation of events on the ground, than a defined imperial vision and purpose.

Nonetheless, the French popular imagination was excited by these tales of glory and discovery. The so-called 'heroic age' of French imperialism, epitomised in Indochina by the exploits of Rivière and Garnier, lived on and was popularised in the proliferation of traveller's tales, military memoirs, the journals of naval officers, and above all the colourful recitation of explorers' exploits in the late nineteenth century. The interest of the metropolitan press was attracted to Indochina by the news of the voyages of Jean Dupuis and Doudart de Lagrée in the 1880s. Descriptions of their charting of the Red River appeared in the *Le Moniteur Universel*, *Le National* and *Le Temps*. Columns chronicling the exploration of Tonkin appeared in *Le Figaro*, *Le Petit Parisien* and *Le Globe*. Following Francis Garnier's expedition and the conquest of the remaining territories of Indochina, most large newspapers started to send foreign correspondants to the area.[11] Harmand's anthropological voyages to unexplored provinces of Indochina, and Henri Mouhot's description of his 'discovery' of the Angkor Wat temple site brought the weight of science alongside the tales of heroic conquest, fuelled the French popular imagination and assisted in the mythologising of the conquest of Indochina.[12]

Jules Harmand[13] for instance, popularised and legitimised the image of the metropolitan explorer: collecting and collating knowledge about the indigenous populations, and charting the geography of these unknown areas. Flowers, fruits, animals and insects, all were collected and displayed in the *Musée de produits coloniaux* at the *Palais de l'Industrie* of which he was nominated curator on his return from Indochina in 1877.

But the scientist also had his eye on future imperial action, demonstrating the complicity of geography and exploration in the imperial project. Travelling in areas of Indochina yet to come under French tutelage, Harmand noted:

Toutes ces choses sont pour nous de la plus grande importance au point de vue de l'avenir de notre colonisation en Indo-Chine, et il n'est pas inutile pour un Français quelque peu soucieux de notre influence future en Extrême-Orient d'y arrêter un instant sa pensée. Le jour ne peut être éloigné où la nécessité s'imposera aux moins clairvoyants d'étendre notre domination à l'empire d'Annam tout entier, dont la Cochinchine française ne forme qu'une faible partie. Ce jour-là, la connaissance des faits que je rapporte ici aura un certain intérêt.[14]

The conquest of Indochina had opened up a new space into which French science and reason could enter and explore. Indochina was a virgin territory to be discovered, explored and understood: a field in which to test and puruse scientific knowledge, the empty space to be comprehended and understood. Harmand's work thus helped to legitimise conquest as the pursuit of knowledge and science. Harmand's writings also demonstrate the psychological appeal to the individual of the empty space of the colony, for his words convey the sense that he was monarch of all he surveyed: 'De la plate-forme de ma petite cuse, en me tournant vers l'oeust, ma vue embrassait tout le panorama des montagnes de Bassac.'[15] Harmand's personal sense of discovery and his enjoyment of being alone in his domination and surveillance of a territory lead him as an individual to contemplate colonisation: 'Si j'étais riche, j'achèterais au roi de Bangkok ce coin perdu de ses immenses possessions et je viendrais m'y établir avec quelques Français. Il n'y a pas de parc qui vaudrait celui-ci.'[16]

Fictional versions of this heroic age tended to emerge later, and relied heavily on the findings which had emerged from the tales of exploration and discovery. Mimicking these more scientific tales of discovery, they often took the form of a pseudo ethnography in their attempts to build up an image of Indochina for readers in the mainland. They contained descriptions of peoples, languages, customs, flora and fauna, religion, practices etc. They were filled with the traditional tropes of exoticist writing, alongside hyperbolic portrayals of the epic quality of explorations and battles. Indochina was a hero's adventure playground, where he underwent physical trials and tested his courage and stamina.

A literary shorthand rapidly emerged with which writers could evoke Indochina quickly and succinctly. These stereotypes usually involved what were perceived as the most unusual and disconcerting features of France's South-East Asian empire. Indochina was thus evoked through references to its physical features: its crops, *hévéas*, *riz*; its deltas and its *arroyos*. The emphasis was firmly placed on the bizarre, the comic, or the seductive characteristics of Indochina. By the turn of the century these very contrasts and differences had been assimilated into metropolitan imaginations as signalling 'Indochina'. Alongside science and exploration, literary portraits of Indochina thus served to construct its identity, and to reinforce an intellectual sense of containment and comprehensibility of the Indochinese Other.

By the turn of the century, however, once pacification had been largely accomplished, representations and interpretations of the conquest, imbued with the Ferryist vision of imperial design, invariably sought to portray the French conquest of Indochina as the result of a pre-designated plan and design. This new focus coincides with the attempt, on the part of the Third Republic in France, to establish and reinforce a sense of national identity which would now base itself on the idea of France as an imperial nation. The codification of the Ferryist vision of French imperial purpose in South-East Asia was accompanied just a couple of decades later by a shift in native policy from assimilation to association – a move which epitomised the way in which the nation attempted to distance itself from the violence of conquest and establish a new legitimacy of empire. This ideological move from conquest and violence to protection and development began relatively early, and is perhaps best embodied in the following quotation from Lyautey, who quotes Galliéni's *Instructions* (1898) in his *Lettres du Tonkin et de Madagascar*. Lyautey notes:

> Le meilleur moyen pour arriver à la pacification dans notre nouvelle colonie est d'employer l'action combinée de la force et de la politique. Il faut nous rappeler que dans les luttes coloniales nous ne devons détruire qu'à la dernière extrémité, et, dans ce cas encore, ne détruire que pour mieux bâtir. Toujours nous devons ménager le pays et les habitants, puisque celui-là est destiné à recevoir nos entreprises de colonisation future et que ceux-ci seront nos principaux agents et collaborateurs pour mener à bien nos entreprises.[17]

Lyautey's interpretation of colonial action shows that he intended that force be used in a limited way, and that native customs, institutions and organisation be respected as far as possible. Galliéni and Lyautey thus straddle the period between conquest and the more humanitarian-minded colonial policies which were to follow. The doctrine of association was officially endorsed in 1905 by then Minister for Colonies, Etienne Clémentel. The policy was finally given sanction in a resolution of the Chamber of Deputies in 1917. The move from assimilatory approaches to a policy of association thus codified the move from the violence of conquest towards a more conciliatory colonial policy, and a new imperial focus for France.[18]

If the nineteenth century had been dominated by concerns to demonstrate economic and military prowess through the acquistion of a colonial empire, then the early twentieth century was marked by a desire to legitimise that acquisition, and to express national prestige through the beneficial contribution of French rule to colonised territories. The merging of these two concerns finds its clearest expression in educational policy and in the concerns of educationalists of the period. Once the nation's imperial identity had become the most convincing means through which to express national grandeur and prestige, it clearly became necessary not only to promote the Empire, but more importantly that sense of French imperial identity, purpose and tradition amongst generations to come. This ideological and historiographical shift is nowhere more evident than in the Republic's educational curriculum.

In the Republic's schools then, the objective of legitimisation was achieved firstly through the presentation of colonisation as a 'natural' policy or stance on the part of European nations. The history and geography sections of the curriculum established a narrative in which colonialism was presented as a right of the French nation, and as a traditional impulse of European nations. Imperialism was thus presented as both a national and a European prerogative, doubly legitimising the French colonial enterprise. Discussions concerning the extent and nature of contemporary French colonialism tended to be situated within a historical background. The majority of school manuals were at pains to emphasise the historical precedent of more recent colonial acts and conquests, and to place these events within a French tradition of colonisation. This narrative of imperial design is invoked in many manuals in their references to the 'old' empire, or the 'first' French Empire. Ferrand for instance, in a manual dating from 1904, relates the following:

> La France a été parmi les premières nations qui aient acquis des colonies. (...) Un moment, sous Louis XV, Dupleix, gouverneur aux Indes, pensa nous conquérir de sujets, mais Louis XV perdit toute l'Inde moins 5 villes, et tout ce qui nous restait encore du Canada (1763). Les guerres de la Révolution et de Napoléon achevèrent la ruine de notre empire colonial dont les Anglais recueillirent les meilleurs morceaux. Elles ne nous laissèrent que quelques îles, la Guyane, les 5 villes de l'Inde et quelques comptoirs en Afrique. Depuis ces désastres, la France s'est remise patiemment à l'oeuvre. En moins d'un siècle, elle s'est refait un empire colonial.[19]

This account of the French imperial past places the colonising act within an unacknowledged political or ideological movement promoting the acquisition of overseas territories. The moral value of this movement, whose other partisans are not mentioned, is clearly implicated in the competitive angle with which Ferrand slants the statement: France was one of the first countries to succeed in creating an empire; the loss of this 'first' empire is regretted, and blame apportioned in the choice of terms such as 'la ruine' and 'ces désastres'. Thus, without discussing either the implications of the imperial act, or even mentioning the overseas populations, Ferrand valorises French colonial aggression as 'une oeuvre'. Furthermore, in introducing an element of competitiveness to this expansive impulse (the references to British recuperation of French colonial territory, the insistence on France being 'parmi les premières nations', and the emphasis on the struggle to regain an empire), he situates French imperialism within a framework of national grandeur and status.

Foucart and Grigault, in their manual of 1909, not only refer to the acquisition of colonial territories as a traditional element of French foreign policy, but also, more specifically than Ferrand, place this gesture within the framework of a competitive pan-European movement of expansion:

En donnant à son empire colonial l'extension qu'il a aujourd'hui, la France n'a pas seulement obéi au mouvement qui, pendant la seconde moitié du XIXème siècle a poussé presque tous les pays d'Europe à s'emparer de nouveaux territoires: revenant à une politique traditionnelle, elle a, en même temps, reconstitué avec d'autres éléments un domaine extérieur que des guerres malheureuses lui avait fait perdre.[20]

The desire to place the 'new' Empire within the context of a French imperial tradition, or even within a European tradition, can, to a certain extent, be perceived as a response to change. To use Hobsbawm's term, this 'invention of tradition' may be seen as a reaction to a novel situation which takes the form of a reference to old situations.[21] The 'old' model of the former Empire is used for the new purpose of establishing structure, continuity and some sense of the invariance of national motives and intent. The repetition here establishes a sense of national social continuity and community of purpose. The new Empire was thus presented as a reconstitution of the first.

This notion of reconstitution allows writers and educators to posit the precedent of the former Empire. The very existence of this former Empire is then used as irrefutable grounds for approval of the reacquisition of a colonial domain. By citing the existence of a colonial precedent, and by valorising that precedent, these writers avoid having to engage in the imperial debate, and having to justify the imperial act. Indeed, nowhere in these manuals is there an objective discussion of the anti-imperial argument. The omission of the reasons for, or justifications of, these expansive acts, coupled with the lack of a counter-balancing argument, presents the legitimacy of the French Empire as beyond contestation. French colonialism, the reader is given to understand, is inherently justifiable.

Although by this juncture heroic accounts of impetuous and ambitious individuals in Indochina were thus largely confined to popular fiction (for example, Malraux's rather anachronistic *La Voie Royale*),[22] where these renegade explorers and soldiers were discussed in school manuals, their actions were brought firmly into line with the retrospectively coherent reworking of French action in Indochina. The famous names of the Indochinese conquest were rehabilitated through the realignment of their action with the revised colonial values of protection and benevolence. Thus the protagonists of the conquest are elevated to the status of national *héros* or *martyrs*, represented as making an ultimate sacrifice in the name of the nation, and thereby as embodying the values of the nation:

Voilà une colonie qui nous a coûté cher, dit Louis, quand son frère eut fermé le livre. Garnier, Rivière, Courbet, Paul Bert, que d'hommes illustres ont payé de leur existence l'acquisition du Tonkin!
- Ils ont donné leur vie sans marchander, lui dit le capitaine, parce qu'ils avaient foi dans l'avenir de ce pays, l'un des plus riches du globe. C'est à nous de marcher sur la

voie que ces grands morts nous ont ouverte, c'est à nous qu'il appartient de relever en Extrême-Orient le prestige de la France, tombé en bas depuis que l'Angleterre est la maîtresse incontestée des Grandes Indes.[23]

Expansionist actions and the war of conquest are thus presented as abstract gestures relating solely to the prestige of the French nation. These narratives of heroism deflect attention from the bellicosity and violence of the French imperial adventure, and add a different moral and historical weight and importance to what was in fact a disorganised series of events.

This desire to redress the balance in favour of a pragmatic and altruistic rather than an indisciplined, self-seeking yet heroic version of France's motives for intervention in South-East Asia is due in no small measure to imperial rivalry and issues of international status. Comparative interpretations of French intervention in South-East Asia emphasised the debt owed by the Vietnamese to the French conquerers, and were marked by comparisons with France's imperial rivals, in particular Great Britain. In the following quotation, the distinguishing feature of French colonialism is its generosity:

> Les grands colonisateurs des autres pays n'ont pas agi aussi généreusement que les explorateurs français. L'Anglais Stanley, au service de la Belgique, traita les Noirs sans pitié.[24]

By contrast,

> La France a pacifié ses colonies: elle a chassé les pirates et empêché les différentes tribus de se battre entre elles; elle a supprimé l'esclavage, ainsi que la traite, c'est-à-dire la vente des nègres esclaves. Grâce à la paix apportée par les Français, les indigènes ont pu travailler et s'enrichir.[25]

The result of French colonialism is therefore to allow the indigenous populations to embrace capitalism and to adopt the French national characteristics of industry and application. However, this interest in the economics of colonialism is not attributed to the colonising nation:

> Beaucoup de nations européennes considèrent seulement les colonies comme un moyen de gagner de l'argent. Les Français ont voulu faire mieux: ils ont cherché à civiliser les peuples protégés. Ils ont respecté les coutumes, les religions, les habitants et les usages indigènes.[26]

This quotation pitches economic concerns against concerns to share the benefits of French civilisation. In distancing France from economic or acquisitive aspects of imperialism to concentrate on the humanitarian vocation of French colonialism, school manuals thus reworked the narrative of conquest in order to attentuate its haphazard and violent nature. The conquest was now represented without fail as a reactive gesture: a response to Chinese aggression, Siamese 'encroachments', or other, often less specific, 'problems':

> En Indochine, des difficultés avec l'Annam, à l'occasion de l'établissement d'un négociant français à Hanoi provoquèrent la prise de cette ville par des troupes envoyées au Tonkin. Le traité de 1874, qui mit fin au conflit, plaçait l'Annam sous notre protectorat; ce protectorat, assez vaguement défini, ne devint effectif qu'en 1883, après une nouvelle intervention au Tonkin pour y faire cesser des troubles causés par des irréguliers chinois.[27]

> Des empiètements que faisait systématiquement le Siam sur des territoires dépendant de l'Annam, notre protégé, et que n'avait pas arrêtés le traité de 1886, nécessitèrent en 1893 l'envoi de troupes au Laos et de forces navales devant Bangkok. Le Siam céda et évacua la rive gauche du Mékong, nous laissant la libre disposition du Laos.[28]

The use of vocabulary such as 'nécessitèrent', 'céda', 'nous laissant la libre disposition', removes motivation and agency from the French conquerors. France's role in the conquest is thus reworked, and is now described using terms which suggest arbitration and protection.

As Barthes noted of the evocation of war in French official colonial discourse:

> GUERRE: Le but est de nier la chose. On dispose pour cela de deux moyens: ou bien la nommer le moins possible (procédé le plus fréquent); ou bien lui donner le sens de son propre contraire (procédé plus retors, qui est à la base de presque toutes les mystifications du langage bourgeois). *Guerre* est alors employé dans le sens de *paix* et *pacification* dans le sens de *guerre*.[29]

Indeed, and as Norindr has suggested, these narratives of creation, and the naming of Indochina, were 'designed to erase from the collective memory the bloody history of its foundation'.[30] Presenting French intervention in Indochina as a reaction to some maleficent force then enables these texts to describe that intervention in terms of purely altruistic intent. France, rather than being represented as yet another aggressor, is treated in these texts as a protector. Conquest becomes pacification, war becomes protection. The sword is replaced by the *drapeau*. By the early decades of the twentieth century, the fetish of the national flag has replaced the sword and the cannon as figures of the French conquest of Indochina.

Metropolitan France's role in Indochina was imagined along lines which followed the same trajectory as demonstrated by reinscriptions of the conquest: liberation and protection from maleficent and domineering exterior forces. Josset's depiction of French colonialism in Cambodia thus focuses upon both interior and exterior aggressions which have provoked the political and cultural decline of the Khmer peoples:

Le despotisme aveugle des souverains a fait de ce peuple, si bien doué, un peuple d'esclaves. Pressurés sans cesse par leurs rois, habitués à courber le dos sous le joug, les Cambodgiens n'ont plus aujourd'hui d'autre force que la force d'inertie. Ils ont succombé sous les coups des Siamois qui leur ont pris Angkor, et des Annamites, qui leur avaient enlevé la Cochinchine. Depuis que la France a établi son protectorat sur le Cambodge, la décadence politique des Kmers (sic) s'est arrêtée. Le Siam, possesseur d'Angkor n'ira plus loin.[31]

Again, as in the case of the conquest, narratives concerning French action in Indochina often present intervention as a reactive gesture; here in response to despotism and local annexations.

French intervention was further reformulated as a form of cultural protection and preservation. The temple site at Angkor, which at the time the manual was written had not yet passed into French hands, served as the symbol of the motivations and value of French colonialism.

-Il est regrettable que cette belle pagode ne soit pas en territoire français, dit Louis.

-Je le déplore comme toi, mon ami. Nous veillerons à la conservation de ce monument mieux que ne le font les Siamois.[32]

In the above quotation it is implied that Angkor, the symbol of past Khmer glory, can be protected, restored and *mise en valeur* by the careful application of the principles of French colonialism. Thus the colonised Indochinese are not only protected by French colonialism, they are also perceived to gain stature and prestige through their association with metropolitan France. French colonialism is thus presented as a mutually beneficial project: the metropole increases its own grandeur in its possession of an empire; Indochina gains reflected glory through its association with the metropole.

This notion of mutually reflected grandeur and prestige exemplifies yet another inconsistency within French colonial discourse. Having justified expansion through the use of Republican and patriotic discourses which assert the great tradition and heritage of the mainland, these manuals simultaneously suggest that France can be great only through the addition of extra-metropolitan countries to the nation. In order to deflect attention from the mainland's need, that very need is displaced and relocated to the colony. These manuals thus elaborate a discourse of generosity in order that the prestige France aspires to will not be tarnished by its own lack.

Rather than embodying military might, the French Empire now represented *ralliement*. Allusions to acquistion and conquest are replaced with discourses of incorporation and inclusion: the incorporation of the 'outside' territories to the Motherland, and the extension of the *hexagone*'s national boundaries to include the far-flung acquisitions of the French Empire. To this end, Josset's manual, for example, takes three brothers on an imaginary trip around the world through the remembered anecdotes of 'Oncle Martin' who served in the colonies:

> si vous êtes capables de m'écouter plusieurs jours de suite, je vous conduirai successive-
> ment dans les cinq parties du monde, dans ces contrées très différentes, habitées par des
> peuples noirs, jaunes ou rouges. Sur toutes ces contrées flotte cependant le même drapeau:
> le drapeau de la France.[33]

Here, the national flag, the symbiosis of the Republic and the French nation, provides a visible symbol of *ralliement*. The *tricolore*, incarnating 'une certaine conception unitaire et conciliatrice du destin national',[34] demonstrates the transplantation of the myth of foundation and unity to the colonies. The French national flag asserts a notion of permanence and cohesion which in fact masks dispersion and disunity.

Conflicting historiographical visions of French imperialism thus emerge from the textual sources of the period. The heroicised version of the solitary male adventurer is abandoned in favour of a myth of imperial purpose, which involves describing the French nation as rallied as one behind the conquest. By the turn of the century, the Ferryist version of French imperial purpose was becoming the most widely accepted version of French interest in Indochina. It replaced the heroic version of conquest which had shored up France's prestige in the imperial game of one-upmanship the nation imagined itself to be engaged in. The Ferryist narrative of imperial design was promoted in a more systematic and institutionalised way through educational programmes, and by the turn of the century seemed to have replaced any lingering suspicions that the creation of the *Union indochinoise* had essentially been an accidental or incidental result of independently imperial-minded *militaires* and *marins*.

In creating a system of colonial government in Indochina, France melded together the old and the new. The system was a hotch-potch of traditional Vietnamese institutions onto which were superimposed modern French ones. In Cochinchine, which was the only full colony, a Governor General ruled from Saigon, and French law was applicable. Annam and Tonkin, and later Cambodia and Laos, each had the status of protectorate. Annam and Tonkin were governed by the Hanoi Governor General, and by two French *résidants supérieurs*, one in Hanoi and one in Hué. Nonetheless, the Vietnamese monarchy at Hué and precolonial bureaucracy were allowed to survive (in a circumscribed and subordinate way); and each province in Annam and Tonkin had two parallel administrations: one led by a French chief, and another led by a Vietnamese chief. There was little difference between the two systems. Appointed by the Minister for Colonies, the Governor General of Indochina could suspend all local councils if he deemed it necessary. In almost all facts of colonial life he ruled by personal decree, with the approval of Paris. The Governor General had power over the entire political federation known as *l'Union indochinoise.*

The conquest was completed, pacification accomplished, and the administrative machinery was set in place in order to govern Indochina. What remained to be realised was the construction and anchoring of Indochina's new identity as part of the French Empire. As we shall see, this objective was pursued not only through the concrete transformation of Indochina, but also through the political and cultural reinforcement of the notion of *Indochine française.*

Notes

1. Alexandre de Rhodes is perhaps best known for his transcription of Annamese into a Latinised script known as *quoc ngu.* The publication of his Annamese-Portuguese-Latin dictionary in 1651 facilitated the spread of Christianity in Indochina.
2. Made formal in Minh Mang's edicts of 1833 and 1836.
3. Franchini, P., *Les Guerres d'Indochine* (Paris: Pygmalion, 1988), p. 77.
4. Chasseloup-Laubat was Minister for Colonies between 1858–1867, and is often viewed as the inspiration behind French expansion into South-East Asia.
5. Taboulet, G., *La Geste française en Indochine: Histoire par les textes de la France en Indochine des origines à 1914: Tome II* (Paris: Maisonneuve, 1956), p. 700.
6. Quoted by Franchini, *Les Guerres d'Indochine*, p. 100.
7. From *Le Temps*, quoted by Brocheux, P., and Hémery, D., *Indochine: la colonisation ambiguë* (Paris: La Découverte, 1995), p. 53.
8. Robiquet, P., *Discours et opinions de Jules Ferry, tome 5: Discours sur la politique extérieure et coloniale* (Paris: Armand Colin, 1897), p. 182.
9. Ibid., p. 186.
10. Ibid., p. 220.
11. Paul Bourde accompanied the *Corps expéditionnaire* for *Le Temps*; Paul Bonnetain was the correspondant for *Le Figaro*. Both later published their collected articles: Bonnetain, *Au Tonkin* (Paris: 1885), Bourde, *De Paris au Tonkin* (Paris: 1885).
12. See Mouhot, H., *Voyages dans les royaumes de Siam de Cambodge et de Laos* (Paris: Hachette, 1868), (repr. Geneva: Olizane, 1989).
13. Jules Harmand was born in 1845. A military physician, he was stationed in Cochinchina in 1866 as an auxiliary with the French Navy. He was posted to Cambodia in 1873. In France he was nominated curator for the *Musée des*

produits coloniaux, and put in charge of the Indochinese section of the *Exposition universelle* of 1883. In 1883 he was also made *Commissaire général du gouvernement du Tonkin* and negotiated the French treaty with the Imperial Court at Hué which imposed a protectorate on Annam. In 1885 he was made *chargé de mission* on behalf of the *Ministère de l'Instruction publique* and the *Société de géographie*. He attempted an expedition upriver to Tonkin which was aborted, and during the same year undertook an expedition to the unexplored area between the Mekong delta and Toulé-Sap. His main voyage in Indochina was undertaken in 1877.

14. Harmand, J., *L'Homme du Mékong: un voyageur solitaire à travers l'Indochine inconnue* (Paris: Phébus, 1994), p. 211.
15. Ibid., p. 15.
16. Ibid., p. 34.
17. Lyautey, *Lettres du Tonkin et de Madagascar 1894–1899* (Paris: Armand Colin, 1933), p. 638.
18. See Betts, R., *Assimilation and Association in French Colonial Theory 1890–1914* (London: Columbia University Press, 1961).
19. Ferrand, L-H., *Géographie de la France et de ses colonies* (Cours moyen, préparation au certificat d'études), (Paris: Cornély, 1904), p. 75.
20. Foucart, G., and Grigault, M., *La Géographie au brevet élémentaire: La France et ses colonies* (Paris: Delagrave, 1909), p. 254.
21. See Hobsbawm, E. (ed.), *The Invention of Tradition* (Cambridge: CUP, 1983); particularly Hobsbawm's introduction in which he discusses his approach, pp. 1–14.
22. Malraux, A., *La Voie royale* (Paris: Grasset, 1930).
23. Josset, E., *A Travers nos colonies: livre de lectures sur l'histoire, la géographie, les sciences et la morale* (Cours moyen et supérieur), (Paris: Armand Colin, 1901). p. 261.
24. Paquier, P., *Histoire de France à l'usage des élèves du cours supérieur des écoles franco-annamites et des candidates au certificat d'études primaires franco-indigènes* (Hanoi: Editions Tan-Dan, 1932), p. 137.
25. Ibid.
26. Ibid.
27. Foucart, G., and Grigault, M., *La Géographie au brevet élémentaire: La France et ses colonies*, p. 258.
28. Ibid., p. 259.
29. Barthes, R., *Mythologies* (Paris: Seuil, 1957), p. 139.
30. Norindr, P., 'Representing Indochina: the French colonial fantasmatic and the Exposition Coloniale de Paris', in *French Cultural Studies*, vi, February 1995, pp. 35–60.
31. Josset, *A Travers nos colonies*, p. 273.

32. Ibid.

33. Ibid., pp. 9–10.

34. Girardet, R., 'Les Trois couleurs', in Nora, P., *Les Lieux de mémoire 1: La République* (Paris: Gallimard, 1984), p. 32.

—2—

Mise en Valeur: **Building Indochina**

Mise en valeur is a term which connotes not only economic development of the kind pursued by other capitalist imperial nations, but also the moral and cultural improvement to be wrought in the colonies. This emphasis on the moral and cultural dimension stemmed from the French belief in the universal value of its civilisation which in turn found its roots in the nation's revolutionary legacy. Both an ideology underpinning the French colonial doctrine, and a set of policies, *mise en valeur* is a polyfunctional concept which was much cited and invoked in the defence of French colonialism. *Mise en valeur* could be put forward as an example of the beneficial value of French colonial action, and thus served as a form of autolegiti-mation for imperial France. *Mise en valeur* came to be one of the pillars of French colonial ideology, a touchstone, and a means through which to measure and display the beneficial impact of the French enterprise abroad. It was the policy through which France quite literally constructed Indochina.

Although the forcible stamping of a visible reminder of the French presence in Indochina was tempered by the gradual adoption of the policy of association, building works and engineering projects remained a crucial point of reference for colonial apologists throughout the duration of colonial rule in Indochina. Once colonialism had been drawn onto the international stage following the First World War (and particularly in the light of the creation of the *Société des Nations*) the developmental aspects of French colonial policy became a vital factor in the defence and promotion of French colonial action. As a response to the scrutiny of the international community, the focus of pro-colonial ideology and propaganda in France changed. The desire to distance France from the bloody legacy of conquest and pacification and to represent colonialism as a more ethically-based project required France's colonial apologists to find worthy points of emphasis which would epitomise the humanitarian and developmental aspects of French action abroad. The notion of *mise en valeur* lent itself readily as an example of an ethically based colonial goal with a beneficial outcome. In colonial texts from the turn of the century onwards, but most particularly in the post World War One period, one can see an increasing emphasis on *mise en valeur* as a defining figure of successful and ethical French colonialism.

Through the careful application of a policy (or set of policies) of *mise en valeur*, France sought to bring Indochina into the era of progress. France certainly transformed Indochina: politically, economically, culturally and physically. With French rule came a capitalist economy, a building programme which transformed cities and brought industry to both urban and agricultural regions. Indochina grew, evolved, and as France's colonial lobby would have it, progressed. Indochina's growth in production output between 1899 and 1923 was estimated at 50 per cent. The economy was modernised, and Indochina was hauled into the era of industrialisation.

Mines, rice production networks, rubber plantations, cotton, tobacco, and sugar production were improved and modernised. Further industries grew out of the development of Indochina's cities and the arrival of settler populations: electricity power stations, service industries to the ports and harbours etc. (Figure 3) The *Travaux publics* section of the colonial government set about an intense programme of transport provision, creating a modern infrastructure throughout the *Union indochinoise*. Between 1891 and 1898, the Programme Doumer oversaw the beginnings of a modern rail network throughout Indochina; and the *Transindo-chinois* network was completed and opened in sections between 1905 and 1936. (Figure 4) In 1911, the road development programme was launched, to include the famous *Route Coloniale 1* (RC1 following the old Route Mandarine, and stretching some 1,200 kilometres from Hanoi to the border with Siam). The ports of Saigon and Haiphong were developed to meet the demands of the flourishing import-export businesses.

The objectives of *mise en valeur* extended to science and technology, with the creation of research centres and technological services in Indochina: the *Service*

Figure 3. Cement works, Haiphong

Figure 4. Section of railway, Yunnan

géologique was created in 1918; the *Institut océanographique* in 1922; the *Institut d'agronomie coloniale* in 1918; a *Bureau de climatologie et de météorologie agricole* in 1927; the *Office indochinois du riz* in 1930; and in 1940 *the Institut du caoutchouc*. The cultural impact of French rule was evident in the changing cityscapes throughout the *Union indochinoise*. Schools and hospitals were constructed; colonial villas and government buildings were built; features of French urban life appeared around Indochina: theatres, sanatoria, hotels, cafés, bars, race courses, gardens and parks, operas, churches and cathedrals.

Ideologically, however, quite apart from producing these tangible results, *mise en valeur* functioned conceptually as a distinguishing feature of French colonialism. Having distanced the nation from the acquistive and bloody legacy of the conquest, France had sought instead to promote an ethical version of its intervention in Indochina. This ethical vision reposed upon what might be conceived as a trinity of values and principles which were to embody the nation's vision of its colonial role – generosity, benevolence, protection. Through the invocation of *mise en valeur*, the move from violence to development could be further codified. Writing at the time of the *Exposition coloniale de Vincennes* of 1931, Albert Sarraut, former governor of Indochina and Minister for Colonies, retrospectively conceded that colonialism had originally been a primitive act of force, but asserted that this initially violent confrontation could be transformed into a collective triumph of solidarity. The French *doctrine coloniale*, he argued

transfigure les traits originels de l'entreprise coloniale, elle leur donne de l'ampleur et la dignité qui leur manquaient; et parce que, désormais, elle l'établit sur cette idée de solidarité avec toutes ses conséquences, elle fait de la colonisation, acte primitif de force, une admirable création de droit.[1]

He further conceptualised France's role in Indochina through a series of building metaphors which demonstrate not only the ethical emphasis in colonialism which he sought to promote, but also correlate closely with the developmental and constructive focus which French colonial action was seeking to embody:

Elle sait, en effet, cette élite, que c'est la souveraineté française, basée sur le droit du bienfait et du progrès, qui a vraiment fait l'Indochine, fondé la France d'Asie, créé cette union puissante de pays hétérogènes et de peuples divers dans laquelle, comme dans une mutualité fraternelle, l'effort de chaque profite à tous et l'effort de tous à chacun. De ces pays différents, séparés, sans lien, trop faibles avec leurs seuls moyens, plus vulnérables dans leur isolement, condamnés chacun par leur solitude à ne devenir, dans le grand tourbillon de la vie moderne, que les satellites obscurs et serviles d'autres Etats.[2]

La souveraineté française est ici comme l'armature puissante qui encercle et soutient les pièces d'un échafaudage. Qu'on l'enlève, et tout s'effondre; il n'y a plus, jonchant le sol, qu'un amas de fragments dispersés. Sans la souveraineté française il n'y a plus d'Indochine.[3]

Sarraut legitimised France's position in Indochina through a myth of unity which homogenises the disparate nations and cultures which made up the *Union indochinoise*. His image of scaffolding suggests that the construction of French Indochina is not yet completed, and posits the coloniser not as a conqueror, but as an agent of improvement and constructive action. More importantly however, Sarraut's foundational myth justifies continued French presence, and emphasises the importance of the integrity of the *Union*. Although he believed that enlightened emancipation would be the ultimate gift of France to her colonies, Sarraut's apocalyptic vision of Indochina without French rule allows him to envisage this future as distant.

Likewise, the metropolitan 'energy' which had resulted in the conquest and pacification of Indochina had, according to the revised version of France's imperial role, been harnessed and contained, and channelled into new projects. The concept of the heroic male imperialist was re-established but in a reworked form: the French colonialist was no longer presented as an explorer or a conquistador, but as an engineer, a builder of roads and bridges. Where previously the French male's colonial role had been the exploration, penetration and domination of the (feminised) colonies, this male energy was now to be channelled into future action and future improvements. As Lyautey noted, at the Exposition of 1931:

Il reste encore sur la terre de vastes champs à défricher, de pacifiques batailles à livrer à la misère, à l'ignorance, à toutes les forces mauvaises de la nature. En montrant l'immense labeur déjà accompli par les nations colonisatrices, l'Exposition montrera par surcroît, qu'il reste beaucoup à faire.[4]

Because the colony tends to function in the imperial imagination as an empty space awaiting European intervention and development, the French notion of *mise en valeur* thus provided the perfect outlet for surplus (and potentially violent) energy. In the above quotation, the correlation between violence and development becomes evident. Military power and forcible subjugation have been replaced by 'peaceful' battles to be fought in the name of civilisation and development. This sentiment is echoed in the literature of the 1931 colonial exhibition, where Western colonialism was said to find in the fight against sickness and death its newest enemy to be overcome and vanquished:

l'Occident ne renonce pas à poursuivre dans le monde sa mission, où il y a encore de grandes et belles batailles à livrer, et à gagner contre la maladie, la sorcellerie, contre la mort.[5]

Similarly, in the Republic's schools, the perceived justice and benevolence of the French colonial method was evoked through an emphasis on *mise en valeur*, particularly in the context of comparative evaluations which naturally eulogised French colonialism in contrast to the colonial attitudes of the nation's imperial rivals. Lavisse, in his influential, not to say ubiquitous *Histoire de la France*, hurries over economic matters, preferring to evoke at much greater length the protective, and developmental aspects of the colonial relationship:

A quoi servent les colonies? Les colonies sont très utiles au commerce et à l'industrie de la France. Nous y vendons beaucoup de nos produits, ce qui augmente la richesse nationale. Nous y achetons les produits dont nous avons besoin.
Mais un noble pays comme la France ne pense pas qu'à gagner de l'argent. En Indo-Chine, la France a mis fin aux ravages de bandits venus de Chine. Partout elle enseigne aux populations le travail. Elle crée des routes, des chemins de fer, des lignes télégraphiques.[6]

Lavisse's emphasis on the generous and humanitarian aspects of France's action in Indochina demonstrates his clear attempt to distance France from a solely economic rationale of colonialism. This reveals not only a desire to differentiate France from its imperial rivals in Europe, but more importantly, it points to the unspoken need to formulate and reinforce that ethical basis which helped to mask the essentially exploitative character of the colonial project.

Fictional works also often simply reinforced and reiterated official France's emphasis on *mise en valeur*. The figure of 'le colon bâtisseur', which proliferated in fictional colonial works of the 1920s and 1930s, personifies France in its role of constructive developer in Indochina. It dramatises the channelling of colonial energy into useful projects and tangible monuments to the benevolence of French colonial rule. In George Groslier's *Le Retour à l'argile* (1910),[7] and Henry Daguerches' *Le Kilomètre 83* (1913),[8] the male protagonists conform to this stereotype of the *colon bâtisseur*. The male colonial settler or administrator who is, above all, concerned with the implementation in the colony of the metropolitan ideals of progress, development and technology. In Groslier's novel, Rollin is the chief engineer of the construction of a new bridge in Cambodia; Bertrand is a plantation owner. Both characters embody the stated aims of the French doctrine of *mise en valeur*. Their role in the colonies is focused upon the improvement of the colony, the turning of its natural resources to economic advantage, ensuring the endowment of French technology and science to the colony.

This concern with the tangible economic and technological advantages of French colonialism is articulated most clearly in Daguerches' novel, whose date of publication correlates most closely with the period of construction and *mise en valeur* in Indochina. As its very title suggests, *Le Kilomètre 83* is a novel which dramatises the process of building a section of railway. The buildings and edifices that Daguerches' engineers construct serve throughout the novel as a metaphor for French colonial action in Indochina. The construction of the section of railway serves as an example of the beneficial effect of French colonialism:[9] the new railway line serves as a visible symbol of the French colonial *oeuvre*, which glorifies modernity and the modern metropolitan nation, and also benefits the subject peoples. Through the character Tourange, Daguerches presents the view of an archetypal colonial pragmatist, imbued with the righteousness of the *colon bâtisseur*: 'Quand vous me dites: "Toute la Cochinchine est à fond de boue", je réponds: "Ce qui m'intéresse, c'est que, dans cette boue, on ait pu porter des ponts!"'[10]

The colony is represented in Daguerches' novel, as elsewhere, as a domain for male action *par excellence*: 'Nous avons eu besoin ni des femmes, ni des aïeux, ni des dieux !'[11] This opinion mirrors the perceived virtue of 'virilité' evoked in much official rhetoric of the 1920s and 1930s concerning the role and status of male metropolitan *colons* in Indochina. A pacified Indochina can thus continue to figure as a haven for the solitary male; a space in which he can prove his masculinity. Here, the male settler is omnipotent, above even the gods in his power and authority within the colony.[12] Furthermore, Moutier appears to speak for a generation of male European settlers when he states:

Et nous sommes satisfaits, notre conscience est en repos, si nous l'avons au moins consacré, ce labeur d'une vie, à quelque chose qui dépasse la vie humaine![13]

Visual manifestations or monuments of national prestige and superiority are deemed an adequate recompense for a life's work. Once the section of railway has been finished, Tourange contemplates it with a mixture of personal, racial and national pride: 'J'écoutais chanter avec orgueil, la force de mon sang, la force de ma race!'[14] Colonialism, or more specifically, the physical by-products of colonial government, become the legacy of a generation. A stamp of permanence on a foreign soil (a railway line, a monument, an impressive building) becomes the enduring headstone of the male settler. The tendency towards phallic descriptions of the railway line, which accompany Tourange's outburst of pride, complete the picture of an exclusively male domain:

> C'était droit, net, d'un trait, comme notre volonté tendue, comme les lignes de nos épures. C'était plat comme une table, et cela portait tout le bouquet resplendissant du ciel. Et je savais que c'était solide, durable, pas en toc (. . .) j'étais content, c'était notre oeuvre.[15]

The ideal of the male metropolitan settler depicted in Daguerches' novel is replete with masculine 'virtues': he is enterprising, active, energetic, persistent and devoted to science and progress. The correlation between the now outmoded conquistador and his newer manifestation, the *colon bâtisseur*, are once again clear: the work of Daguerches' engineers is likened to that of soldiers, and the time spent in the building of the *kilomètre 83*, to that of the duration of a war.[16] Thus the *oeuvre* of French colonialism is celebrated as an heroically masculine pursuit, a 'peaceful battle' to recall Lyautey, but glorious in its accomplishment.

This masculinised version of settler society in Indochina thus replicates the official reworking of the heroic explorer figure whose legitimacy is now in question. The heroic qualities of the conqueror or soldier are displaced onto his more peaceful homologue: the engineer or builder. His masculine characteristics are rearticulated in the more acceptable form of the *colon bâtisseur*, and the pacifying action of the conquistador is displaced by the peaceful development undertaken by the engineer or builder.

The codification of *mise en valeur* as a defining feature of French colonialism was thus pursued through a variety of means: world and colonial exhibitions, fictional and educational sources. The propagandist value of *mise en valeur* worked on two levels: national and international. On the national scale the notion of imperial France as a bestower of such gifts was widely disseminated in order to anchor and popularise France's imperial identity; on the international scale, France's emphasis on *mise en valeur* served to shore up France's prestige, and distinguish the nation's colonial project from that of its imperial rivals.

However, the policy of *mise en valeur* was not, of course, without its limits. One of the most striking paradoxes of French colonialism finds expression in this desire to develop and improve both colony and colonised: for, to endow the colonies with the benefits of French civilisation through the policy of *mise en valeur* is to enable the colonised, ultimately, to reach a level of civilisation which would render obsolete the need for further French intervention. The logical outcome of a successful implementation of *mise en valeur* was the end of the French Empire. The application of *mise en valeur*, most particularly in relation to the intellectual 'development' of the native populations, was thus often tempered by a desire to confine the Indochinese peoples to an inferior position, and thereby to perpetuate colonial rule.

These restrictions are most obvious in the educational policies and reforms which successive administrations put into place in Indochina. They reveal not only the limits of *mise en valeur*, but also highlight the often ambivalent approach to colonial rule contained within the nation's official rhetoric. French attitudes towards the *mise en valeur* of the Indochinese populations – to the native populations' access to education, their right to study in France, and to their entry into positions of (relative) authority in Indochina, thus provide telling insights into the limits of *mise en valeur*. Colonial educational policy in Indochina was thus marked by the tension between French cultural universalism and racial elitism. (Figure 5)

Unrest in Indochina had often been fed, sometimes engendered, by the mandarin teachers who had traditionally been at the forefront of opposition to colonial rule. This was particularly true during the early days of metropolitan intervention in Indochina. In the nineteenth century, Indochinese schools had been perceived as recruiting grounds for anti-French agitators, and the mandarins were viewed as capable of mobilising political opinion againt French rule. Consequently, the French education system had been most highly organised in places where Indochinese resistance was strongest. Additionally, education reform arose from the concern that rival empires and nations, particularly Japan and China, would influence Vietnamese education if the French did nothing. As Anderson has noted, French educational policy was intended to break the existing politico-cultural ties between the colonised peoples and the immediate extra-Indochinese world, most particularly China, but also (in the case of Laos and Cambodia), Siam.[17] The implementation of education programmes in the nineteeth century can thus be regarded as a reactive and controlling gesture on the part of French administrations.

By the 1920s and 1930s however, the French drive for educational reform in Indochina arose from somewhat different criteria. Ostensibly, the improvement of the education system in Indochina was a prime example of the *mise en valeur* of the natives themselves.[18] The newer imperatives of associationist policies also meant that there was a certain realisation that the metropolitan system could not be transported wholesale to Indochina.[19] Teaching methods and curricula had to be adapted to the peculiarities of the *milieux*.

Figure 5. Franco-Cambodian school

Il faut, dans chaque colonie, adapter au caractère spécial du milieu, aux besoins locaux comme aux mentalités de races très distinctes, la souple variété des programmes d'enseignement et de méthodes pédagogiques dont une application identique et uniforme en tout lieu serait une lourde erreur, déjà condamnée par l'expérience.[20]

Concerns over the state of indigenous education in Indochina were raised by the *Résident supérieur* of Indochina in 1919. It was thought that the system currently in place was outdated and no longer sufficient 'pour les besoins de la vie sociale actuelle'.[21]

A series of reforms was therefore carried out between 1924 and 1926.[22] The reformed *Code de l'Instruction publique* provided a breadth of schooling ranging from elementary to university education. Elementary education consisted of a three-year programme (*cours enfantin, cours préparatoire, cours élementaire*), followed by a three-year primary cycle (*cours moyen 1, cours moyen 2, cours supérieur*). This in turn was followed by a four-year primary superior course and three years of secondary education leading to the Indochinese version of the *baccalauréat*.[22] The Indochinese university, founded in 1907 by Paul Beau, but periodically shut down, and under constant transformation, was the pinnacle of the system.[23]

The *Commission de lettrés* organised a public competition in order to elaborate new school manuals in Indochina.[24] In line with the now accepted doctrine of association, it was decided that different books had to be created for the five different regions within the *Union indochinoise*. Equally, the French administration had to ensure that these books were produced cheaply in order to ensure that they were as accessible as possible to the indigenous populations. The books had to suit a variety of ages and be appropriate to a wide age group (elemetary: 6–10 years; and post-primary: 10–16 years). These manuals were also intended for the use of adults studying at home.

Similarly, a series of initiatives was implemented to create publications aimed at indigenous teachers in Franco-Indochinese schools. These monthly publications were intended to provide the indigenous teachers with material, and also to keep them informed of new educational reforms, and the latest accepted pedagogical methods. They contained model lessons, lesson plans and references. The French administration thus kept a tight rein upon both the material taught and the methods through which it was taught in Franco-indigenous schools. Indochina was thus furnished with a highly centralised education system. An office of Public Instruction supervised the hiring of teachers, their performance, commissioned text books, drew up lists of texts permissable for use in classrooms, published curriculum guides, inspected schools and set exams.

As Albert Sarraut's observations reveal, the *mise en valeur* of the indigenous populations through reform of the education system in Indochina would, it was hoped, provide a two-fold benefit for imperial France – the increased economic viability of the colony, and the creation of an Indochinese elite who would assist the French in their government of the colony:

> L'instruction, en effet, a d'abord pour résultat d'améliorer largement la valeur de la production coloniale en multipliant, dans la foule des travailleurs indigènes, la qualité d'intelligences et le nombre des capacités; elle doit, en outre, parmi la masse laborieuse, dégager et dresser les élites de collaborateurs qui, comme agents techniques, contre-maîtres, surveillants, employés ou commis de direction, suppléeront à l'insuffisance numérique des Européens et satisferont à la demande croissante des entreprises agricoles, industrielles ou commerciales de la colonisation.[25]

These *chefs indigènes* were to act as 'intermédiaires entre nous et populations indigènes',[26] and were to be educated in such a way as to ensure that they diffused 'parmi les éléments de ces troupes, avec la conscience plus claire des bienfaits de notre civilisation, les raisons profondes de la servir et de la défendre.'[27] Their education was clearly intended to be propagandist and to facilitate the dissemination and inculcation of French ideals amongst the Indochinese populations. Thus the first aim of education in Indochina was to be the formation of a second 'tier of influence'. Metropolitan propaganda was to be reinforced by an ideologically loyal section of the indigenous community.

However, whilst education might indeed allow certain sections of the indigenous community to improve their chances of advancement, these *chefs indigènes* would never attain the same status as their colonial masters. Furthermore, for the majority, the reformed education programmes fitted them solely for manual work, and subservience to the colonising elites. Loubet noted of revised school manuals to be adopted following the reform programmes of the 1920s:

> Ils ont été rédigés de manière à assurer au petit paysan ou au petit citadin de condition ouvrière qui quitte l'école pourvu de son certificat d'études élémentaires le minimum indispensable de connaissances dont il aura besoin: lecture, écriture, calcul, langue locale, éléments de français, histoire de l'Indochine, géographie de son canton, de sa province et de sa région, morale traditionnelle, rudiments d'enseignement manuel.[28]

These modest aims reflect the reluctance on the part of many colonial administrators and thinkers to spread ideas from the Enlightenment thinkers, or to allow indigenous populations unsupervised access to the inquisitive tenets of modern science. School manuals held out the promise of an equality of education between the mainland and the colonies, as in the following quotation:

> La France s'efforce d'ouvrir de plus en plus largement devant ses enfants d'Asie comme devant les fils de sa race, le vaste domaine où les fruits du savoir tendent à qui sait cueillir leur nourriture saine et puissante.[29]

But most commentators still considered it dangerous to permit the peoples of Indochina even technical education beyond the most basic level, lest they become 'ambitious'. The educational needs of the colonised Indochinese populations were thus perceived to be rudimentary, and largely of a practical rather than intellectual nature. Education in Indochina thus resembled a form of modest vocational training rather than an education in its traditional and accepted sense.

For the Indochinese social elite, the pursuit of education in mainland France was a highly desirable goal, particularly as they received such a limited education in Indochina. For France, it was something to be discouraged, restricted, and carefully policed. It was feared that too many young Indochinese travelling and studying in France would learn the 'wrong things', as did the most famous of Indochina's exports to France: Ho Chi Minh. According to the *sûreté* there were 1,556 Indochinese students in France in 1930.[30] As early as 1919 however, a circular emanating from the Indochina section of the Ministry for Colonies made clear the threat that this French-educated elite might pose to colonial rule in Indochina.

> Il convient que l'on ne s'engage dans la voie des réformes qu'avec une extrême prudence (. . .) Ce sont précisément les natifs instruits dans nos méthodes et dans nos idées qui sont les ennemis les plus dangereux de notre autorité et les partisans les plus résolus d'un *home rule*, où nous n'aurions plus aucune place. Nul doute, en effet, que l'enseignement donné en France ne corresponde à aucun besoin réel des populations

indigènes, non plus qu'à leur mentalité. Là plus que partout ailleurs, il convient de ne pas ouvrir trop largement le domaine des idées spéculatives, mais de favoriser au contraire l'acquisition des connaissances les plus essentielles.[31]

Some contemporary commentators have perceived this reluctance to offer the Indochinese a more traditional and intellectual education as a means of reasserting difference between colonised and coloniser. As Lebovics[32] has noted, the aim of French education reformers was not to jeopardise French colonial rule by creating a generation of Indochinese whose educational background enabled them to contest French rule, or to contest the superiority of their French rulers. On the contrary, the aim of education in Indochina was, as Lebovics suggests, to 'reroot the Vietnamese in their villages':

> Conservatives' fears for the loss of traditions, and with them of a certain essential identity (. . .) fueled the anxieties and projects of Frenchmen concerned with Indochina. If bad imitations of Frenchmen could be turned once more into good Vietnamese peasants, the disorder of the world would subside.[33]

This limitation of the amplitude of *mise en valeur*, the desire to restrict Indochinese education, and to pare down instruction to a minimum basic level, is reflected in the content of the curriculum of Franco-Indochinese schools as the following chapter will show.

Education thus highlights the political and disciplinary potential often masked behind the rhetoric surrounding the policy of *mise en valeur*. Whilst Indochina was perceived as a fruitful investment in terms of education, France nonetheless severely limited the degree to which the indigenous populations were permitted to advance. The liberty, equality and fraternity which the Republic claimed to extend to *la Plus Grande France* was not only restricted and curbed in political terms, but also in cultural and educational ones. The education policies and programmes adopted by France in Indochina reveal the latent unease of the colonising nation vis-à-vis the potential of its subjugated populations to acquire the tools with which to question colonial authority.

Notes

1. Sarraut, A., *Grandeur et servitudes coloniales* (Paris: Sagittaire, 1931), p. 207.
2. Ibid., p. 265.
3. Ibid., p. 266.

4. Lyautey, quoted by Dagens, B., *Angkor la forêt de pierre* (Paris: Gallimard, 1989), p. 110.
5. *Rapport général vol. 6 (I),* (Paris: Imprimerie nationale, 1932–5), p. 67.
6. Lavisse, E., *Histoire de France* (Cours moyen, préparation au certificat d'études primaires), (Paris: Armand Colin, 1912), p. 244.
7. Groslier, G., *Le Retour à l'argile* (Paris: Emile Paul, 1928), (repr. Paris: Kailash, 1994).
8. Dageurches, H., *Le Kilomètre 83* (Paris: Calmann-Lévy, 1913), (repr. Paris, Kailash, 1993).
9. This is an extremely popular image of French colonialism throughout the French Empire. Betts quotes Gabriel Hanoteaux, for instance, who suggested that the railway station was more valuable than the fort in the process of colonisation, see Betts, R., *Tricouleur: the French Overseas Empire* (London: Gordon and Cremonesi, 1978), p. 29.
10. Daguerches, *Le Kilomètre 83*, p. 173.
11. Ibid., p. 128.
12. Indeed, later, critical, texts were to refer to these all-powerful metropolitans as 'Dieux blancs'. See, for example, Luc Durtain's *Dieux blancs, hommes jaunes* (Paris: Gallimard, 1930).
13. Daguerches, *Le Kilomètre 83*, pp. 213–14.
14. Ibid., p. 317.
15. Ibid., pp. 304–5.
16. Ibid., p. 303.
17. Anderson, B., *Imagined Communities: Reflections on the Origin and Spread of Nationalism* (London: Verso, 1991).
18. See *Plan d'études et programmes de l'enseignement primaire supérieur franco-indigène : réglementation du Diplôme d'études primaires supérieurs franco-indigène* (Hanoi: Imprimerie de l'extrême-Orient, 1928); and Bourotte, B., *La Pénétration scolaire en Annam* (Hanoi: Imprimerie de l'Extrême-Orient, 1930.)
19. See Loubet, *L'Enseignement en Indochine en 1929* (Hanoi: Imprimerie de l'Extrême-Orient, 1929), p. 4.
20. Sarraut, A., *Grandeur et servitude coloniales* (Paris: Sagittaire, 1931), p. 97.
21. Bourotte, *La Pénétration scolaire en Annam*, p. 1.
22. See *Plan des études et programmes de l'Enseignement primaire supérieur franco-indigène: réglementation du Diplôme d'études primaires supérieurs franco-indigène.*
23. Some have argued that the Indochinese university was founded in order to prevent contact between the Indochinese elite and left-leaning students in France. See for example, Marr, D., *Vietnamese Tradition on Trial 1920–45* (Berkeley: University of California Press, 1981).

24. These reforms are set out in detail in *Les Manuels scolaires et les publications pédagogiques de la Direction générale de l'Instruction publique* (Hanoi: Imprimerie de l'Extrême-Orient, 1931).
25. Sarraut, *Grandeur et servitudes coloniales*, p. 95.
26. Ibid., p. 96.
27. Ibid.
28. Loubet, *L'Enseignement en Indochine en 1929*, pp. 5–6.
29. Pham-Dinh Dien and Vu-Nhu'-Lâm, *Manuel d'Histoire d'Annam* (Nam-Dinh: Imprimerie My Thang, 1931), p. 114.
30. The activities of, and French surveillance of, Indochinese in France during the inter-war years is a huge potential area of research which I have identified as a future project, but which is not within the remit and scope of the present work. There is a large archive held by the Archives d'Outre-Mer at Aix-en-Provence, which includes the SLOTFOM series, which would provide a particularly useful and fruitful source of future research on the interaction between French and Indochinese in mainland France, and on the interaction between the future political elites of both France and nationalist movements in Indochina.
31. *Note du Ministère des colonies, service de l'Indochine, pour l'inspection générale de l'Instruction publique*, 11 novembre 1919.
32. Lebovics, H., *True France: the Wars over Cultural Identity 1990–45* (London: Cornell University Press, 1992). See chapter entitled 'Frenchmen into Peasants: Rerooting the Vietnamese in their Villages', pp. 98–134.
33. Ibid., p. 133.

—3—

Making Indochina French

The importance attached to the policy of *mise en valeur*, and more particularly, the visible markers of French presence in buildings and the changing cityscapes of Vietnam, Cambodia and Laos, clearly contributed hugely to France's project of making Indochina French. The gallicisation of the colony, or more particularly the imperative of bringing Indochina within the cultural as well as political sphere of *la plus grande France*, was a goal pursued not only through urban design, but also through educational policies, an emphasis on the indigenous acquisition of the French language, and through the marginalisation of neighbouring Asian influences and pre-colonial Indochinese history.

This last objective was achieved not least by the the the act of drawing together the disparate and culturally different areas of Cambodia, Vietnam and Laos under the umbrella term *Indochine française*. The political term *l'Indochine française* was formally adopted in decrees of 17 and 20 October 1887. As was noted in the Introduction, the metropolitan use of 'Indochine', to signify Vietnam,[1] Cambodia and Laos alerts us to the fact that the geographical space imagined by imperial France was, in fact, an artificial construction. Indochina, as the territory's name suggests, was initially perceived as a hybrid entity. In the early days of conquest and pacification, Indochina was referred to as *Indo-Chine*, with a hyphen reflecting its hybrid status.[2] The nomenclature fixes the territory geographically as 'in between' India and China. The implication of this hyphenated term is that the territory lacked a specific identity of its own. By suppressing its hyphen and adding its own national adjective, imperial France was able to forge a completely new domain of cultural influence. France metaphorically filled the gap. The affix *française* wiped out, in this limited and linguistic sense, Chinese and Indian influence, thereby creating a new territory, *Indochine française*.

Once this homogenisation had been accomplished geographically and politically, France set about rendering Indochina visibly French. As a feature of the policy of *mise en valeur*, construction clearly played a crucial role in the formation of this new identity. Indeed, the greatest impact of this desire to make Indochina French can be seen in the visible stamping of the French presence upon Indochina through the destruction of native cities and the construction of French ones in their place. The spirit of conquest can be discerned in the attitudes towards native cities and in French urban design in the late nineteenth century. Because there was much indigenous resistance to the conquest, the French military had to establish an authoritarian regime which would crush indigenous revolt. Military control was expressed not simply through military buildings, but also in the initial urban plans for the cities which France had conquered. Urban design in the nineteenth century was dominated by spatial concerns which reflected the military imperatives of the conquering French admirals. Pacification was thus partially accomplished through disciplinary building policies.

Indeed, it was a military engineer, Coffyn, in the 1880s, who drew up the first plans for the redevelopment of Saigon.[3] Coffyn's plans were dominated by the concerns of military surveillance: he stressed the need for large open streets which would permit observation, but rejected the creation of large open spaces lest unauthorised indigenous gatherings occur. Coffyn perceived the need for a few ostentatious buildings which were intended to attract European investors. Similarly, he attempted to give a French feel to the city, emphasising the need for symbols of French greatness. (Figures 6 and 7)

The early French policy of assimilation, coupled with these military concerns in Indochina in the nineteenth century led to the destruction of the indigenous city of Saigon. In an attempt to destroy any vestiges of indigenous organisation, the city was razed and rebuilt. This destruction stemmed from an intense dislike of the intrusion of indigenous motifs and references in architecture. Perceived as a transgression against the sanctity of French culture, this *métissage* was rigourously

Figure 6. Lieutenant Governor's Palace, Saigon

Figure 7. Hôtel de Ville, Cholon

avoided. Brébion for instance, praises the soldiers of the conquest for having 'tiré pour nous Saigon de sa brousse et de sa vase',[4] and goes on to say:

> Il était souhaitable (. . .) que la ville européenne fût aussi homogène que possible pour éviter ces constructions en un style que nous qualifierons de métis.[5]

The rebuilding which took place after the destruction of Saigon was therefore intended to assert a domineering and inviolable image of the imperial nation. Buildings were formalist and grandiose: their ornementation made reference to classical and baroque monuments. They represented a visible expression of the universality of Western concepts of beauty and order. Much was made of the connection between the prestige of Paris and Saigon: for some, Saigon was a symbol of magnificence – an embodiment of French cultural superiority. Percieved as the *Paris de l'Extrême-Orient*, Saigon became a symbol of French prestige and cultural hegemony:

> -Est-ce que Saigon ressemble vraiment à Paris? demanda Louis, nous n'y sommes établis pourtant que depuis 1859.

> -C'est vrai. On ne peut songer sans admiration au petit nombre d'années qu'il a fallu à la France pour faire d'une ville malsaine, aux canaux marécageux, une cité élégante, aux riches édifices, aux rues larges, aérées, bien ombragées.[6]

Figure 8. Theatre, Saigon

However, urbanism and construction in late nineteenth-century Saigon was of a largely superficial nature. The French built an 800-seater theatre, a racetrack, countless pavement cafés, yet failed to modernise the defective water supply system. (Figure 8) Often, the buildings constructed were also inappropriate to the tropical climate in Indochina. Saigon's *Notre-Dame* cathedral for instance (completed in 1880 by the architect Jules Bourard), was a red brick construction with Gothic vaulting. Its ventilation system was more suited to a Northern European climate than the heat and humidity of Indochina. As Wright notes, it was not until 1942 that the French were to concede finally 'the need to pierce additional openings in the lateral chapels, following more or less the traditional Vietnamese practice for ventilating pagodas'.[7] The initial metropolitan rebuilding of Saigon and Hanoi demonstrated, in effect, the inadvisability of assimilative policies. The wholesale export of metropolitan principles of town planning and design had resulted in inappropriate buildings which were ill-suited to Indochina.

The move towards a more associationist spirit in urban planning and design was embodied in Indochina in the appointment of a professional *urbaniste* to oversee its development.[8] Maurice Long succeeded Albert Sarraut as Governor General in 1919. His period of office saw the systematisation and further implementation of the politics of association. In 1920, he requested funds for a new technical council in Indochina, to be headed by a professional urbanist. He admired the urban accomplishments of Lyautey and Prost in Morocco,[9] and felt that

Indochina would benefit from this type of concerted urban policy, rather than merely the random, individual policy towards public building which had prevailed until then. Indeed, Long hoped to create in Indochina an aesthetic in the associationist spirit.

The decision was thus taken to bring to Indochina a professional urbanist as a government advisor. Long appointed Ernest Hébrard, a member of the *Société française des Urbanistes*, in 1921. Long also created an official urbanism department in Indochina in 1923 and made Hébrard the director of the *service d'urbanisme*, which was part of the *Inspection générale des Travaux Publics*. Hébrard's first task was to be the redevelopment of the *quartier du Gouvernement général* in Hanoi. Maurice Long had been unfavourably impressed by the construction of a large *lycée* right next to the *Palais du Gouvernement*, and hoped to repair this fault by buying up from a credit company the surrounding land with the intention of creating a government administrative *quartier* there. This *quartier* would regroup all the governmental departments, which were at that time scattered throughout the city. Hébrard's plan for this development was approved in 1924 by Long's successor, Governor General Merlin, and construction began the following year with the financial and registry buildings.[10] (Figure 9)

During his career in Indochina, Hébrard undertook a wide variety of redevelopment and building works, the construction of the *Institut Pasteur* (completed 1930), and the *Musée Louis Finot*, the museum of the *Ecole française d'Extrême-Orient*

Figure 9. Governor General's Palace, Hanoi

in Hanoi (completed 1931), being just two of the most prominent. Hébrard's largest project however was the creation of a 'model city': Dalat. Referred to as a 'ville d'agrément et de repos pour les Européens fatigués par le climat tropical',[11] Dalat was designed as a summer seat of government, and a retreat for the metropolitan elite. It was conceived as a highly controlled environment: Dalat was intended to inspire governmental efficiency, high-minded leisure, and the health of body and mind, through its site and its design.

One might imagine that reinforcing the identity of *l'Indochine française* in the context of urban design and planning was dealt a blow by the gradual adoption of the policy of association which rejected the wholesale destruction of indigenous cities in order that they be made French. Nonetheless, the spectre of assimilation appears to have lived on in Ernest Hébrard's conception of his role as *urbaniste* in Indochina, and in his works of the 1920s and 1930s. Hébrard's speeches and texts on his urban ideals are all marked by concerns which were born out of the move towards association. However, Hébrard's background equally inclined him to a universalist view of urban design. In his formative years he had been involved in the conception of a 'ville mondiale':[12] a universalist vision of a global city. Hébrard believed he had isolated the universal principles of urban planification in this design, and tried to refute the notion that his global plan would have to be adapted to local milieux. This rationalising, universalist and essentially modernist vision sat uncomfortably alongside the imperatives of association. Yet nevertheless, Hébrard's own stated ideals concerning urbanism in Indochina propelled him towards the adaptation of buildings to local conditions. This fundamental tension is constantly played out in Hébrard's vision of town-planning in Indochina. The lure of assimilatory and universalist principles undercuts and undermines the drive towards association in urban planning. Hébrard's dilemma in Indochina thus reflects the conflict between difference and homogeneity which characterises so much of French colonial discourses.

For colonial urbanism continued, up to the 1930s at the very least,[13] to be viewed as a privileged means of asserting the metropole's grandeur and prestige as an imperial nation. This very sense of prestige, manifested through grandiose monuments and public buildings, posits the visual impact of colonial urbanism as an aggressive gesture: visible manifestations of imperial prestige were used as a means of perpetuating control over indigenous populations. As Vivier de Streel noted at the *Congrès de l'urbanisme* (1931),

C'est par l'éclat de leurs monuments et de leurs travaux d'urbanisme que les Grands Etats ont conquis, de tout temps, le prestige qui était leur principal instrument de domination sur les populations soumises à leur souveraineté.[14]

Reinforcing this latter notion in a comparison with the impact of Roman urbanism, Vivier de Streel continues:

> là se sont affirmées, de façon saisissante, non seulement la force mais aussi la supériorité intellectuelle et morale.[15]

Colonial urbanism is clearly viewed as a means of asserting coercive force and reinforcing cultural and economic superiority over the colonised peoples of the French Empire. In addition, colonial urbanism was perceived as a valuable asset in France's competitive vision of her status amongst fellow imperial powers:

> ils [les pouvoirs publics] doivent avoir celui [le souci] de remplir leur devoir vis-à-vis des sujets et protégés français, et de ne pas entendre dans leurs bouches des comparaisons peu flatteuses entre l'effort français et celui des autres puissances coloniales.[16]

Thus, in spite of the proliferation of the rhetoric of association from the first decade of the twentieth century onwards, urbanism and city-planning in Indochina were concomitantly used by imperial France as a means of reasserting its imperial identity and colonial ideal. Embodied in the plans, the construction and the visual impact of the cities, edifices and monuments created in the 1920s and 1930s in Indochina, was a codified version of France's *doctrine coloniale*. As Vivier de Streel concluded,

> C'est qu'en effet l'urbanisme est l'une des formes les plus nobles de la civilisation puisqu'il satisfait à deux préoccupations également élevées: l'amour du prochain, se manifestant par la mise à sa portée de la santé, de la salubrité, du confort de l'habitation; les satisfactions esthétiques obtenues par les grandes réalisations architecturales, l'embellissement du foyer, de la cité et de ses alentours.[17]

By covertly marrying assimilation and association in urban planning, France could reinforce its political objectives in Indochina. The recognition of indigenous architecture in colonial building projects, for example, had a political pay-off for imperial France; it would engage

> la sympathie des indigènes en leur affirmant notre respect pour leurs ouvrages et en les associant à nos travaux. Ainsi, peu à peu, se gagne le coeur des indigènes et se conquiert cette sympathie qu'il est du devoir des colonisateurs d'obtenir.[18]

In keeping with these tenets of associationist colonial policy, Hébrard's intention was to create an 'Indochinese style'. He stated:

L'architecture en Indochine devrait tenir compte des caractéristiques du peuple, de ses habitudes et de ses traditions. Il devrait se baser sur des études des monuments indochinois sans les copier.[19]

However, this acknowledgement of local conditions and styles was to be accompanied by new 'forms':

Il est bien entendu que l'adoption des moyens modernes de construction facilitera la mise en oeuvre de formes nouvelles qui devront toujours être adaptées aux conditions du pays.[20]

It was the conception of these 'new forms' which constituted the more radical side to Hébrard's approach, and also one which mitigated his acceptance of the tenets of association.

In a practical sense, this gesture of respect and tolerance was to be highlighted by the use of indigenous craftsmen in building projects. Hébrard's urban 'ideal' for Indochina involved the production, invention, or 'guided evolution' of a new style which would be specific to the Indochinese:

au lieu d'élever en Indochine des pastiches d'européen, pourquoi ne pas diriger les indigènes dans une voie qui s'accorde bien avec leurs traditions, leurs tempéraments et leurs aptitudes, et les faire évoluer normalement vers un art moderne, qui leur restera bien particulier.[21]

Hébrard's own use of language here clearly indicates the extent to which this 'style' was to be manufactured by metropolitan overseers: the verbs 'diriger' and 'faire évoluer' effectively wrest aesthetic control from the indigenous artists and architects. It was, it appears, inconceivable that local traditions and styles might be left intact to evolve at their own pace, or that this evolution might be generated from the Indochinese populations themselves.

In addition, Hébrard's perception of an Indochinese style is premised upon the fact that this style would be distinguished, selected, and put into practice under the guidance of French experts. Advocating the use of indigenous artisans in order to arouse their *sympathie* towards imperial France, Marrast states:

On ne saurait mieux y parvenir qu'en confiant, dans une très large mesure aux artisans indigènes l'ornementation, leur laissant toute liberté dans des limites définies.[22]

The perceived necessity of limitation and guidance of the indigenous workers demonstrates the extent to which the associationist discourses of the 1920s and 1930s were nevertheless underscored by a desire to assert metropolitan controls and aesthetic hierarchies. Thus, although French officialdom in Indochina attempted to demonstrate a democratisation of artistic expression by using indigenous artisans, censorship played an important part in their work. The hands of indigenous artisans were guided and censored by the *service d'urbanisme*.

Hébrard further attempted to implement the principles of association in the design and execution of his buildings by making architectural allusions to South-East Asian cultures. In order to discern and delimit this Indochinese style, Hébrard spent much time photographing and studying indigenous architecture – Angkor Wat, Buddhist pagodas, simple rural dwellings. He similarly studied the principles of site planning, ventilation and choice of materials which prevailed in the Far East, and attempted to use Indochinese technical mastery over the environment (stilts, verandas, thinner walls etc.) in his building design. Hébrard's principal aim was to find local antecedents for official structures, and to strike a balance between tradition and modernism, industrial growth and cultural respect.

In spite of his painstaking research of local architectural designs, Hébrard seemed oblivious to centuries-old cultural rivalries between the different countries which made up the Indochinese Union. As the *Musée Louis Finot* demonstrates, Hébrard freely mixed elements from different regions and also from countries outside the Indochinese Union in order to generate his ideal of an innovative, adaptive aesthetic. As a result, the museum, and many of his other buildings resembled a pastiche of exotic details superimposed upon a *Beaux-Arts* plan, rather than the more radical change in direction which he advocated.

The *Musée Louis Finot*, a museum designed to house the *Ecole française d'Extrême-Orient* and its collections, presented, as Wright has noted,[23] an eclectic mix of architectural motifs. Its facade evoked Japanese Shinto temples; its steep-tiled porch roofs recalled Hindu temples in India; the two-tiered roof of the central core alluded to Siamese, Cambodian and Laotian temple structures. Although the museum appealed to the EFEO's scholars' knowledge of a diverse range of oriental stylistic traditions, the blurring of national cultural references and styles neverthe-less signals the imposition of metropolitan cultural and aesthetic values, and the subsumation of separate Indochinese identities under a homogenising Orientalist and imperial vision of the identity of Indochina under colonial rule.

Hébrard's desire to create an 'Indochinese style' had further repercussions in that it effectively marked a break with indigenous architectural continuity. The historical break which French colonialism had itself effected was used to create an entirely new and modern architectural and urban model in Indochina. This model would serve not only to anchor the notion of new cultural and historical status for *Indochine française*, but would also present a long-lasting acknowledgement of French intervention in South-East Asia. Not only a permanent visual testament to French reinterpretations of indigenous cultural and political identity, Hébrard's 'Indochinese style' also functioned as a long-lasting influence on any future developments in indigenous architecture. In 'inventing' an 'Indochinese style', by not using French exemplar, nor rigidly preserving traditional models, Hébrard effectively created a hybrid architectural style, peculiar to French Indochina, which reflected its colonial status.

Hébrard's concern to create and use in his designs an 'Indochinese style' thus reflects the new directives of associationist policy, but also underlines the tensions and conflicts which its adoption highlighted. For while France had attempted to break all Indochina's ties with neighbouring cultures in an attempt to establish more firmly the identity of *French* Indochina, the move towards association, particularly in urban design, seems, at first glance, to work against this desire, and on the contrary to revive and to reintroduce these Asian cultural references and traditions.

The creation of an 'Indochinese style' nonetheless has a similar intention in that colonial urbanism in Indochina was undeniably linked to the political aim of implanting a French identity amongst the Indochinese populations. Not only were the territory's regions and countries blurred into the French construction of *l'Union indochinoise*, but more importantly, distinctions were further effaced and masked by Hébrard's plundering of neighbouring cultures for artistic and architectural references.

By the 1930s then Indochina had become an eclectic pot pourri of nineteenth-century French buildings, newer ones embodying the Indochinese style, and traditional indigenous villages and dwellings. Indochina was irrevocably transformed: architectural and historical ties with the past were severed, and the imprint of French rule was ubiquitous. Indochina's landscapes and cityscapes everywhere bore testimony to France's cultural and political impact and authority.

A more overtly propagandist approach to the objective of making Indochina French was undertaken through the means of education in Indochina. Where, in metropolitan France a successful form of colonial education was highly desirable if France were to establish and anchor a new sense of imperial identity and to popularise Empire amongst a generation of youth, in the colonies it was clearly imperative. Education is a crucial way in which to maintain and strengthen domination over a colonised people. It is a pillar of national identity: education props up and underpins national identity, and reflects the nation's sense of self. In the case of the colonised/coloniser relationship, education is also a superlative form of control. It is the means through which the colonising nation asserts its desire to appropriate the past in order to regulate the present. Educating the colonised is to gain privileged access to (and ultimately ownership of) their culture, heritage and national history. It should not be surprising therefore, that the 1920s and 1930s witnessed a significant *effort scolaire* in Indochina.

As we have seen, the educational reforms of the 1920s in Indochina were in part intended to break former ties with neighbouring Asian cultures. One of the ways in which this was achieved was to eradicate historical linguistic links through the systematic use of French in an educational context. The reformed school programmes were thus intended to ensure the diffusion of the French language, just as had Ferry's reforms in mainland France during the 1880s. Language was perceived as a crucial vehicle for the propagation of French ideals of Franco-Indochinese cultural identity:

> Le développement de l'enseignement du français correspond trop aux voeux des indigènes et aux besoins de notre pénétration pour que la Direction générale de l'Instruction publique ne considère pas comme son principal devoir de l'assurer par tous les moyens.[24]

French language was not only to be used as a propaganda tool, it was also to have an extremely important role in the homogenisation of Indochina. The creation of a coherent linguistic area would facilitate the indigenous acceptance of the reformulated geographical and political entity of *l'Indochine française*. It was thus equally the intention of manuals to render the various dialects within the various countries and regions of Indochina uniform:

> Il est incontestable que cet effort d'unification du vocabulaire doublé d'un effort identique en ce qui concerne la syntaxe et la fixation de l'orthographe, aura pour effet de répandre dans les contrées proprement annamites l'usage d'une sorte de langue commune que ces livres généraliseront.[25]

A much smaller place was to be given to the teaching of indigenous languages – a minimum of two hours and a maximum of three – thus ensuring the gradual adoption of French as the language of common communication in Indochina.

This reformed education system and programme in Indochina thus embodied France's political, cultural and ideological aims in Indochina. Offset against the colonial ideals of protection, benevolence, progress and development which the French nation believed it both embodied and exported to the colonies, existed a mirror image of qualities which colonial education abroad was intended to engender: gratitude, loyalty, duty and submission to a greater cultural and political power. The propagandist value of education thus served a two-fold purpose: it was the means through which the empire was 'sold' to the colonised, but it also served the political purpose of averting dissension, promoting loyalty to the French Republic, and thus assuaging potential rebellion. These two goals were married in the overarching aim to 'make Indochina French'.

Popularising the notion of *l'Indochine française* meant forging new cultural and political loyalties amongst the Indochinese. Points of comparison and cultural models in the reformed educational programmes thus all took metropolitan France as their central point of reference, creating an identity which placed the Indochinese populations firmly within the political, cultural and historical sphere of influence of *la Plus Grande France*. The concern to eradicate influences from neighbouring Asian cultures, to dissolve those former attachments and references, and to 'make Indochina French' thus resulted in an overweening emphasis on the history and qualities of the French nation in Indochinese school manuals. These descriptions fall into two categories: the status and specificity of France within the global arena, and the nation's role in Indochina as a colonial power. Both hold up France as a model to be emulated and revered.

Vaunting the values of mainland France thus became a means through which a *French* Indochina too could be popularised. In the following extract, (which is reminiscent of Lavisse's catechistic section entitled 'Les devoirs patriotiques' in which 'la France est la plus juste, la plus libre, la plus humaine des patries'),[26] France is described in superlative terms as a superior nation:

> La France est habitée par un peuple actif, industrieux et bon. C'est un des pays de la terre où la civilisation a atteint son plus haut degré. La France a mis tout son génie à améliorer les conditions de l'existence humaine. La France a toujours cherché à répandre ses bienfaits dans le monde entier.[27]

Once more emphasising the humanitarian and universalist tradition of Republican France, this type of narrative allows for negative comparisons which place Indochina in an inferior position. The quotation draws on traditional Orientalist myths of Asia as passive and slothful by implying a series of antitheses which posit the French as active, industrious and good, and the Indochinese populations as passive, lazy and bad. More important, however, is the carrot held out to the effect that a close relationship with France will result in the endowment to Indochina of those 'bienfaits' and 'améliorations' which such a civilisation can bestow. Indochina alone, it is implied, cannot compare with France, but yoked to France and that nation's 'génie' as *l'Indochine française*, Indochina could also gain status in the world.

Some school manuals were even more blatant in their enumeration of the attributes and attitudes which made France a worthy and desirable colonising force. Indeed, they reveal much about France's sense of self (as an imperial nation), and serve as a form of national self-justification, as an apology for imperialism:

> La France se montre généreuse et juste; elle est humaine, elle a pitié des peuples arriérés et malheureux; elle leur prodigue ses soins et ses bienfaits sans compter.
> Pour l'Indochine, ces bienfaits sont immenses. Les troupes françaises protègent nos frontières, contre les ennemis du dehors et débarrassent notre pays des bandes de pirates et de brigands. Le paysan vit heureux et tranquille, il peut vaquer à ses travaux sans être inquiété.

La France nous apporte la science occidentale. Elle nous fait bénéficier des profits de cette culture pratique et cherche toujours à élever notre niveau intellectuel. Sous la bienveillante direction de savants maîtres qu'elle envoie, l'Indochine fait figure aujourd'hui parmi les pays les plus civilisés de l'Extrême-Orient.

La France se préoccupe aussi de notre éducation morale. Les bons exemples qu'elle nous donne et le bien-être matériel qu'elle nous procure contribuent à nous rendre meilleurs.[28]

France is thus held up as a model on both a national and international scale. In comparison with other imperial powers, the very qualities embodied in France's national identity and heritage render its colonising role and actions more ethical and altruistic. France's imperial identity and role are thus justified through reference to unimpeachable national characteristics. The inherent superiority of the nation's civilisation, and its generous sharing of its scientific, cultural and economic wealth coupled with its humanitarian 'pitié' can but render the miserable and backward Indochinese 'meilleurs', and *l'Indochine française* 'plus civilisée'.

The elevation of French models and the 'selling' of French culture to Indochinese youth through education also involved tampering with Indochinese history. The archetypal rhetorical method of positing a turbulent, catastrophic past (as in the last quotation) in contrast with a prosperous present was widely employed in many school manuals. The past/present dialectic allowed for the redescription of Indochina, and the rewriting of (or at least the reworking of elements of) Indochinese history. In school manuals at least, Indochina was to be understood only within the totalising schema of historicist imperial ideology and essentialist universalism.

According to the reformed education programme, history lessons were to focus upon two main features: 'Notions d'histoire locale, et de celle du pays de l'Union où se trouve l'école. L'oeuvre française en Indochine.'[29] This recommendation demonstrates once more the importance accorded to the colonising nation in the history of the colony itself. In Altbach's and Kelly's comparative work on educational policy in colonised countries, the authors make the general observation that the teaching of the history of colonised territories tended to avoid the evocation of pre-colonial history as far as possible:

What history was taught revealed a devaluation of indigenous cultures. History, in the main, if it touched on the colonized's past, was only the history of the colonized since they were ruled by Europeans. If precolonial history was touched on, it usually emphasized, through chronology, civil wars, tribal conflicts, famines, and barbarism in order to contrast them with the peace and orderly progress under colonial domination.[30]

Indeed, the pre-colonial history of Indochina is presented in school manuals in extremely limited, general and underdeveloped terms, as the following extracts demonstrate:

> Le Viet-Nam existe depuis plusieurs milliers d'années. Il a été sous la domination chinoise et il a beaucoup souffert. Mais ses souffrances n'ont pas été vaines, car elles l'ont fait aimer davantage de ses enfants qui travaillent sans cesse à le rendre plus riche et plus puissant.
> Le Viet-Nam a beaucoup prospéré depuis qu'il est placé sous le protectorat de la France. Cependant, il est encore peu de chose à côté des Grandes Puissances du monde. Il faut pour le classer parmi elles, que ses habitants redoublent d'efforts physiques et intellectuels.[31]

Given the need of the colonising nation to maintain and strengthen its control over the indigenous populations, it is not surprising that school manuals based their 'history' of Indochina around an axis which contrasted a negative view of the period before colonial rule, with a laudatory narrative of the country's situation since colonial rule began. Here, as elsewhere, the *autrefois/maintenant* formulation of Indochinese history highlights past suffering and repression under Chinese domination in contrast with the benevolent protection offered by the French nation. 'History' in Indochinese school manuals thus mirrors the view of French colonialism as protective, and reactive: a response to aggression and disorder.

This *autrefois/maintenant* dichotomy operated in many forms and was extended to most domains in these manuals. Descriptive texts, for example, always noted the improvements to indigenous life that French changes had wrought.

> La maison commune de mon village a été remise à neuf l'année dernière. Elle est grande et belle.[32]

> Une grande route traverse mon village. Mon père m'a dit qu'autrefois il y avait à la place un sentier étroit et mal entretenu. On ne pouvait y marcher qu'à la file. La moindre pluie le rendait boueux et glissant. Maintenant, c'est une route large, propre, empierrée et bordée d'arbres.[33]

> Hanoi est la capitale du Tonkin. Cette ville, construite à la française, est maintenant la plus jolie.[34]

> Le Viet-Nam a beaucoup prospéré depuis qu'il est placé sous le protectorat de la France.[35]

Although these improvements are not always specifically attributed to French colonisation, the contrast between 'autrefois' and 'maintenant' clearly pitches previous backwardness, poverty, or lack of prestige against current progress, development and prosperity.

Often, these contrasts are more overtly articulated to the detriment of pre-colonial Indochina. A section in one manual on 'l'Assistance médicale' for example eulogises the work of the Pasteur Institute in Indochina, whilst denigrating the Indochinese medical resources in place before the arrival of the French:

> Avant l'arrivée des Français, les malades n'avaient aucune ressource. Les médecins étaient rarement bons; la plupart étaient des charlatans qui tuaient plutôt leurs clients avec leurs médicaments douteux. [36]

Although Indochina clearly did benefit from some of the technological advances which colonial rule brought with it, this comparative axis nevertheless strips the pre-colonial society of any cultural value, thus once more rendering a *French* Indochina more desirable. The purpose of the *autrefois/maintenant* axis is clear: through the systematic denigration of Indochinese history and society, and the equally systematic portrayal of an exemplary French nation and people, the new French identity of Indochina could be made popular and sought after - thus anchoring *l'Indochine française* in young minds as a rightful repository of their patriotic affection.

In return for the gifts of French protection and generosity, educational texts sought to implant the notion of reciprocated duty. Many school manuals took the form of moralistic fables, which exhorted young members of the indigenous community to work hard at school, not to cheat, or to be lazy. During the first year of their *cours moyen*, indigenous students were to be taught *la morale*, which comprised 'devoirs de l'enfant dans la famille, à l'école, hors de l'école et après l'école, envers lui-même et envers autrui'.[37]

Alongside personal and community morality, most school manuals sought to extend their influence into cultural and political domains, an aim which had been mooted in the reform programme:

> Dès maintenant, à côté de la presse indigène, les manuels contribueront à former l'opinion populaire.

> Il convient aussi d'escompter que ces manuels, en combattant certaines habitudes néfastes et certaines routines finiront par exercer une influence bienfaisante sur l'hygiène et les moeurs des populations.[38]

Moreover, these 'leçons de morale' were also to include sections on loyalty to France, and the instruction of what Indochina owed to France. This ideologically-orientated propagandist tool, masquerading as moral education, enabled educators to influence, if not transform, not only the customs and practices native to Indochina, but also the political and ideological mindset of generations of Indochinese.

Many of the texts used in Indochinese schools contained veiled threats: either of a return to past disorder, former poverty or pre-colonial conflict. The school manuals therefore consistently present Indochina as occupying a weak, inferior, and potentially dangerous position, should French colonialism be removed. Although, as a previous quotation showed, France claimed to 'prodigue[r] ses soins et ses bienfaits sans compter', most texts clearly made a reciprocated duty on the part of the Indochinese a requirement of continued French protection, aid and generosity.

> En reconnaissance de tous ses services, nous devons aimer la France, notre patrie d'adoption, d'un même amour que nous avons pour notre propre pays.[39]

> Nous lui devons encore du respect et ce respect nous oblige à nous conformer aux ordres du Gouvernement qui la représente ici, à nous instruire à l'Ecole française, et à lui vouer une grande fidélité.[40]

In the above extract, that required duty is at once political and ideological. It demands loyalty and patriotism, conformity and obedience. In spite of France's seeming confidence in its own civilising mission and sense of imperial identity, threatening discourses − implicit or explicit, blatant or comparatively subtle − resurface with regularity and undermine those apparent certainties. If France's belief were so unshakeable, would it be necessary, as this last quotation shows, to bolster the French and to denigrate the Indochinese so overtly?

> Ce Monsieur est français, il est plus fort que celui-ci qui est annamite. Il faut protéger les personnes faibles.[41]

Education is obviously a domain where propaganda (imperial or otherwise) is often at its most overt. Aimed at an impressionable and untutored audience, school texts are unnuanced and unfiltered, simplified and schematic. Their narrative of the colonial relationship therefore provides telling insights into the nation's ideal image of its colonial role. Indeed, 'colonial history' in school manuals reveals far more about the imperial nation than it does about the colonised territory. The educative texts under discussion presented a validation of French imperial identity and of colonial action, serving as a form of self-promotion on the part of imperial France.

Indigenous peoples of Indochina were taught a limited amount about their own culture and their own countries. What they were taught about their own history was clearly a metropolitan view of that history. For school manuals rewrote the history of Indochina in such a way as to emphasise the beneficial influence of French colonialism, and the altruistic motives which purportedly lay behind imperial gestures. These narratives operate principally around an axis which contrasts former disorder, poverty and susceptibility to aggression, with present order, progress and prosperity under French protection. In school manuals, Indochina was thus totally defined by the presence/absence of the colonising nation.

The implantation of both the political and cultural notion of French Indochina had to be achieved amongst the populations both at home and abroad. At home, French Indochina had to be legitimised and popularised as part of a more widespread attempt to forge and maintain France's imperial identity. The Third Republic had set great store by education as a means of propagating and diffusing state-created notions of national identity within the *hexagone*. By the turn of the century, once France had accumulated its vast overseas empire, it became necessary to extend national identity in order to incorporate its new possessions into that very sense of nationhood. The notion of *la plus grande France*, stretching out the *hexagone*'s limits to envelop the overseas territories, required a significant shift in the composition of the Third Republic's sense of nationhood. The reworked sense of national identity which the Third Republic now sought to popularise meant not simply an inward-looking sense of what it was to belong to metropolitan France, it involved an understanding and appreciation of the implications of France's role and status as an imperial nation. In order to circumvent any residual anti-colonial sentiment such as had emerged during the parliamentary debates over colonialism of the late nineteenth century, educationalists promoted colonialism through the extension of patriotism and the notion of *la plus grande France*. The following quotation, taken from the introduction to a school manual of 1901, typifies these aims:

> Il importe de préparer nos fils à cette tâche colossale: il faut leur faire connaître nos possessions lointaines et les leur faire aimer comme leur propre patrie (. . .) il faut enfin, par des exemples probants, réfuter cette erreur funeste qui veut que le Français ne soit pas colonisateur, et inspirer à la jeune génération cette confiance en soi qui fait les peuples forts.[42]

National identity, in other words, had now to encompass and complement a *conscience impériale*.[43] Thus, making Indochina French was evidently part of a larger, more ambitious, imperial project: the creation, promotion and popularisation of *la plus grande France*.

From the turn of the century onwards, but most notably in the 1920s and 1930s, successive governments, supported by the *parti colonial*,[44] made the dissemination of this new sense of national identity one of their prime educational aims. This imbrication of national and imperial identity is demonstrated in the observations Messimy made in 1933 on the education of metropolitan French schoolchildren:

il est indispensable qu'ils sachent exactement ce qu'est la France, qu'ils voient nettement la place qu'elle occupe dans le monde, qu'ils comprennent que seule, est désormais une grande puissance la nation qui possède dans toutes les parties du monde des bases de départ pour le développement de son influence morale et de son commerce matériel, que, seule, est une nation véritablement mondiale, un Etat qui n'est pas limité entre les étroites frontières qui morcellent la petite Europe.[45]

At a time when France could not expect to expand its frontiers on a European scale, French national identity is viewed as reposing upon extra-national factors, and extra-European influence. Messimy further stressed that

tout l'Enseignement en France doit être imprégné, dans ses diverses modalités appropriées, de la pensée coloniale qui est liée étroitement à la mission de la France dans le monde.[46]

A clear link can thus be established between education and the diffusion of state-created notions of national identity. Just as it had at its outset, the Third Republic continued to place emphasis upon the inclusion in educational curricula of specific ideals of national prestige and grandeur. By the period now under discussion, the French Empire had become the most convincing means of demonstrating and exemplifying national prestige.

The notion of Greater France was consolidated and disseminated through a variety of means both at home and abroad: colonial exhibitions, the didactic work of the *parti colonial*, educational policy and the like. School textbooks, which contain both deliberate propaganda and also indirect reflections of the relatively conservative mind-set of metropolitan educationalists, thus illustrate both educational policy and the 'official' vision of French colonialism of the era. Precisely because they were aimed at an unsophisticated audience, the school manuals under discussion present a schematised, unnuanced and largely unfiltered overview of France's role as an imperial nation in Indochina. Indeed, they present the reader with the basic founding principles of French colonial discourses. Sections within history and geography textbooks which dealt with the French Empire set state-produced notions of the imperial nation alongside state-produced representations of the Indochinese Union. The patriotism which had previously been directed solely towards the Motherland was therefore to be extended to include the overseas territories.

Because a youthful audience is far more impressionable than its adult counter-part, French government officials had far greater liberty in setting the terms and boundaries of their own representations of French imperialism in school manuals than they would have encountered elsewhere. By inculcating into a generation of metropolitan French youth chosen tenets of government imperial ideology, the nation was not only ensuring short-term support for its imperial designs, but was furthermore ensuring that the spirit of Empire would be instilled in generations yet to come. As August has noted, 'Lessons learned in childhood remain for a lifetime. The socialisation of one set of youth forms the cultural inheritance of the following generation'.[47] School children were the most fertile ground on which to sow the seeds of imperial propaganda:

C'est sur l'enseignement primaire qu'il faut avant tout compter pour donner à la France cette conscience coloniale qui lui a manqué jusqu'ici.[48]

The metropole's version of Chamberlain's drive to encourage the British to 'learn to think imperially', was thus encapsulated by the discourses of colonialism present in school manuals from the turn of the century onwards. Thus colonial propaganda served to anchor the idea of France as an imperial power, and also the political and cultural notion of *l'Indochine française*, in both the metropolitan imagination and amongst the colonised populations of Indochina.

The popularisation and reinforcement of French Indochina amongst the mainland population was pursued through educational texts, the *parti colonial*'s propaganda, and perhaps most importantly, as we shall see shortly, through the presence of Indochina in colonial exhibitions.

Notes

1. Which itself was comprised of three different areas: Annam, Tonkin and Cochinchina.
2. The etymology of this term is unclear. Norindr has traced the hyphenated orthography to the Danish geographer Conrad Malte-Brun in the early nineteenth century. See Norindr, P., 'Representing Indochina: the French colonial fantasmatic and the Exposition Coloniale de Paris', in *French Cultural Studies*, vi, February 1995, pp. 35–60. The OED however, asserts that the name 'Indo-China' was coined by John Leydon (1775-1811), a Scottish poet and Orientalist. Nor is it clear when the hyphen disappeared from current French usage. It seems to have gradually been dropped from the late nineteenth century onwards. Norindr however, suggests that the hyphen disappears 'at the very moment French fantasies of Indochina take hold of the French popular imagination' (p. 39).
3. See Brébion, J., 'La Naissance et les premières années de Saigon, ville française', *Bulletin de la Société des Etudes indochinoises*, vol. 2, no. 2, 1927, pp. 63–138.

4. Ibid., p. 83.

5. Ibid., p. 100.

6. Josset, E., *A Travers nos colonies: livre de lectures sur l'histoire, la géographie, les sciences et la morale* (Cours moyen et supérieur), (Paris: Armand Colin, 1901), p. 262.

7. Wright, *The Politics of Design in French Colonial Urbanism*, (London: University of Chicago Press, 1991), p. 176.

8. A version of the present work on colonial urbanism was first published in French Cultural Studies, and I am grateful for permission to rework that material here. See Cooper, N., 'Urban Planning and Architecture in Colonial Indochina', French Cultural Studies, vol. 11, part 1, no. 31, February 2000, pp. 75–99.

9. For a commentary on Prost's work in Morocco see: Rabinow, P., 'Colonialism, Modernity: The French in Morocco', pp. 167–82, in AlSayyad, N., *Forms of Dominance: On the Architecture and Urbanism of the Colonial Enterprise* (Aldershot: Avebury, 1992).

10. Education, justice and agricultural departmental buildings were to follow, but economic cut-backs prevented their construction.

11. 'L'Urbanisme en Indochine', *L'Architecture*, vol. 36, no. 7, (1923), p. 97.

12. Hébrard collaborated in this project with Henrik Christian Anderson, an American sculptor.The plan of this project was published in English in 1912 and in French in 1913.

13. These views were consistently reiterated at the *Congrès de l'urbanisme* which took place in 1931.

14. Vivier de Streel, M., 'Urbanisme et colonisation', pp. 2–4, in Royer, J., *L'Urbanisme aux colonies,* vol. 2 (Paris: Editions d'Urbanisme, 1935), p. 4.

15. Ibid.

16. Ibid.

17. Ibid.

18. Marrast, M., 'Dans quelle mesure faut-il faire appel aux arts indigènes dans la construction des édifices?', in Royer, *L'Urbanisme aux colonies*, vol. 2, p. 24.

19. Hébrard, E., 'L'Architecture locale et les questions d'esthétique en Indochine', in Royer, *L'Urbanisme aux colonies*, vol. 2, p. 34.

20. Ibid.

21. Ibid.

22. Marrast, J., 'Dans quelle mesure faut-il faire appel aux arts indigènes dans la construction des édifices ?' in Royer, *L'Urbanisme aux colonies*, vol. 2, p. 24.

23. See Wright's chapter on Indochina entitled 'La Folie des grandeurs', in *The Politics of Design in French Colonial Urbanism*.

24. Barthélémy, P., (Inspecteur de l'Instruction publique), Direction de l'Instruction publique, *L'Enseignement du Français à l'école franco-indigène* (Hanoi: Imprimerie de l'Extrême-orient, 1927), p. 3.

25. Ibid., p. 22.
26. Lavisse, E., 'Le Devoir patriotique', in *Histoire de la France – cours moyen – préparation au certificat d'études primaires* (Paris: Armand Colin, 1912), p. 246.
27. Nguyen Duc Bao, *Pour nos jeunes écoliers: lecture courante et expliquée* (Hanoi: Tan-Dan Thu Quan, 1925), p. 192.
28. Pham-Dinh-Dien and Vu-Nhu'-Lâm, *Manuel d'Histoire d'Annam* (Nam-Dinh: Imprimerie My Thang, 1931), p. 116.
29. Barthélémy, *L'Enseignement du Français à l'école franco-indigène*, p. 11.
30. Altbach, P., and Kelly, G. (eds) *Education and the Colonial Experience* (2nd revised edition) (London: Transaction Books, 1984), p. 14.
31. Nguyen Duc Bao, *Pour nos jeunes écoliers*, p. 190.
32. Ibid., p. 70.
33. Ibid., p. 76.
34. Ibid., p. 128.
35. Ibid., p. 190.
36. Pham-Dinh-Dien and Vu-Nhu'-Lâm, *Manuel d'Histoire d'Annam*, p. 110.
37. Ibid., p. 11.
38. Gouvernement général de l'Indochine, Direction de l'Instruction publique, *Plan d'études et programmes de l'enseignement primaire supérieure franco-indigène: réglementation du diplôme d'études primaires supérieures franco-indigènes* (Arrêtés des 26 décembre 1924, 16 janvier 1925, 13 mars 1926, 1 juin 1926, 23 novembre 1926), (Hanoi: Imprimerie de l'Extrême-Orient, 1928), p. 22.
39. Pham-Dinh Dien and Vu-Nhu'-Lâm, *Manuel d'Histoire d'Annam*, p. 116.
40. Ibid., p. 117.
41. *Méthode de langage français et annamite destinée aux Ecoles de l'Indochine* (Quinhon: Imprimerie de Quinhon, 1923), p. 69.
42. Josset, E., *A Travers les Colonies*, preface.
43. Thirty eight hours were given over to colonial education in the mainland following the reforms of 1925. Many commentators still believed this to be too little.
44. The composition and action of the *parti colonial* under the Third Republic is documented by Ageron, C-H., *France colonial ou parti colonial?* (Paris: PUF, 1978), and Andrew, C., 'The French Colonialist Movement during the Third Republic: the unofficial mind of imperialism', *Transactions of the Royal Historical Society*, Fifth Series, vol. 26, 1976.
45. *Rapport Général*, vol. 6 (i), (Paris: Imprimerie nationale, 1932–5), p. 82.
46. Ibid., p. 80.
47. August, T., *The Selling of Empire: British and French Imperialist Propaganda 1890-1940* (London: Greenwood, 1985), p. 107.
48. *Rapport Général*, vol. 6 (i), p. 81.

—4—

Exhibiting Indochina

The identity constructed for Indochina by imperial France found its fullest expression at the *Exposition coloniale de Vincennes* of 1931. Most commentators agree that the 1931 Colonial Exhibition marked the apogee of France's colonial Empire. The *parti colonial's* strenuous efforts had at last come to fruition, and the Empire was, for the duration of the exhibition at least, the primary focus of the metropolitan media and imagination. The exhibition also allowed Indochina to be revealed and displayed to the masses. The predominence of Indochina at the exhibition thus reflects the desire to popularise the notion of French Indochina and to legitimise France's colonial role in South-East Asia. The *Exposition* triggered an unprecedented proliferation of works discussing French colonialism: journalism, exhibition literature and works published by prominent colonial thinkers and administrators to coincide with the exhibition; it generated a nine-volume work which exhaustively describes the organisation of the exhibition, the exhibits, and also reproduces the speeches and comments of the leading figures involved in its conception and organisation.

The high profile accorded to the exhibition clearly provided an important occasion to reassert France's colonial ideal. The exhibition provided France with an opportunity to express its colonial views and demonstrate its imperial prowess on an international stage. The exhibition was a forum in which the specificity of French colonialism could be laid before both the metropolitan public and France's international imperial competitors. By the 1930s, conquest and pacification had become a distant memory, and French presence, government and administration were firmly established in the component parts of her diverse Empire. Confidence in Empire was at its height. From this secure position, ideals of Empire could now be subtly reworked to present French colonialism in its maturity. The *Exposition* provided an opportune moment to reassess the *génie* of French colonialism in comparison with that of France's imperial rivals.

Although the *Exposition coloniale* of 1931 was not the first nor the last of France's colonial exhibitions[1] it was arguably the most significant. The largest of France's colonial exhibitions, covering 110 hectares between *Porte dorée* and the *Bois de Vincennes* to the East of Paris, the exhibition of 1931 was inclusive and exhaustive: it sought to represent not only each and every one of France's colonies and protectorates, but equally included a substantial section representing France itself.

Furthermore, the 1931 exhibition opened its arms to its imperial competitors. The exhibition was ostensibly given over to the glorification of 'la grandeur des empires', but while other colonial powers (Denmark, Portugal, Belgium, the Netherlands amongst others) did play a part in this great spectacle, France dominated it. Significantly, Great Britain declined to participate,[2] leaving France free rein to emphasise its prestige and status in South-East Asia. France's predominance was thus symbolised not least by the immense reconstruction of the Cambodian Khmer temples of Angkor Wat, which towered over the other constructions evoking the splendours of the colonies.

The culmination of the uniquely colonial propaganda which had first found expression in the embryonic Marseille exhibitions of 1906 and 1922, the Vincennes exhibition was intended, according to Albert Sarraut, to constitute 'la vivante apothéose de l'expansion extérieure de la France sous la Troisième République'.[3] The importance attached to this colonial manifestation was reflected in the choice of France's capital city as host. Although the Marseille exhibitions had been successful, they had not constituted a reflection of France's colonial greatness in its maturity. By the 1930s, a period often described as the apogee of French colonialism, it was argued that it was only fitting that Paris be the stage. Governor General Olivier noted that the exhibition would confer international status upon France's capital:

> La capitale de la France, grâce à l'Exposition, sera plus que jamais la capitale de l'intelligence humaine.[4]

Thus, although ostensibly a *colonial* exhibition, focus was, from the exhibition's inception, firmly placed upon the colonising nation. Similarly, although the exhibition included the word *internationale* in its official title, prestige and attention were firmly focused upon the French metropole.

The *Exposition de Vincennes* was to be both a 'fête populaire' and a 'spectacle d'art', appealing to all levels of French society. Lyautey even went as far as imagining the event as a force for social cohesion amongst the poor, communist-inclined masses of Eastern Paris.[5] Its organisers envisaged the exhibition as a great forum for international debate: the exhibition was to be a 'foyer intellectuel intense où les savants, les écrivains, les philosophes, les sociologues de tous les pays viendront confronter leurs thèses ou exposer leurs travaux'.[6]

The exhibition's role was not solely that of a forum for debate: it was equally intended as a seductive and picturesque entertainment. Hailed as the 'événement de l'année',[7] the exhibition dominated both the daily and popular press. There was a prolific output of literature and images concerning the exhibition: guides, newspaper and journal articles, posters, even songs. According to many historians, the exhibition had a profound and lasting effect on its visitors:

> Le retentissement fut énorme (. . .) nombre d'enfants trouvèrent à tout le moins dans ce grand spectacle l'écho et la confirmation imagée des immenses plages roses dévolues à l'empire sur les cartes scolaires, et de l'idéologie impériale déjà véhiculée par les chapitres coloniaux du fameux manuel d'histoire des classes élémentaires de la Troisième République ou *Petit Lavisse*.[8]

The Exhibition was thus to be a lesson in the legitimacy of France's notions of its own self-worth as a colonising power. It was also an exercise in unification and community. Paul Reynaud asserted that

> Il faut que chacun de nous se sente citoyen de la grande France, celle des cinq parties du monde.[9]

The metropolitan French population were thus exhorted to take possession of, and to appropriate the colonies for themselves as a national community; to feel their collective power as members of a nation which had extended its influence across five continents.

A wealth of information pertaining to both the colonies themelves, and to metropolitan action, was provided for the visitor. One of the principal educational sites of the exhibition was the newly-constructed *Musée colonial*,[10] a permanent structure, which along with the zoo and aquarium, were to remain after the exhibition's closure. Its impressive facade, created by the sculptor Janniot, sported an immense fresco purporting to represent: 'l'apport de biens terrestres de l'Empire à la mère patrie'.[11] The fresco bore the inscription: 'A ses fils qui ont étendu l'Empire de son génie et fait aimer son nom au-delà des mers, la France reconnaissante',[12] and depicted allegories of abundance, peace and prosperity.

The *Musée colonial* gave a symbolic infrastructure to France's colonial power. Within its walls, it contained a retrospective of France's colonial past beginning with a historical survey of the Empire under the monarchy and the Second Empire. A further *section de synthèse* gave a historical overview of France's empire from 1870. This section was intended to 'en dégager dans son ensemble l'oeuvre de la France dans ses colonies et la somme de la puissance que représentent pour elle leurs activités totalisées'.[13] The *section de synthèse* was in particular supposed to render 'ainsi sensibles les réalités incluses dans cette formule généreuse de la plus grande France, demeurée si vague pour la plupart des Français'.[14] Thus the aim of the museum, and, as we shall see, the exhibition as a whole, was to render the 'myth' of the French Empire a more tangible reality:

En France, la notion d'un empire colonial, loin d'être familière aux hommes privés, n'a même pas été clairement exprimée dans la vie publique. (. . .) La section de synthèse, en faisant surgir, vivante et palpable, l'image même de 'l'empire' a, plus qu'aucune autre, préparé cet avènement.[15]

These didactic aspects of the exhibition were coupled, however, with attractions and entertainments designed to draw in the less educationally-minded crowds. Thus a visitor to the *Exposition* could choose to ride around the immense *Parc de Vincennes* either by the scenic railway or by elephant or camel. S/he might take a trip round Lake Daumesnil in an indigenous boat; sample indigenous food at one of the many restaurants representing each colony; marvel at the spectacular light and water shows or the exotic flora and fauna in the purpose-built Vincennes zoo. As Panivong Norindr has pointed out, these attractions formed part of the exhibition's design to 'ravish' and 'arouse desires' for the colonies.[16]

The exhibition abounded with metaphors which extended the controlling, colonising gaze to a wider French public. These metaphors concerned the possession and consumption of the colony, and involved the importance of the visual impact of the exhibition as a spectacle. In poster and publicity campains, the exhibition's principal slogan was: 'le tour du monde en un jour'. The allusion to Jules Verne's *Le Tour du monde en quatre-vingt jours*, emphasised the elements of adventure and exploration inherent in the colonising act, and enabled the general public to share in that 'virilité' which was embodied by the early colonisers and explorers. The slogan also points to progress: rather than in eighty days, the exhibition allowed the Empire to be colonised in a single day; and allowed the visitor vicariously to become a coloniser. Here was an Empire in miniature: the marvels of a perceived colonial golden age were spread out before the public, to whose commanding, colonising gaze they offered both aesthetic pleasure, and also information and power. In an age of media colonialism, the emphasis was not on the penetration of unknown continents, but on the surveillance of the appropriated. The exhibition conferred upon the public the position of authority at the centre of the Panopticon which Foucault recalled in his discussion of the intimate relationship between power and visual surveillance. The observed Empire was thus trapped and fixed by the authoritative gaze of the dominating power. The exhibition also reinforced the myth of unity: it suggested order and purpose that in fact belied the reality of France's Empire, scattered as it was over five continents. It was a world that had been selected, collected, ordered and relocated by Western powers; and which had been contextualised and given value according to a Western value system. The exhibition was a representation of the colonised world, an artificial and mythical embodiment of a Western view of the colonial territories. Filtered through the imperial eyes of France's colonial ministers and the historians of the

Third Republic, the Empire, in all its diversity, was homogenised as a simple extension of the Motherland.

Although all of France's overseas possessions were amply represented at the exhibition, it was Indochina which dominated.[17] Britain's absence from the Paris exhibition allowed French Asia to shine, and not to be outshone by British India. The metropole's *perle de l'Extrême-Orient* stepped out of the shadow of her rival's 'jewel in the crown'. The specificity and importance of the Indochinese Empire to the mainland was emblematised by the predominence of Angkor Wat.

The temple of Angkor Wat was just one part of the remaining Khmer ruins in Cambodia. The site in fact covers 50km from east to west and includes a walled city, further smaller temples, and an impressive irrigation system.[18] Nevertheless, Angkor Wat was, and remains,[19] a peculiarly fascinating archeological marvel for French scholars. The interest generated by the site lies partly in the fact that for centuries it remained relatively invisible to the West. Built between the ninth and twelfth centuries, Angkor and its surroundings were abandoned, not forgotten, but allowed to fall into ruin. The departure of the Khmer dynasty following a Chinese invasion meant that the site gradually succumbed to the encroachment of the Cambodian forest. Although Spanish and Portuguese explorers stumbled upon the ruins in the seventeenth century, it was not until two centuries later, on the publication of Henri Mouhot's *carnets de voyage* that this impressive site became the focus of concerted Western attention.

Mouhot, a naturalist, visited Angkor briefly, and died a year later in Laos. The posthumous publication of his travel diaries and sketches, *Voyages dans les royaumes de Siam, de Cambodge et de Laos*,[20] was a media event and created something of a cult around his name. The diaries were published in 1863, coinciding with the formal establishment of the French protectorate over Cambodia. The diaries had a considerable impact as they were first published over fourteen weeks in *Le Tour du Monde*, complete with drawings and engravings transformed from Mouhot's sketches.

In an era when the West was absorbed by mapping, charting, classifying and collecting, building a global archive, and pushing back the frontiers of geographical and historical knowledge, France gained prestige from claiming to have discovered this important site, and brought it to European attention. Angkor Wat thus played a significant role in France's early relationship with Indochina. The assertion that France, through the person of Henri Mouhot, had discovered Angkor, awakened curiosity and encouraged explorers, archeologists and photographers to take an interest in the Indochinese peninsula.[21] Further visits and explorations took place throughout the late nineteenth and early twentieth centuries: the expeditions of Garnier, Delaporte and Doudart de Lagrée helped to turn metropolitan attention towards these vestiges of an ancient Khmer dynasty.

The role of the *Ecole française d'Extrême-Orient* (EFEO) in the dissemination of information concerning France's Asian possessions was of course significant. The exploration, classification and description of this 'marvel' had helped to legitimise colonial intervention in terms of scientific advancement and the protection of native cultures. Its appropriation and *mise en valeur* by the *Ecole Française d'Extrême Orient* further strengthened the case for technological intervention, and encouraged tourism in Indochina. Although France had established a protectorate over Cambodia in 1863, the regions in which the Angkor site was situated had been ceded from Cambodia to Siam. France strenuously endeavoured to wrest these territories from Siam, and finally succeeded in 1907. The involvement of the EFEO in French attempts to gain control of the Angkor site demonstrates the complicity of science and scholarship in the colonial project.

The various 'voyages of discovery' to Angkor fuelled an already-present desire for the mysterious and exotic in metropolitan France. The fact that it had long been hidden by the surrounding jungle only added to Angkor's mystery and mythology. The temples became a feature of much literature, both factual and fictional: Groslier, Malraux, Dorgelès, Claudel, and Loti all drew on the 'mystery' of Angkor in their works.[22] Angkor simultaneously embodied the fairy tale or legend and the key to ancient historical secrets: it was 'la ville au bois dormant',[23] and 'le refuge des antiques mystères'.[24]

However, the replication of the site at the *Exposition coloniale* brought the temples to a far broader spectrum of the metropolitan population. Hailed as 'l'oeuvre maîtresse', 'la clef' of the exhibition,[25] the immense reconstruction of the Cambodian temples of Angkor Wat dominated the exhibition. The temples of Angkor Wat had featured in previous exhibitions of the late-nineteenth and early-twentieth centuries, and most successfully at the Marseille exhibition of 1922. The 1931 exhibition, however, was dominated by these towering Cambodian structures: Angkor Wat occupied 5,000 square metres at the 1931 exhibition, and its central tower rose to a height of 55 metres. (Figures 10, 11 and 12)

The re-creation of the temples at the exhibition, however, symbolised the most valuable attribute of French colonialism: French intervention had retrieved the temples from obscurity and had enabled the public (*humanité*, mankind in general) to share rightfully in the enjoyment of this colonial wealth. In spite of the exhibition's professed internationalist agenda, and the attempts of many officials to integrate colonialism into an ideal of *rapprochement* and international cooperation, the reconstruction of Angkor Wat served to set France apart from the other colonial powers at the exhibition. Indeed, the exhibition was intended to affirm 'aux yeux du monde, la grandeur de l'oeuvre coloniale de la Troisième République'.[26] Britain's absence from the exhibition allowed France's South-East Asian marvel to glitter all the more brightly. In a contemporaneous issue of *L'Illustration*, Claude Farrère notes of the temples:

Figure 10. Palais de la Cochinchine, Exhibition, Marseille 1906

En étendant donc le drapeau de la République sur ces débris-là, qui sont aujourd'hui le Cambodge, et en forçant les Siamois à restituer Angkor aux Cambodgiens opprimés et dépouillés, nous avons donc fait oeuvre non pas d'impérialisme, mais d'affranchissement.[27]

Angkor thus comes to occupy a paradigmatic status in terms of French colonialism. It stands for French colonial principles of protection and *mise en valeur*. It functions both as a sign and a myth of French colonialism: it stands for French colonialism everywhere, hence its appearance in ever-increasing volume and stature at exhibitions since the turn of the century.

Reynaud's speech at the exhibition's opening provides further insights into the significance of Angkor, and upon the perceived status of Indochina amongst other French colonies:

En Asie, où nous avons apporté aussi comme premier présent l'ordre et la paix, que nous maintiendrons, nous avons trouvé à son déclin une civilisation millénaire pour laquelle nous avons de l'admiration et du respect.

N'est-ce pas nous qui avons sauvé le temple d'Angkor de l'étreinte meutrière de la forêt vierge qui l'avait envahi?[28]

The Angkor ruins encapsulate what was intended to be understood by allusions to pre-colonial void and disintegration. Yet they also epitomise Indochina's hier-archical advantage amongst France's colonial possessions. France's other colonies

Figure 11. Angkor, Exhibition, Marseille 1922

had nothing to compare with the splendours of Angkor. The culture which, centuries earlier, created the vast site is both admired and respected. The largest and most prominent exhibit, after Angkor, was the pavilion of *l'Afrique occidentale française* (AOF): a reproduction of Djenné's great mosque. However, comparisons between the two were often unfavourable towards AOF, as the following press account reveals. While Angkor is

taillé comme un joyau, couvert sur toute sa surface d'admirables motifs ciselés,

the reproduction mosque, representing a 'pays des tam-tams', is described as

Figure 12. Angkor, Exposition coloniale de Vincennes 1931

un quartier de Djenné, village de l'AOF, où paraissent des cases d'un art sommaire, sommées d'énormes chignons de boue, traversés par des pieux.[29]

Indochina was thus perceived as more 'civilised' in the hierarchy of race and culture which French imperial ideology operated. As Reynaud had noted:

Le secret de la France, c'est d'être une mère généreuse et de ne distinguer entre ses enfants que par le mérite et les talents.[30]

Indochina was thus distinguished and favoured thanks to cultural relics which for several decades had remained outside French control.

The admiration and respect for Angkor was nevertheless unmatched by a similar respect for its ancestors. In keeping with views of pre-colonial Indochina expressed in official discourses of French colonialism, the Cambodian inheritors of Angkor were viewed as in decline. Many allusions to the magnificence of Angkor and the craftsmanship of its Khmer architects were shot through with sentiments which castigated contemporary Cambodians for its decline and degradation. The *décadence* of the Cambodian peoples served to reinforce the perceived necessity of colonial intervention.

Similarly, although this example of indigenous culture was ostensibly admired and respected, Angkor was simultaneously debased through commercialism. The temples featured in innumerable posters, advertisements and postcards. Angkor came to signify luxury, wealth, elegance: Lincoln cars, Gévelot cartridges, Frigéco refridgerators, Rollo and Cyma watches. Its sumptuousness turned back upon itself, and Angkor became a *produit publicitaire*. Its increasing presence in advertisements rendered it a commodity. Endlessly replicated at a series of metropolitan exhibitions, Angkor was divested of its religious and cultural significance and became part of the exhibition's *féerie*.

Furthermore, the reproduction of the Angkor temple at the exhibition was partial and deceptive. The large esplanade in front of the reconstruction of the Angkor temples was a point of concentration for parades and cortèges, and a meeting place for the hordes who gathered on the *jours de fêtes*. The reconstruction of the temples was intended to recreate 'l'impression de grandeur et de majesté que le visiteur éprouve à Angkor Vat'.[31] Reworked and remodelled by architects Blanche and Blanche to suit the needs of the exhibition organisers, the Angkor site was not in fact reproduced in its entirety. The scale of the other pavilions had been reduced in order that Angkor Wat dominate. The complex of temples was simplified to include only the the *massif central* of the site. This central spacing was surrounded by a gallery, which in Angkor itself surrounds all four sides of the site. The gallery was reshaped in such a way as to improve the spectator's view:

> Afin de permettre au public la vision directe du massif central, cette galerie dut être largement échancrée en devant dans l'axe du massif. Ainsi, l'escalier monumental qui escalade le soubassement fut visible de tous les points de la chausée, ce qui permit pendant les grandes fêtes de l'exposition d'y grouper d'imposantes et pittoresques figurations.[32]

Faithful reproduction and authenticity thus gave way to the more imperative needs of spectacle.

Angkor thus appears to take on the qualities of a fetish in the metropolitan imagination. A detached spot of intense visual focus, a material object cut off from the body (Indochina), indeed preferred to the body itself, Angkor becomes the signifier of an absent totality. This reading of the significance of Angkor draws attention to the ambiguous status of Indochina for the metropole which revolves around axes of absence/presence, desire/repudiation, recognition/disavowal. As Bhabha has noted of the colonial fetish or stereotype:

> Within discourse, the fetish represents the simultaneous play between metaphor as substitution (masking absence and difference) and metonymy (which contiguously registers the perceived lack). The fetish or stereotype gives access to an 'identity' which is predicated as much on mastery and pleasure as it is on anxiety and defence, for it is a form of multiple and contradictory belief in its recognition of difference and disavowal of it.[33]

The prominence of the temple of Angkor Wat at the *exposition*, epitomises the ambivalent and contradictory images and representations of Indochina which were prevalent in metropolitan France during this period. Angkor was possessed, admired, copied, and exhibited as desirable. It leant credence to the vision of Indochina as the *perle* of the French Empire. However, Angkor was equally used as a 'proof' of indigenous weakness. Its restoration under French mastery was used to reprimand and castigate its indigenous descendents. Used as a metaphor, Angkor demonstrated the prestige and value of indigenous Indochinese culture. It was a focus of Western admiration, thereby shortening distance and difference between European and non-European cultures. As metonymy, it functioned as a visible sign of indigenous chaos, disorder and passivity; as a sign of the benefit of French protection and development. It held before the indigenous populations, and the world at large, as a tangible monument to continued French colonial intervention.

Apart from this immense reconstruction of the temples of Angkor Wat, the remainder of the Indochinese section represented one-tenth of the whole exhibition. It included a central *palais*, 'pour l'exposition d'ensemble de la colonie';[34] a pavilion for each member of the *Union indochinoise*, and separate pavilions which covered administrative, economic, and historical aspects of the colony.

Two *pavillons d'Annam* recreated the Imperial Palace of Hué; Cambodia was represented by a scaled-down model of the *Musée Albert Sarraut* of Phnom Penh, inside of which a pagoda was built. The Cochinchina pavilion was decorated with contemporary Chinese art inspired by the buildings of Cholon.[35] Tonkin's pavilion was a reproduction of the Balny pagoda (situated near Hanoi), and had installed alongside it indigenous shops and stalls. Laos was represented by a village, comprising a pagoda containing a library and chapel, and an exibition pavilion of four *cases*. Three further buildings (*pavillons forestières*) mounted an exhibition of hunting, fishing and the forests of Indochina. Additionally, there was an Indochinese restaurant built in the style of the Chinese houses of Cochinchina;

Figure 13. Exposition coloniale de Vincennes 1931, Pavillon d'Annam

Figure 14. Exposition coloniale de Vincennes 1931, Pavillon du Cambodge

Figure 15. Exposition coloniale de Vincennes 1931, Pavillon de la Cochinchine

Figure 16. Exposition coloniale de Vincennes 1931, Section indochinoise

housing for the Cambodian dancers; and a *pavillon de la presse indochinoise et coloniale*, once more built after the Chinese style.[36] (Figures 13, 14, 15 and 16)

The following architectural imperatives were expressed by the exhibition's organisers:

> Tous les bâtiments de la section devant être essentiellement évocateurs du milieu indochinois et recréer pour ainsi dire l'ambience exotique, ce fut une obligation impérieuse de se conformer strictement, dans l'établissement des projets, aux types et aux règles de l'architecture locale.[37]

The above quotation employs terminology in which the competing projects of representation and authenticity are clearly at odds. Conformity to the rules of indigenous architecture is juxtaposed with the evocation of an ephemeral exotic atmosphere. What the *section indochinoise* in fact amounted to was remarkably similar to the results of French colonial urbanism: a transfigured vision of indigenous buildings which better conformed to French aesthetics.

Mannequins, 'reproduisant exactement les types ethniques',[38] and wearing traditional costumes were placed inside each pavilion; 'personnages' from the *Cour impériale* were grouped around the Emperor Khai Ding in the Annam pavilion; 'types populaires' were placed within the various rooms of the Cochinchinese pavilion; mandarins and notables populated the Tonkin pavilion.[39] A reconstruction of a Buddhist ceremony was created from drawings from the *Ecole d'Art*. Further visual stimuli were provided within each pavilion through the use of several different display techniques: *cartes lumineuses*, cinematographic films, dioramas, models, graphs and charts, paintings and drawings.

These attractive methods of display can be viewed as a *mise-en-scène*, or a staging of Indochina. Indeed, it was significant part of the exhibition's aim to seduce the visitor:

> Pour attirer les visiteurs et les retenir, il était indispensable de recourir à toutes les séductions du pittoresque et à la magie irrésistible de l'art.[40]

The 'spectacular' aspects of the exhibition, often referred to as 'la féerie de l'exposition', encouraged the fair-goer to position him/herself as a consumer. As Walter Benjamin's work shows, world-fairs and exhibitions such as the Vincennes extravaganza can be viewed as 'sites of pilgrimage to the commodity fetish'.[41] Indeed, the exhibition laid out a panoply of 'exotic' wares for both the literal and metaphorical consumption of the visitor.

The exhibits mounted in the *Palais central* were intended to display Indochina as a whole, and thus demonstrate the ways in which metropolitan France sought to represent Indochina, and also reveal perceptions of the nation's *oeuvre* in the colony. According to the exhibition's *Rapport général*,

L'Indochine devait apparaître, au milieu des colonies françaises et étrangères qui seraient représentées à l'Exposition comme un grand état moderne, avec l'ensemble de son organisation politique, la représentation exacte de sa puissance économique et le tableau complet de son activité sociale et intellectuelle.[42]

The exhibition's aim in relation to Indochina is clearly one of verisimilitude. The representation of Indochina is to be exact and complete, which was further reflected in the exhaustive inventory of articles exhibited. The terminology in the above quotation immediately illustrates the slippage, in the minds of the exhibition's organisers, between the antithetical concepts of representation and exactitude.

Throughout the exhibition, in both its visual artefacts and textual documentation, metropolitan representations of Indochina are posited not as simulacra, but as authentic and 'real'. Imagined, idealised and mythologised versions of Indochina and its indigenous populations were presented to visitors as authentic, unmitigated contexts and inhabitants. The exhibition therefore perpetuated and reinforced images and myths already partially implanted in the collective conscious of a metropolitan population through the popular press, exotic literature, and school manuals. The exhibition reinforced the political action of colonial France in creating the *Union indochinoise* by conflating image with political desire. In the grounds of the Parc de Vincennes, this constructed Indochinese identity became a visible and tangible reality for visitors.

The *Palais central* demonstrates metropolitan France's abiding concern within the context of the exhibition to pay constant homage to herself. Each of the Palais' sub-sections gives an overview of the ways in which official France chose to evoke aspects of colonial Indochina.

Economic policy: outillage économique, production

Four large galleries in the *Palais central* were given over to the evocation of the economic activity and success achieved in Indochina under French auspices. In the section on 'outillage économique', displays showed major public works, the development of rail and road networks; the improvement of the fluvial network; the creation of bridges, and hydraulics. An adjoining section evoked the work of *L'Inspection générale des services agricoles*: the use of raw materials, and alimentary production; progress in creating cultivable lands; the modernisation of agricultural methods and mechanical tools; the standardisation of Indochinese products. A further four rooms were devoted to Indochinese products: alimentary, textiles, and raw industrial materials. Modes of indigenous production were demonstrated alongside contrasting modern methods and techniques. Informative explanations and indications were situated above each exhibit, along with illustrative photographs, slides and dioramas.

The importance of the commercial and economic value to the metropole of this colony rich in natural resources was further emphasised by the inclusion of an entire section devoted to credit and banking services.

As in many of these subsidiary exhibitions, the idea of Indochina was evoked solely through the perceived 'benefits' that the colonising country had brought to the colony. Where indigenous techniques, tools or methods of production were demonstrated, it was in order to provide a compelling portrait of the intrinsic value of the modernising action of metropolitan France.

Tourism and transport

All the large rail, air, maritime and river navigation companies had installations within this pavilion.The ground floor of the building was completely taken over by a *diorama mouvant* which took the spectator on a voyage throughout Indochina: 'un merveilleux voyage, au décors toujours changeants, de France en Indochine, puis autour de l'Indochine, par le navire, la chaloupe, le train, l'automobile et l'avion'.[43] An immense touristic map detailed all the sites and monuments of interest to a Western visitor, indicating routes and hotels along the way.

It is interesting to note that a voyage through Indochina had France as its *point de départ*. Mirroring the mythologised departure for the colonies so often portrayed in the openings of colonial and exotic novels, this diorama rendered this familiar *topos* of popular literature more accessible and 'real'. Moreover, this exhibit can be viewed as a microcosm of the exhibition itself. While *l'expo* had as its slogan 'le tour du monde en un jour', the touristic diorama similarly extended to the visitor the opportunity to 'faire le tour d'Indochine en moins d'un jour'. This appropriative gesture transformed the visitor into a coloniser.

The forestry pavilion

This pavilion contained details, specimens, reproductions and images of local flora and fauna; portraits of various 'typical' landscapes, and traditional sampans and fishing vessels, which, according to the *Rapport général*, 'donnait une impression de vie réelle'.[44] Once more it becomes clear that the exhibition's organisers had complete faith in the role of mimetic displays to represent a colonial reality that was thought to be transparent and accessible. The principal curiosity, it appears, was

la reproduction d'un récif de corail, expédié pièce par pièce de la colonie, présenté en diorama, avec un premier plan donnant l'illusion parfaite de la masse d'eau qui, à marée haute, recouvre le récif.[45]

By expropriating natural phenomena and manipulating it through the use of techniques of spectacle, the organisers attempted to recreate the colony within the confines of the *Parc de Vincennes*. Moreover, the visual immediacy of this peculiar combination of illusion and authenticity operated in such a way as to subsume the 'real' under the fictitious. The 'reality' of Indochina was replaced by the transfiguring metropolitan vision of Indochina.

La Politique indigène

The inclusive and exhaustive ambitions of the exhibition were manifest once more in the administrative section, which was created in order to give the general public 'un aperçu très simple, mais très complet, de l'organisation de notre colonie'.[46] The respective administrative services were represented in schematised graphic charts: financial services, defence, customs and telegraphical services, the judiciary, the police, and *la garde indigène*.

The emphasis was once more placed upon a comparative vision of Indochina in which the indigenous practises of pre-colonial times were understood to be inadequate, subsumed as they were under the unmitigated glorification of metropolitan reorganisation and modification:

> Le public pouvait se rendre compte, en parcourant les galeries consacrées à l'oeuvre administrative, de l'évolution très sensible qu'elle a provoquée au point de vue politique et social.[47]

As metropolitan school manuals had done, the exhibition too tended to eclipse Indochinese history, which became subsumed under the more important task of evoking the action of imperial France.

La Salle historique

'Il suffisait, pour mesurer l'étendue de cette évolution, de parcourir la salle historique,' boasted the *Rapport général*, 'où l'on pouvait se rendre compte à la fois des étapes de l'influence française dans le passé et des grands faits de l'histoire des peuples de l'Indochine.'[48]

This section drew on an immense variety of sources in order to allow the visitor to 'revivre le passé de l'Indochine'. Not only were institutions such as the *Bibliothèque nationale, les Musées nationaux, l'Ecole des langues orientales, les Missions étrangères*, and the *Archives de guerre et de la Marine*, responsible for providing exhibits and information, but this section also drew upon personal collections, and the *témoignages* of representatives from the families of those who had played a significant role in the 'history' of the colony.[49] According to the *Rapport*, with their help

On a pu revivre le passé de l'Indochine et le souvenir de ceux qui ont été les précurseurs et les bons ouvriers de l'action française: missionnaires, soldats, voyageurs etc.[50]

These sources were, evidently, all of metropolitan French origin. Not only was the history of Indochina (as one might imagine, given that 'Indochina' had been imagined and constructed by the French) presented as beginning with the intervention of French explorers and missionaries, but more importantly, the origins of the separate countries of Vietnam, Cambodia and Laos were completely occluded.

By placing emphasis on the testament of explorers, travellers and soldiers (which itself formed the basis of the 'knowledge' classified and catalogued by institutions such as the *Ecole française d'Extrême-Orient*), this retrospective accorded legitimacy to the narratives of conquest and government mythologised in these popularised accounts. Indochina's was clearly a history which could be written by the French alone. Wresting from the indigenous populations their access to the writing of their own past, this exhibition reiterated that Indochina was a fixed space which came into being through the glorious actions of metropolitan explorers, missionaries, administrators and soldiers.

Exposition artistique et scientifique

This reconstitution of modern and contemporary history had a more anthropological focus, and was organised jointly by members of the *Ecole française d'Extrême-Orient* and the *Direction des Archives de l'Indochine*. French archeological work in Indochina made up the third part of this historical overview. Within this section was an ethnographical sub-section displaying skulls and fossils discovered in caves in Tonkin. These exhibits were further embellished with mannequins representing various races, which had been copied from photographs. They were dressed in traditional costumes and were surrounded by scaled-down models of their dwellings and tools. This 'science française', as it was termed in the *Rapport*, had enabled French 'savants' to cast 'quelques clartés sur le mystère qui les entoure [les races], à établir avec précision la chronologie de leur histoire, à retracer les formes successives de leurs civilisations'.[51]

Here too, the claim of French 'science' was the creation of Indochinese cultural history. The indigenous populations were 'reborn' and had their identity reinstated by French historians. Implicit in the absence of indigenous research in ethnography or archeology was the notion that these traces of the past could only be excavated, restored, studied and understood by metropolitan experts.

Oeuvres d'hygiène

This section celebrated the work of metropolitan institutions and organisations to eradicate disease in Indochina, with the three Indochinese branches of the Pasteur Institute taking pride of place. Displays informed visitors about the scientific study of tropical diseases, the preparation of serums and vaccines, and the creation of sanatoria and *stations climatiques*. Charts showed the extent and dispersal of diseases throughout Indochina. Tables revealed the progress made and results obtained in the metropolitan battle against disease. Dioramas showed the interiors of French-built hospitals, and graphic displays presented the 'progression constante des vaccinations contre la variole, le choléra, la peste etc.'.[52]

This scientific modernisation was sharply contrasted with 'backward' indigenous medicinal practises:

> Le contraste entre les méthodes de la science occidentale, avec son arsenal thérapeutique, et la médecine traditionnelle indigène était mis en lumière d'une façon pittoresque par l'installation de deux boutiques de médecins et pharmaciens sino-annamites.[53]

The indigenous pharmacies are relevant and interesting only in the sense that they provide a picturesque tableau for the Western viewer; their worth is neither a pharmacological nor a medical one. On the contrary, the reduction of indigenous medicine to an aesthetic object strips these exhibits of any professional status they might presume, and places metropolitan France, and the exhibition's visitors, in a superior and patriarchal role which communicates in a starkly visual way the inferiority of indigenous science.

Oeuvres d'enseignement

This section provided descriptions of the system of education put into place in Indochina since the arrival of French government.

> Le soin des esprits s'impose aux colonisateurs au même titre que le soin des corps. Aussi dès notre arrivée en Indochine avons-nous considéré l'éducation des races indigènes comme un de nos devoirs primordiaux.[54]

Scaled-down models depicted the school rebuilding programmes; graphics, statistics, and photographs demonstrated how the metropolitan system had been successfully adapted to Indochinese students; and a collection of students' *cahiers* 'permettaient de saisir la vie même de l'enseignement indochinois'.[55]

The benefits of metropolitan educative action is further eulogised in descriptions of a perceived 'renovation' of indigenous art:

Oeuvres d'art et d'inspiration coloniale : il est permis de dire qu'une part dans cette oeuvre de renaissance revient à l'influence des artistes français qui ont séjourné en Indochine, notamment aux boursiers de la colonie, qui, soit par leur enseignement à l'école, soit par les expositions de leurs oeuvres, n'ont pas manqué d'exercer une action sérieuse sur les jeunes artistes annamites.[56]

Not content with claiming control and authorship of Indochina's historical past, the exhibition extended its appropriating arms to the cultural traditions and heritage of the colony.

Les Oeuvres littéraires

A section entitled 'le livre indochinois' was intended to reveal to the metropolitan public 'la place que tient l'Indochine dans notre littérature'.[57] The section exhibited works by 'maîtres de la littérature française', and writers who resided in Indochina, but nowhere present was there the work of an indigenous author.[58] It was precisely during this period, however, that francophone indigenous writing had begun to flourish. The first indigenous creative works of fiction in French had appeared in 1913, and the first novel in French was published in 1921.[59] Indeed, 1930 marked the publication of a collaborative novel between a French writer and an Indochinese author: Truong Dinh Tri, with Albert de Teneuille, published the novel *Ba-Dam*, in Paris.[60] This silencing of the indigenous author allowed metropolitan writers to devise and portray an uncontested image of the colony. Metropolitan writing was to write not only from the colony, but also for the colony.

Les Figurants

The *délégation indigène* from Indochina comprised 409 people of whom 250 belonged to the military contingent (a detachment of *tirailleurs indochinois* stationed in France). According to the *Rapport*, these representatives were made up of 'les types les plus variés et caractéristiques de la société villageoise'.[61] The indigenous *figurants* were, however, not strictly participants in the exhibition in that they functioned as objects to be viewed rather than as actors, agents and the equals of the metropolitan visitors. Alongside the inanimate exhibits, they thus became another part of the *grand spectacle*.

The theatrical aspect of the Indochinese section comprised the music of the *Garde indigène*, the Cambodian ballet, the Laotian ballet and the Cochinchinese theatre. (Figure 17) The Cambodian ballet had already appeared twice, to great acclaim, in metropolitan France (Marseille 1906, and Paris 1922).[62] Of the dancers it was reported that:

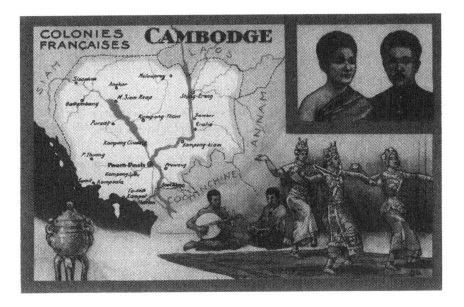

Figure 17. Postcard illustrating Cambodian dancers

Le répertoire avait été soigneusement établi et les pièces interminables dont la représentation dure plusieurs jours à Phnom Penh, avaient fait l'objet d'une sélection, ne laissant subsister que les thèmes principaux et les scènes essentielles reliés par un argument facile à communiquer aux spectateurs étrangers.[63]

The metropolitan audiences were thus presented with a travesty of Cambodian dance. What they witnessed was a carefully edited version of the original, made palatable, comprehensible and containable by French overseers. Similarly, the 'authenticity' of the music provided by the daily concerts of the *Garde indigène* is open to question. It was 'created' by Governor General Pasquier (*Résident supérieur* in Hué), and the musicians were directed by a *chef français* (Maurice Fournier).

All these spectacles were presented to the metropolitan public as authentic examples of indigenous art, culture and lifestyle. In fact, all the original elements had been reworked by French leaders: choreographers, artistic directors, conductors. They represented not 'traditional indigenous culture', but rather reflect the imposition of a metropolitan system of values.

The metropolitan visitors were firmly placed in a voyeuristic and vicarious position. Pastoral scenes, and evocations of everyday indigenous life were fixed and framed for the consumption of the visitor. The Laotians, for example,

qui venaient faire leurs dévotions à la pagode lui fournissaient une figuration vivante des plus pittoresques.[64]

The *Guide officiel* reinforced this subject/object dichotomy between Western fair-goers and indigenous *figurants*:

Penchez-vous sur leur oeuvre. Regardez-les agir. Ecoutez leur chants et leur musique, goûtez aussi des mets nationaux qu'ils vous offrent pour un prix facile.[65]

Along with their music, dance, even food, the Indochinese populations were classified and exhibited as objects.

The indigenous populations were framed by the metropolitan view. As the following quotation demonstrates, the image of Indochina and its inhabitants which the exhibition produced was intended to inform the metropolitan public and provide the visitors with a definitive and unified portrayal of France's Indochinese empire:

Il est incontestable que les Indochinois retireront un profit réel des grandes assises de Vincennes. Ils en sortent mieux connus et mieux appréciés par l'opinion métropolitaine.[66]

The importance of the exhibition for the Indochinese participants was thus evaluated according to a schema of metropolitan knowledge. The scopic desires of metropolitan exhibition-goers are viewed as conferring status upon the indigenous populations of Indochina:

Tous les Français de la Métropole avec qui ils ont été en contact ont été frappés, non seulement par leur instruction générale et leur connaissance de notre langue et de notre culture, mais par la clarté de leurs idées, de leur esprit pratique, leur conception de notre rôle colonisateur, leur désir sincère de collaboration.[67]

This desire to gaze, and therefore know, remains circumscribed by the disciplinary nature of the Franco-Indochinese colonial relationship. Metropolitan opinions concerning the Indochinese hinged upon indigenous acceptance and complicity in French colonialism. Metropolitan approbation remained predicated upon indigenous ability to assimilate French culture and practices.

Indochina figured in the exhibition as a site of ambivalence. Lauded as an advanced society and a worthy recipient of French colonial action, the goal of continued French rule was only possible if this image were tempered with a simultaneous view of Indochina as chaotic and weak, a needy inferior clamouring for French intervention and aid.

These dual narratives of success/disaster, value/ambivalence are repeated in the visual discourses of the exhibition. The *Exposition coloniale de Vincennes* demonstrates the importance of Indochina to the French nation and empire. Brought out of the shadow of Britain's 'jewel', France's *perle* was *mise en relief*, framed by, and overshadowing the nation's other colonial possessions. Central to Indochina's special status was Angkor Wat, a marvel unrivalled by the architectural features of any of France's other colonial possessions. Indeed, this special status functioned as a feature, a weapon even, in ongoing French imperial rivalry with Great Britain. A symbol of France's strong presence in Asia, Angkor served to underline French prestige, and confirmed its international status as an equal player alongside the greatest imperial power in the world.

As a symbol of French ideals of protection and *mise en valeur*, Angkor Wat nevertheless also functioned as proof of metropolitan superiority over decadent and inferior native populations. The 'special place' Indochina was accorded at the exhibition is nonetheless undermined by discourses which deny its very specificity and tend towards a blurring of the diversity of the respective colonies by conflating all the component parts of the French Empire.

The exhibition thus reveals the ambivalence with which the colony was viewed. Displayed to advantage and held up for admiration, Indochina was nonetheless debased and commodified, its populations simultaneously applauded and reprimanded. The spectacle of otherness, amply demonstrated by the *Exposition coloniale*, reveals the double-faced ambivalence of French colonial discourses in relation to Indochina.

Admiration for Indochinese culture thus nevertheless remained at odds with colonial discourses which emphasised Indochina's inferiority to her colonial protectors. Although within the context of the *exposition*, it was hoped that Indochina would appear as 'une métropole seconde, foyer d'influence française, poste avancé de notre commerce et de notre industrie',[68] although it was simultaneously necessary to temper this vision of technological and commercial success with an ominous portent of Indochina if bereft of French involvement. The exhibition thus reiterated the dual narrative of success and disaster in its vision of Indochina.

Notes

1. Notable others include *l'Exposition Coloniale de Marseille*, 1922; *l'Exposition générale du centenaire de la conquête d'Algérie*, 1930; *le Salon de la France d'outre-mer*, 1933; *l'Exposition du tricentenaire du rattachement des Antilles à la France*, 1935; *le Quarantenaire de la conquête de Madagascar*, 1935.
2. Britain excused itself on the grounds that it was still paying off the debt incurred through the staging of the British Empire Exhibition of 1924.

3. *Rapport général*, vol. 1 (Paris: Imprimerie nationale, 1932–5), p. 340.
4. Ibid.
5. 'Je suis convaincu que l'exposition peut etre un grand facteur de paix sociale dans cette region de Paris', quoted in Hodeir, C., and Pierre, M., *L'Exposition coloniale* (Brussels: Editions complexe, 1991), p. 26.
6. Ibid.
7. *Le Temps*, 6 January 1931.
8. Coquery-Vidrovitch, C., in Tobie et al, *Histoire de la France coloniale 1914–1990* (Paris: Armand Colin, 1990), p. 214.
9. Reynaud, P., *L'Empire français* (discours prononcé à l'inauguration de l'Exposition coloniale), (Paris: Guillemot et Lamothe, [n.d.]), p. 19.
10. Its architects were Jaussely and Laprade.
11. *Rapport général*, vol. 2, p. 68.
12. Ibid., p. 68.
13. *Rapport général*, vol. 5 (i), 'Les Sections coloniales', p. 9.
14. Ibid.
15. Ibid.
16. Norindr, P., 'Representing Indochina: the French colonial fantasmatic and the Exposition Coloniale de Paris', in *French Cultural Studies*, vi, February 1995, p. 37.
17. For a more detailed overview of exhibits relating to territories other than Indochina, see Hodeir, C., and Pierre, M., *L'Exposition coloniale*.
18. For a full description of the site see Dagens, B., *Angkor: la forêt de pierre* (Paris: Gallimard, 1989).
19. A major exhibition, 'Angkor et dix siècles d'art khmer', took place in Paris as recently as February-May 1997. It is interesting to note that although this exhibition alluded frequently to the work of the EFEO in Cambodia, no mention was made of the fact that the country had been a part of the French Indochinese Empire. The language of the 1997 exhibition nevertheless remained remarkably similar to that used during the period of French colonisation, particularly in its insistence on the date of the 'discovery' of the Bantreay Srei temple as 1914.
20. Mouhot, H., *Voyages dans les royaumes de Siam, de Cambodge et de Laos* (Paris: Binbliothèque rose, 1868), (repr. Genève: Olizane, 1989).
21. Charles Bouillevaux, a French missionary, had in fact visited the temples several years before, in the 1850s. For an interesting discussion of the way in which the 'discovery' of Angkor was appropriated by the French media, see Barnett, A., "Cambodia will never disappear", *New Left Review*, no. 180, 1990, pp. 101–25.
22. Malraux, A., *La Voie Royale* (Paris: Grasset, 1930); Loti, P., *Un Pèlerin d'Angkor* (Paris: Calmann-Lévy, 1912)(repr. Paris: Kailash, 1994); Claudel,

P., *Oeuvres complètes de Paul Claudel: Tome 4, Extrême-Orient* (Paris: Gallimard, 1952); Groslier, G., *A l'Ombre d'Angkor* (Paris: Emile Paul, 1916); Dorgelès, R., *La Route mandarine* (Paris: Albin Michel, 1925), (repr. Paris: Kailash, 1994).

23. See Dagens, *Angkor: la forêt de pierre*, p. 85. See also Daney, C., 'Angkor au bois dormant', *Histoire*, special issue, 'Le Temps des colonies', no. 69, 1984, pp. 37–9.

24. Loti, P., *Un Pèlerin d'Angkor* (Paris: Calmann-Levy, 1912), p. 73.

25. *Rapport général*, vol. 2, p. 110.

26. Coquery-Vidrovitch, in Tobie et al, *Histoire de la France coloniale 1914-1990*, p. 117.

27. Farrère, C., 'Angkor et l'Indochine', *L'Illustration*, Album hors série sur l'Exposition coloniale, no. 4603, 23 May 1931.

28. Reynaud, *L'Empire français*, p. 25.

29. Quoted by Hodeir and Pierre, *L'Exposition coloniale*, p. 44.

30. Reynaud, *L'Empire français*, p. 29.

31. *Rapport général*, vol. 5 (ii), p. 670.

32. Ibid.

33. Bhabha, H., 'Difference, Discrimination and the Discourse of Colonialism', pp. 194-211, in Barker, F., et al, *The Politics of Theory* (Colchester: Essex Conference of the Sociology of Literature, 1982), p. 202.

34. *Rapport général*, vol. 5 (ii), p. 658.

35. Cholon is the name of the Chinese commercial district within the city of Saigon.

36. These details are laid out in the *Rapport général*, vol 2.

37. *Rapport général*, vol. 5 (ii), p. 670.

38. Ibid., p. 691.

39. Ibid.

40. de Beauplan, R., 'Les Palais de l'Indochine', *Illustration*, no. 4612, juillet 1931 (pages non-numérotées).

41. Benjamin, W., 'Paris, Capital of the Nineteenth-century', *Reflections* (New York: Schocken, 1976), p. 152.

42. *Rapport général*, vol. 5 (ii), p. 660.

43. *Rapport général*, vol. 6 (i), p. 698.

44. Ibid., p. 699.

45. Ibid.

46. Ibid., p. 700.

47. Ibid.

48. Ibid.

49. Representatives from the Garnier, Chasseloup-Laubat, Pavie, and Delaporte families.

50. *Rapport général*, vol. 6 (i), p. 701.
51. Ibid., p. 702.
52. Ibid,. p. 704.
53. Ibid.
54. Ibid., p. 705.
55. Ibid., p. 706.
56. Ibid., p. 709.
57. Ibid., p. 710.
58. For a detailed account of indigenous literature in French, see Yeager, J., *The Vietnamese Novel in French; a Literary Response to Colonialism* (Hanover: University Press of New England, 1987).
59. Nguyen, P., *Le Roman de Mademoiselle Lys* (Hanoi: L'Imprimerie tonkinoise, 1921).
60. *Ba-Dam* (Paris: Fasquelle, 1930).
61. *Rapport général*, vol 5 (ii), p. 720.
62. The Cambodian ballet was also the subject of a series of sketches by Rodin, who followed the company on their tour of France in the 1920s. See Dagens, *Angkor: la forêt de pierre*, p. 81.
63. *Rapport général*, vol. 5 (ii), p. 725.
64. *Rapport général*, vol. 6 (i), p. 717.
65. Demaison, A., *L'Exposition coloniale internationale 1931 Guide officiel* (Paris: Mayeux, 1931), p. 20.
66. Ibid.
67. *Rapport général*, vol. 5 (ii), p. 750.
68. Demaison, *L'Exposition coloniale internationale 1931 Guide officiel*, p. 20.

5

Rebellion and Uprising in Indochina: Responses from France

As we have seen, France had attempted to construct a coherent, stable and homogenising image of both Indochina, and of its own role in this South-East Asian empire. French faith in these images was put to the test in the 1930s, when rebellion and anti-French sentiment in Indochina reached a peak, and when critical views of French colonial rule in Indochina began to emerge. The growing troubles in Indochina provoked an unprecedented inquest into French colonialism, and provided perhaps the sternest test of the nation's belief in its colonial doctrine. The nation's colonial management of Indochina was metaphorically put on trial.

During the inter-war years, very few groups or individuals expressed the desire to see the colonial system entirely overthrown. For the most part, critics of colonialism questioned the system's application rather than the system itself. Having, ostensibly at least, rejected the disciplinary assimilationist approach to colonial rule, the majority of French colonial administrators felt confident that the associationist policies they were implementing in the colonies demonstrated a reformist disposition, and a colonial policy of cooperation rather than domination. As previous chapters have shown, the inter-war years were marked by a firmly held belief in France's 'humanisme colonial'. Furthermore, and especially following the First World War, the crucial financial contribution of the colonies to the national war effort, and the participation of colonial troops in the salvation of the Motherland made it difficult for a weakened France not to cling to the notion that it was the possession of a vast colonial Empire which provided the nation with a sense of international prestige and grandeur.

Although the *Ligue contre l'Oppression Coloniale et l'Impérialisme* had been founded in Brussels in 1927, the movement broke up after only a few years: its actions were curtailed by the rise of Fascism, and its members were divided over policy. While its communist members had pushed for a global condemnation of colonialism, and envisaged involving the *Ligue* in revolutionary action, its non-communist associates were simply interested in guarding against the system's excesses and abuses. Criticism of colonialism as a system during this period in metropolitan France was almost exclusively the preserve of the *Parti communiste français* (PCF), and individuals associated with the Surrealist movement.

The PCF's most ferocious attacks on French colonial policy began in response to the bloody oppression of the Rif War,[1] and reached new heights over the repression in Indochina following the Yen Bay uprising. The anti-imperial struggle was to remain one of the main objectives of the Communists until 1935, when the changes in world politics brought the party a more immediately menacing enemy in the shape of Fascism. Furthermore, the PCF's violent attacks on French colonial policy were abandoned in favour of maintaining unity once the *Front populaire* came to power in 1936.

The Communist stand against the oppression of the indigenous 'proletariat' was echoed in 1931 by members of the Surrealist movement.[2] Mounting an attack on the *Exposition coloniale de Vincennes*, they attempted to organise a counter exhibition[3] which was intended to draw custom away from the main exhibition.[4] It is a measure of the predominance and pervasiveness of the colonial ideal propagated by the *parti colonial* in the 1930s, and of the irresistible attraction of the *Exposition coloniale* itself, that the counter exhibition received fewer than 2,500 visitors as opposed to the eight million who attended the Vincennes extravaganza.

André Malraux might be viewed by some as the most constant critic of French colonialism in Indochina. However, his journalism was published exclusively within Indochina and therefore had little or no effect upon dominant colonial or anti-colonial sentiment in the metropole. Writing on Paul Monin's newspaper *L'Indochine*[5] from 1925, Malraux endeavoured to expose corruption within the colonial administration and to encourage Franco-Indochinese *rapprochement* and reconciliation.[6] As Raymond has noted, Malraux's criticism of the colonial situation in Indochina was 'fired by an idealistic passion rather than an ideologically defined set of convictions'.[7] Like many of his period, Malraux's critical view of colonial government in Indochina remained circumscribed by a strong belief that to discard colonialism would be to deprive the indigenous populations of Indochina of their 'opportunity of acquiring the identity to be found in that great cultural, supra-national polity whose centre was France'.[8]

During the inter-war years anti-colonial thought in metropolitan France was thus limited to a small section of the political community. Many of the most vehement and committed voices raised against France's colonial 'vocation' were those of relatively marginal figures. However, although the colonial exhibition of 1931 provided the most confident assertion of the perceived rectitude of France's colonial mission, there were nonetheless signs that all was not well in the Empire. In Indochina, economic hardship and recession had gradually led to growing discontent and dissatisfaction amongst the indigenous populations, which found expression in a series of revolts and rebellions. Nationalist movements in Indochina, it seemed, were becoming more organised; and the growing elite of French-educated Indochinese appeared to be turning the Republic's own legacy of revolutionary principles against France itself. Suddenly it seemed, a vision of unruly natives had begun to provide a counterpoint to the positive images of placid, docile and complicit natives disseminated by official France.

The late 1920s and early 1930s saw an increase in literary output which expressed a growing concern and unease with the situation in Indochina.[9] These works, which prefigure the texts which are the main focus of this chapter, acted as something of a corrective to the official version of France's role in, and relationship with, Indochina. In 1925, Roland Dorgelès had begun to question this view: in his *Sur la route mandarine*, he examined the contradictions which had begun to become apparent between the metropole's colonial 'ideal' and the state of justice, development and capitalist exploitation in the colony.[10] Similarly, in *Les Jauniers*, Paul Monet perceived the contradiction between what he witnessed, and the ideal proclaimed by official organisms in the metropole, but concluded finally with an acceptance of those contradictions.[11] In spite of his lucid accounts of colonial mismanagement and ill-treatment of the native workforce, he believed that conflict between action and ideal could be resolved through a return to that very ideal. Monet expressed a pragmatic view of the colonial situation in Indochina. He believed wholeheartedly in the French justice system, and believed that unjust practices could, and would, be remedied in favour of the indigenous populations. Luc Durtain's influential account of his visit to Indochina, *Dieux blancs, hommes jaunes*, encapsulates his critical stance in its very title. Denouncing the way in which the native workforce were treated by their French masters, Durtain produced a compelling portrait of colonial malpractice and exploitation in Indochina.[12] These often jaundiced portrayals of the Franco-Indochinese relationship of the late 1920s and early 1930s started to alert the metropolitan public to the worsening situation in Indochina, and prefigured the types of criticism which were to emerge just a few years later. For in 1930, as the mainland was gearing up to staging its greatest colonial extravaganza the following year, it was Indochina, France's showcase colony, which threatened to overturn the applecart and reveal an altogether different face of French colonialism.

These worrying developments in 1920s Indochina did not however prepare opinion in the mainland for what was the most serious rebellion in Franco-Indochinese history: the Yen Bay uprising of 9-10 February 1930. While the mainland was celebrating its colonial *génie* at the 1931 colonial exhibition, Indochina was still suffering the after-shock of the Yen Bay uprising. While partisans of French colonialism were congratulating themselves on the generous, humanitarian and benevolent doctrine which the metropole had developed vis-à-vis its colonised peoples, the Indochinese were being submitted to probably the most severe repression the territory had yet seen under French rule.[13]

The uprising itself occurred when the Vietnamese nationalist movement (VNQDD – Viet Nam Quoc Dan Dang) attacked the French garrison post at Yen Bay. Joined by a significant number of indigenous troops stationed there, they seized the arms depot and killed a number of French officers.[14] Although the uprising was part of a series of rebellions, demonstrations, attacks and protests, the fact that French officers were killed in number called for a show of strength on the part of the colonial authorities. Eighty-three indigenous 'rebels' were sentenced to death, thirteen of whom were guillotined in June 1930 after a distinctly undemocratic trial.[15] The French air force pursued sympathisers into the surrounding country, indiscriminately bombing assembled crowds and 'suspect' villages.

Reports of the uprising and its suppression led to a renewed interest in travel journalism, as writers hastened to Indochina to investigate the situation which had led to such a shocking reversal of the official vision of the Franco-Indochinese relationship. Louis Roubaud, having worked for some time as the colonial correspondent for *Le Petit Parisien*, travelled to Indochina in the wake of the uprising in order to assess the extent of nationalist sentiment in Vietnam and to interview some of the movement's leaders; to discover whether these nascent movements had come under the influence of communism (as was being suggested in press reporting in the mainland): his *Vietnam: la tragédie indochinoise* was published in 1930.[16] Andrée Viollis visited Indochina in the last three months of 1931, as a journalist attached to Paul Reynaud's entourage. On her return, extracts from her travel diaries were published in the left-leaning journal *Esprit*, and were then collected in a single volume entitled: *SOS Indochine*.[17]

Reports of the uprising and the manner of its repression had clearly shocked contemporary commentators. As Roubaud noted in the introduction to *Vietnam: la tragédie indochinoise*:

> Que se passait-il? Rien, absolument rien, n'avait pu faire pressentir à l'opinion métropolitaine de pareils événements.[18]

This vision of French colonialism, which pitted disaffected natives against merciless European masters, was not easily reconciled to the notions of 'devoir', 'responsabilité' and 'solidarité fraternelle', which were being expounded by all of French colonialism's major apologists. Reports of the repressive action of the French colonial administration in Indochina undermined accepted notions of French colonialism as enlightened, benevolent and humanitarian, gratefully embraced by a loyal, subject people.

Moreover, news of the repression in Indochina had acted as a catalyst for protest on the part of Indochinese students in Paris. Indochina's problems, it seemed, were being played out in the mainland, much to the consternation of a puzzled public. Inaugurating the *Maison de l'Indochine* at the *Cité universitaire*, Gaston Doumergue (President) was heckled with cries of 'Libérez les prisonniers de Yen Bay'. Applications for places were retracted by the students, and tracts distributed:

Vous ne vous laisserez pas fasciner par la somptuosité de la maison indochinoise. Vous vous méfierez de cette philanthropie coloniale . . . Vous n'accepterez rien de ceux qui nous exploitent . . . Dénonçons toutes les amitiés hypocrites . . . Combattons toutes les tentatives de corruption! Adoptons pour mot d'ordre le boycottage de la Maison des étudiants de l'Indochine.[19]

If the image of the Yen Bay mutineers had seemed distant and perhaps largely unconnected to the mainland, here those Indochinese who had most benefitted from France's cultural 'generosity' were displaying an unprecedented lack of gratitude, and using the metropolitan capital as their stage. What did this emerging elite find to support in the nationalist protests? The disjunction between official images of Indochina, and the seeming reality of anti-French sentiment in Indochina, was all the more shocking when it was played out visibly in this way in the mainland.

Félicien Challaye's dismay over events at Yen Bay, (which prompted his re-publication of his travel diaries containing a reassessment of his views of French colonialism) reveals the extent to which the official rhetoric of French colonialism was the dominant and most widely accepted version of France's colonial history:

je croyais naïvement ce qu'on m'avait enseigné dans les écoles de la République. Je croyais que la colonisation est une entreprise humanitaire, destinée à faire progresser des peuples de race inférieure au contact de la civilisation blanche. Je croyais que ces peuples arriérés sollicitent le secours des blancs, et qu'ils leur sont reconnaissants de cette aide dévouée. Je croyais que la France est la plus bienveillante de toutes les puissances colonisatrices et que le loyalisme de ses sujets témoigne de leur gratitude.[20]

Furthermore, images of the indigenous populations which had been prevalent until this uprising did not equate with the representation of these 'rebels' as fanatical nationalists opposed to French rule. The Indochinese had often been represented as model colonial subjects. At the *Exposition coloniale de Vincennes*, the Indo-chinese *figurants* had been viewed as placid and docile, willing collaborators in French colonial rule. In the exhibition's posters, they were represented as hardworking and industrious. Reports from Yen Bay effectively shattered these comforting views.

It is therefore at this period in the Franco-Indochinese relationship that one might legitimately expect to discern a *remise en cause* of the principles of French colonialism in Indochina. Indeed, these writers have been viewed by critics as representative of a burgeoning anti-colonial voice in France.[21] However, my purpose here is to contend that although at times critical of the colonial administra-tions in Indochina, the conclusions these writers draw more often than not underwrite and reinforce the colonial rhetoric and ambitions of the period. I will argue that although critical of certain colonial practices in Indochina, these texts helped to perpetuate the strong sense of France's *mission civilisatrice* in Indochina.

Although initially reluctant to believe that the repressive and inhumane reaction of the French colonial authorities to the Yen Bay uprising was anything more than a singular aberration, the writers who travelled to Indochina in the early 1930s were steadily bombarded with indications and attestations to the contrary.[22] A large proportion of Challaye's, Viollis' and Roubaud's work is taken up with 'revelations' of colonial abuses: the torture of political prisoners, the failures of the French rice distribution networks, press censorship and so on. All three writers report sympathetically on the demands of the indigenous peoples, adopting a reformist attitude towards the problems in Indochina.

Their sympathetic views are nonetheless deeply marked by fundamental principles of colonial ideology. One of the most noticeable examples of this tendency is revealed in the proliferation of anecdotes which relate instances where Vietnamese 'de bonne famille' have been humiliated or insulted by French settlers in Indochina. Although Viollis advocates equality between coloniser and colonised,[23] it becomes clear that this equality is desirable only between peoples judged to belong to the same social class. Discussing young Vietnamese students who had returned from school in France, she says:

> en France ils étaient traités en égaux par des hommes éminents: ici des fonctionnaires sans éducation ni culture font aucune différence entre les Annamites de bonne famille, instruits, et les boys qu'ils traitent Dieu ne sait comment.[24]

Viollis thus suggests that a hierarchy of cooperation, based on class, should operate between the French and indigenous populations.

Her concept of 'equality' is reminiscent of the hierarchy of humanity which was a fundamental tenet of colonial ideology. This system of classification graded populations between the two poles of civilisation and savagery, and served to demonstrate the fundamental justice of the colonial enterprise by ranking peoples according to their relative degree of technical, political or cultural sophistication as seen from a European point of view. Operating this same principle Challaye can allow himself to react sympathetically to the Vietnamese, who rank, for him, relatively high in this evolutionary scale:

> Or ce peuple d'une intelligence si fine, d'une sensibilité si délicate, d'une civilisation si avancée, les Français d'Indochine le traitent aussi mal qu'ils auraient traité n'importe quelle peuplade nègre du centre de l'Afrique.[25]

Thus although at times critical of colonial policy in Indochina (Viollis in particular is scathing towards Paul Reynaud who refused to raise the problems of

rice distribution and the amnesty of political prisoners before the *Parlement*),[26] these documents cannot be viewed as political tracts against colonisation. For the most part, the critical views of French colonial policy in Indochina expressed in these texts remain circumscribed by the cultural assumption that the legacy of French civilisation was of intrinsic value, but that its colonial heirs had betrayed it.

The ideals of French colonialism represented in the official texts of the colonial exhibition and by writers such as Sarraut appear to have reflected (and exerted) a pervading influence on attitudes towards French colonialism. Not only were Roubaud and Viollis reluctant to shed this image of benevolent colonialism, but when provided with proof to the contrary they sought not to denounce the principle of colonialism (Viollis says: 'je ne veux pas discuter ici le principe de la colonisation. Il est ce qu'il est'),[27] but to point to the corruption of that perfect ideal.

The discovery that colonial rule in Indochina was not always managed according to the principles of human solidarity, paternal protection and nurturing enlightenement was mitigated by the adoption of a view which asserted that in the past, French colonial policy had been exemplary. Disappointment was thus transformed into nostalgia for a lost, glorious past.

Former relations between France and Indochina, which were never more specifically dated than 'autrefois', or 'avant', began to assume a paradigmatic status in these texts. This vague and utopian notion of the past was held up as an archetype of 'good' colonialism, which had to be recuperated. Thus, visiting Thanh-Hoa, Viollis remarked on the French-built dam which had allowed the surrounding area to be irrigated:

> Voilà du beau travail. Aussi la région ne souffre-t-elle pas de famines comparables à celle de la province de Vinh, et n'y parle-t-on point de troubles. Pourquoi avant tant d'autres dépenses inutiles, ne pas poursuivre cette oeuvre indispensable et l'étendre à d'autres provinces?[28]

This comment not only oversimplifies the causes of the 'troubles' in a particularly patronising way, but also reveals a specific notion of the type of French colonialism which Viollis admired and hoped to see re-established in Indochina. This notion encompassed the same themes which dominated the Colonial Exhibition: economic and moral progress, the channelling of colonial 'energy' into visibly successful projects which would be objects of national pride, and symbols of French prestige.

Viollis' vision was one of benevolent pastoralism: she envisaged an ideal of domestic order and tranquillity which had been brought about by the thoughtful application of European technology to an impoverished people. The Pasteur Institute in Indochina was cited as another example of 'good' colonialism: its 'admirable travail' was, however, thwarted by colonial administrators who viewed

the Institute's work in terms of manufacturing profit and loss. Viollis thus quotes a doctor from the Institute:

> Les autorités ne comprennent et ne secondent pas toujours nos efforts, me dit l'un d'eux en souriant. Comme nous voulions envoyer une mission dans une région particulièrement impaludée: 'Pourquoi faire?' nous répondit ingénument un grand chef. 'Il n'y a dans ce district ni usines, ni plantations'.[29]

Viollis articulates the clash between the economic reality of colonialism and her own ideological faith through a 'them' and 'us' opposition ('les autorités', 'un grand chef'), which attributes the nefarious effects of colonialism to the capitalist and individualist forces of the modern era. The old 'human' relationship between coloniser and colonised has, for Viollis, been debased by materialism. She resolves the evident conflict through the myth of 'autrefois': visiting a small French enclave in Southern India, Viollis notes that the natives 'nous témoignent (. . .) une véritable sympathie . . . preuve que notre ancienne méthode coloniale de coopération n'était pas si mauvaise'.[30]

Throughout these texts, former relationships between colonised and coloniser are viewed as exemplifying 'entente', 'coopération' and 'compréhension'. Viollis uses the words of a former *résidant* of Laos to indicate the harmony that previously existed between the French and the Indochinese:

> Autrefois nous voyagions à cheval dans les sentiers de la brousse: nous descendions le soir dans les villages, et, reçus par les notables, nous arrivions à nous comprendre mutuellement, à nous estimer. Depuis le règne de l'auto, les administrateurs passent en trombe sur les grandes routes, devant des dos courbés par le respect. Ils ignorent tout ce qui se passe dans leur district. Nous étions des pionniers, presque des explorateurs. Eux, ce sont des bureaucrates.[31]

Former colonial administrations are here viewed as sustaining solidarity between colonised and coloniser, thus allowing a harmonious order to prevail. The past compliance of the colonised (in contrast with their present rebelliousness) is presented as affirming a familial bond between France and Indochina, whilst it is implied that the current troubles have been provoked by the disintegration of the familial order.

Viollis thus reproduces a romantic narrative which plays upon a myth of social integrity and harmony, and regrets the destruction of a proto-social community. She contrasts a pastoral simplicity with urban bureaucracy through the emblematisation of the modes of transport preferred in each era. Although, ideologically, France was expounding ideas of progress, writers such as Viollis seemed to advocate a return to a pre-modern era, in which the distinct power structures are more reminiscent of a feudal model. The myth of *autrefois* would thus appear to represent French Indochina as the last outpost in which aristocratic values survived. The *colon*, innately superior by birth, nationality and class, commanded immediate respect from his underlings through his very bearing and demeanour.

In the above quotations, it begins to become clear that if this 'golden age' of French colonialism has disappeared, then it is the new settler community who are to blame for its disappearance. Portrayals of an undesirable 'new style' of colonial administrator are taken up with alacrity in the texts under discussion. Viollis, for example, quotes the *Chef de la Sûrêté* in Annam:

> Tous ces troubles, d'Annam, dit-il, sont dus à l'incroyable négligence, à la nullité du personnel des services civils (. . .) au lieu d'envoyer dans les pays en fermentation des hommes de valeur et d'expérience, qui ont fait leurs armes et leurs preuves dans des services où ils ont été en contact avec les indigènes – des fonctionnaires des douanes, des ponts-et-chaussées, des docteurs, des ingénieurs etc. – on nomme des jeunes gens, frais émoulus de l'Ecole Coloniale. Ils sont vaniteux, satisfaits de leurs connaissances toutes théoriques, uniquement préoccupés de leur confort: glace, ventilateurs, boys. Ils ne font que rarement des tournées et négligent à ce point leurs devoirs que certains villages passent quinze ans, vingt ans sans avoir jamais vu un seul Français. (. . .) Ces administrateurs savent même pas l'annamite.[32]

In the above quotation, activity is contrasted with passivity; theory with practice; a consumerist, egotistical and feminised society with a pioneering, selfless and masculinised one. It praises the warrior-like qualities of an elite male order ('des hommes de valeur et d'expérience, qui ont fait leurs armes et leurs preuves'), contrasting this mythical, almost chivalric, fraternal community with a feminised bureaucracy. It reveals preoccupations which emerged from the conflicting perceptions of the colonial settler seen in the exhibition rhetoric: the need for the dissuasive power of a forceful masculine presence, but the hope that indigenous peoples would simply accept and comply with this situation rather than testing French authority.

In Laos, Viollis comes across yet more administrators who fail to meet the exacting standards of *autrefois*:

> Nous nous arrêtons dans quelques résidences. Je suis stupéfaite par les propos de table de certains administrateurs, leur égoïsme, leur puérilité. Il n'est question que d'avancement, d'indemnités, de retour en France, de ragots. Est-ce possible? Ces gens sont-ils aveugles? N'ont-ils aucun souci de leur devoir, ni des problèmes qui se posent ici?[33]

In both quotations a distinction is made between the maturity of the old-style colonial administrator and the puerility or immaturity of their younger counterparts. Given the tendency to view the colonial relationship in terms of gendered roles, it appears that Viollis and her interviewees are lamenting the disappearance of the hierarchy which distinguished the 'parent' country from the 'child' colony. French and Indochinese appeared to cooperate because the distance between the two communities was clearly demarcated, and hierarchy was immediate. The immaturity of the colonial officials now in office in Indochina allows the indigenous population to shorten the distance separating colonised and coloniser; the superiority of the French, which justified their continued presence in Indochina, is no longer immediately apparent.

Further descriptions of members of the newer settler community highlight an anxiety that distance and hierarchy between coloniser and colonised are not being maintained. Roubaud, for example, regrets that the colony has become a sort of 'dumping-ground', receiving unwanted elements of the metropolitan community:[34]

> Le commis européen est souvent (. . .) un jeune cancre que sa famille a expédié ici (. . .) faute d'avoir pu lui trouver une place dans la métropole.[35]

The qualities of former settlers ensured that French power and authority were immediately recognisable. Their aristocratic social position, their breeding, stature and class, demanded and obtained respect. This community of nobles, it is implied, has been polluted and thus degraded by the influx of the masses. French cultural and moral superiority, which Sarraut had cited as imperative to the maintenance of colonial rule in Indochina, has been undermined by the arrival of sections of the metropolitan population who demonstrate moral standards which are little better (if not worse) than those of the indigenous populations they are intended to dominate.

For Viollis and Roubaud, one of the most abhorrent manifestations of this unappealing face of French colonialism is what they term 'l'esprit colon'. Albert Sarraut defined 'l'esprit colon' as 'la fâcheuse survivance du sentiment de conquête'.[36] This, one supposes, indicates the attitude of domination, superiority and force which Sarraut believed had since been transformed into a collective triumph of human solidarity. In these texts it appears that the women settlers are the principal perpetrators of this despised 'esprit colon'. The beginnings of the corruption of the idealised period of harmony, order and respect of the coloniser is posited with the arrival *en masse* of metropolitan French women to Indochina in the 1920s. Indeed, this is a view which persits to this day. Franchini, a contemporary historian of Indochina states:

> dans l'ensemble, leur présence a pour effet de figer la société dans ses hiérarchies, ses clivages, ses préjugés, et d'aggraver généralement l'incompréhension qui mine les rapports entre colons et colonisés.[37]

Roubaud similarly notes of the female settlers in Indochina

> celles – trop multipliées depuis dix ans – qui ayant quitté le petit logement du 5ème, où les heures de ménage étaient chichement comptées se sont trouvées brusquement dans un hôtel particulier, à la tête d'un personnel domestique (. . .) Ainsi, les petites bourgeoises de quartier ayant gagné, en vingt-huit jours de traversée, leurs nouveaux quartiers de noblesse coloniale, ont importé ici le mépris de l'indigène sans distinction de classe ni de culture.[38]

He emphasises the artificiality of their newly acquired bourgeois lifestyle, regretting that class superiority is no longer inherent in the French community, but has to be proved through ostentation and overt displays of power.

The unproductiveness and passivity of the women settlers is implicitly contrasted with the desired values of the masculinised community of *autrefois*: activity, creative energy, virility. Viollis and Roubaud contrast a passive, narcissistic attitude with the rough, pioneering outlook of the past. Women appear in these texts as a debased substitute for the Motherland; Viollis describes the women settlers she meets in the following terms:

> J'ai souffert du vide de leur cerveau, de leur âme, de leur vie! Pas une qui semblât consciente de ses responsabilités, des douloureux problèmes qui se posent là-bas, qui vit dans les Annamites autre chose que des inférieurs à exploiter. Pas une qui se soit élevée contre les abus monstrueux qui auraient dû révolter sinon leur coeur, du moins leur nerfs. Je les ai vues sincèrement ahuries quand je leur demandais, dans les villes, si elles fréquentaient des femmes de la société annamite, dans les campagnes, si elles se préoccupaient de la santé, de l'hygiène des familles paysannes et surtout des enfants. Non, il faut le dire, le répéter, les femmes françaises, en Indochine, ne sont pas à la hauteur de leur tâche qui pourrait être si belle.[39]

She regrets that the female settlers are unable to offer the nurturing, protection and education which the Motherland should confer upon the indigenous populations. She implicitly calls for a form of patriarchal feminism, in which the French women in Indochina would undertake to perform the role of moral tutors to the 'uncivilised' natives ('si elles se préoccupaient de la santé, de l'hygiène'); and a return to the former relationship of *entente*, and (ostensible) mutual respect, in which there was contact between coloniser and colonised of a similar social class ('si elles fréquentaient les femmes de la société annamite'). The women that Viollis met appeared to subscribe to the materialistic and exploitative values that the *grands chefs* and new administrators had upheld ('Pas une . . . qui vit dans les annamites autre chose que des inférieurs à exploiter').

Official discourses of colonialism mirror these concerns. A 1927 publication of the Colonial Army urging the foundation of metropolitan families abroad, observed that the presence of metropolitan French women in Indochina should improve conditions in the colony.[40] Its prescriptive view of the role of metropolitan women in the colonies presents the sort of 'ideal' from which Viollis clearly felt the women she encountered had fallen. The presence of European wives, the pamphlet asserted, should play a considerable part in raising moral standards in the colony: European women saved men from debauchery, and the ignominy of creating a 'temporary marriage' with an indigenous woman; they furthermore reinstated in male minds the benefits of a stable home life. European women, it was said, also encouraged the technological improvement of the colony: they were perceived as catalysts for improvements such as the electricity and water supplies, the creation of public gardens.

It appears that, for these authors, the arrival of women and the consequent feminisation of the settler community in Indochina marks the beginnings of an artificial, consumerist society which spelled the ruin of the earlier, more authentic and creative masculine society. The idyllic era of the aristocratic and heroic *broussard* was thus corrupted, polluted and undermined by the combination of materialism, inferior colonial personnel, the sheer number of metropolitan immigrants from an 'undesirable' social class, and women who were unwilling or incapable of performing the duties required of a benevolent French patriarchy.

The assessment that these writers presented of the situation in Indochina in the 1930s was one which viewed the civil disobedience of the indigenous populations as a response to colonial mismanagement rather than a legitimate protest against French presence. Their criticism of certain aspects of French colonial policy in Indochina was not, therefore, formulated as an attack on the the fundamental justice of the entire system, but as a springboard for future action. By pinpointing the various and numerous instances of colonial mismanagement and abuse, Viollis and Roubaud provided a challenge to the authorities to right these problems. Heirs to the humanitarian view of French colonialism, and concerned for the suffering of the Indochinese, they thus envisaged remedying the unrest with reformist measures. Roubaud stated:

> Il ne faudra point céder à la révolte, et, lorsque l'apaisement sera établi, que nous devrons nous rappeler nos promesses, les réaliser sans brusquerie.[41]

Furthermore, the reformist agenda present in these texts underwrote the view that Indochina continued to remain a field for French action, an area for development. The 'catastrophic Orient' becomes a realm which is understood to be culturally apart, 'out there', contained and localised, but demanding the intervention of a technologically and morally superior benefactor. Viollis, for example, here describes the degeneration, degradation, sickness and pollution of the indigenous populations in depersonalised terms:

Dans un immense enclos, entouré de barrières de bois, 3 à 4000 créatures humaines, vêtues de loques brunes, sont si entassées et pressées qu'elles ne forment plus qu'une seule masse, agitée de remous, hérissée de bras de sarment, noueux et desséchées, qui tendent des corbeilles de jonc. Dans chaque être toutes les tares, toutes les déchéances: faces bouffies ou décharnées, dents absentes, prunelles éteintes ou chassieuses, plaies ulcérées. Sont-ce des hommes, des femmes, ont-ils vingt ans, soixante ans? On ne sait pas. Plus d'âge, plus de sexe, rien qu'une mortelle misère qui, par des milliers de bouches noires, pousse d'horribles cris d'animaux.[42]

It is a portrayal which recalls Sarraut's assertion that without French intervention, the Indochinese would have remained abandoned to misery and abjection, decimated by famine and disease in the midst of unexploited wealth.[43] Viollis' description is clearly a restatement of a discourse of abjection which qualifies territories without, or lacking adequate Western intervention, as chaotic and unstable.

Viollis' portrait also reveals an element of fear and loathing which can be attributed to the coloniser: the moral and physical degradation of the natives is clearly fixed and located as *ailleurs*, and the natives themselves are inhuman, an animal-like Other. At a time when the value of Western 'civilisation' was being called into question, and the Indochinese nationalists were testing the authority and strength of French rule, it became doubly important to emphasise the superiority of French morals, culture and technology. If the superior qualities of the metropolitan French settler in Indochina were not asserted, if the boundaries and limits of difference were not upheld, then the risk of defilement and contamination would further threaten the French position in Indochina The impulse to reform and to remedy suffering can thus can be viewed as a renewal of the French colonial mission: Viollis and Roubaud were not appealing for the right of the Indochinese to govern themselves, but for a reinforcement of French 'civilising' action in Indochina.

Throughout their texts, these writers refer to the 'devoir' and 'responsabilité' that the metropolitan French settlers in Indochina were no longer fulfilling: Viollis' criticism of women settlers ends with the assertion that '[elles] ne sont pas à la hauteur de leur tâche qui pourrait être si belle'. The preoccupation with these moral and humanitarian duties indicates not simply a desire that French colonial rule be perpetuated, but that France's civilising mission be intensified. Roubaud noted:

La France n'a pas achevé l'oeuvre indochinoise. Toutefois, par ses propres bienfaits, le bienfaiteur se créé des devoirs. La France n'a pas fini. Il ne faut pas qu'elle soit arrêtée dans son travail généreux par l'ingratitude de quelques-uns et l'égoïsme de quelques autres.[44]

The vilification of the newer members of the settler community (above: 'l'égoïsme de quelques autres') enabled Roubaud and Viollis to envisage the redemptive return of the aristocratic *colon*, whose authority and stature would ensure that the lines of difference between colonised and coloniser were redrawn and reinstated.[45] Their texts can therefore be read as reaffirmations of the hierarchies and disequilibrium of traditional French colonial ideology.

At face value, the conclusions Challaye reaches in his additional, updated comments to his visits to Indochina differ from Roubaud and Viollis in that he openly criticises the concept of colonisation itself (from a pacifist and Marxist standpoint).[46] However, having stated in his conclusion that

> Les avantages de la colonisation ne suffisent pas à compenser les injustices, les violences, les crimes de toute sorte qu'elle entraîne (. . .) Il faut mettre fin à ces maux. Il faut étendre aux peuples dits de couleur le droit à la libre disposition d'eux-mêmes, travailler à la libération des colonies.[47]

Challaye then goes on to say:

> Il faut admettre que cette évolution révolutionnaire se fera par étapes.[48]

Not only does Challaye qualify his assertion in such a way as to mitigate his criticism of colonisation, the very language of his criticism is impregnated with colonial ideology. The 'étapes' he envisages are reformist measures, not designed to overthrow French rule, but to ameliorate the condition of the indigenous peoples. His plea for the end of colonisation is made using vocabulary which itself suggests the colonising act: 'étendre aux peuples . . . le droit'. Furthermore, his comments on the Indochinese peoples reinforce the notion of French colonialism as bestowing 'les lumières de la civilisation' on an ignorant population:

> Ils comprennent avec une rare vivacité tout ce qu'on se donne la peine de leur expliquer.[49]

Even Challaye, in spite of his Marxist rhetoric, thus subscribed to the view that Western culture was innately superior and therefore of value to populations implicitly viewed as inferior. While his restatement of the French civilising mission is markedly less overt than that of Viollis and Roubaud, he nevertheless endorses certain key concepts of colonial ideology: he reinforces notions of evolutionary hierarchies, and implies that ultimate emancipation will be achieved only through the continuing assistance of a French colonising presence.

The ideal of colonialism and the repressive or abusive face it presented to these writers in the wake of the Yen Bay uprising were reconciled through the myth of *autrefois* and the vilification of the settler community. There were striking similarities between the 'official rhetoric' of colonialism and the future (redeemed) situation of Indochina envisaged by these writers. Both parties remained convinced of the enlightening potential of France's *mission civilisatrice*, and emphasised that this philanthropic work had yet to be completed; both were equally insistent that distance and hierarchy between coloniser and colonised should be reasserted in order that French authority be maintained. The revalorisation of the *colon* in official texts, was mirrored in Viollis' and Roubaud's nostalgia for the heroic and aristocratic *broussard*, and their repudiation of the contemporary settler community.

The travel journalism of the 1930s thus not only presented a case for the perpetuation of French colonial presence in Indochina, it did so by adopting the rhetoric and ideology which underwrote official versions of France's *doctrine coloniale*. Far from legitimising the Indochinese nationalists' demands through their portrayals of colonial abuse, and thus introducing an anti-colonial perspective to the Indochinese debate after Yen Bay, these writers remained firmly convinced that the legacy of French civilisation was of value to overseas populations, and that the slippage from this ideal was temporary and simply attributable to the incompetence or inferiority of the incumbent administrations.

Notes

1. For an account of the Rif War, see Thobie, J., et al, *Histoire de la France coloniale 1914–1990* (Paris: Armand Colin, 1990), pp. 190–1.
2. The principal figures involved included André Breton, Paul Eluard, René Char and Louis Aragon.
3. The official title of the *contre-expo* was 'La Vérité sur les colonies'.
4. For an account of the *contre-expo*'s exhibits and an overview of the anti-colonial position of its principal organisers, see Hodeir, C., and Pierre, M., *L'Exposition coloniale* (Brussels: Editions complexe, 1991), pp. 111–34. Herman Lebovics also provides a short account of the counter exhibition in *True France: The Wars over Cultural Identity 1900–1945* (London: Cornell University Press, 1992), pp. 105–10.
5. Later renamed *Indochine enchaînée*.
6. For an account of Malraux's participation in *L'Indochine* and his time in Indochina, see Langlois, W., *André Malraux: L'Aventure indochinoise* (translated from the English by Jean-René Major, 1967), (Paris: Mercure de France, 1966).
7. Raymond, G., 'French Culture and the Politics of Self-esteem; the Vietnam Experience', in Melling, P., and Roper, J., *America, France and Vietnam: Cultural History and Ideas of Conflict* (Aldershot: Avebury, 1991), p. 62.

8. Ibid., p. 63.
9. These concerns were also expressed in relation to other colonial territories by works such as Gide's *Voyage au Congo, retour du Tchad* (Paris: Gallimard, 1927).
10. Dorgelès, R., *Sur la route mandarine* (Paris: Albin Michel, 1925), (repr. Paris: Kailash, 1994).
11. Monet, P., *Les Jauniers, histoire vraie* (Paris: Gallimard, 1930).
12. Durtain, L., *Dieux blancs, hommes jaunes* (Paris: Gallimard, 1930).
13. For an account of indigenous rebellion and French repression in Indochina, see Van, N., *Viêt-nam 1920–1945: révolution et contre-révolution sous la domination coloniale* (Paris: L'Insomniaque, 1996).
14. This was intended as part of a more widespread rebellion to include the fledgling Indochinese Communist Party (founded 1930), but communications failed, and the Yen Bay 'mutineers' found themselves isolated.
15. See Viollis' appendices transcribing the trial.
16. Roubaud, L., *Vietnam: la tragédie indochinoise* (Paris: Valois, 1931).
17. Viollis, A., *SOS Indochine* (Paris: Gallimard, 1935); the articles appeared in *Esprit* in December 1933.
18. Roubaud, *Vietnam: la tragédie indochinoise*, p. 9.
19. Ibid., p. 11.
20. Challaye, F., *Souvenirs sur la colonisation* (Paris: Picart, 1935), pp. 3–4.
21. See for example, Girardet, R., *L'Idée coloniale en France de 1871 à 1962* (Paris: La Table ronde, 1972), pp. 218–20.
22. See for example Viollis, *SOS Indochine*, p. 19: 'Je ne voulais, je ne pouvais y croire, mais mes hôtes me donnèrent des détails si précis, si complets que la conviction peu à peu s'imposa.'
23. Ibid., pp. 35–6.
24. Ibid., p. 17.
25. Challaye, *Souvenirs sur la colonisation*, p. 20.
26. Viollis, *SOS Indochine*, p. 60.
27. Ibid., p. 23.
28. Ibid., p. 60.
29. Ibid., p. 37.
30. Ibid., p. 6.
31. Ibid., p. 124.
32. Ibid., pp. 128–9.
33. Ibid., p. 124.
34. Albert Sarraut uses the same metaphor, referring to certain elements of the settler community as 'déchets'. See *Grandeur et servitudes coloniales* (Paris: Sagittaire, 1931), p. 210.
35. Roubaud, *Vietnam: la tragédie indochinoise*, p. 246.

36. Sarraut, *Grandeur et servitudes coloniales*, p. 207.
37. Franchini, P., 'La Cité blanche', in Franchini, P. (ed.), *Saigon 1925–45: de la 'Belle Colonie' à l'éclosion révolutionnaire ou la fin des dieux blancs* (Paris: Les Editions Autrement/série mémoires, no. 17, 1992), p. 44.
38. Roubaud, *Vietnam: la tragédie indochinoise*, pp. 243–4.
39. Viollis, *SOS Indochine*, p. 35.
40. *Le rôle et la situation de la famille française aux colonies* (Paris: Editions du journal des coloniaux et de l'Armée coloniale réunis, 1927).
41. Roubaud, *Vietnam: la tragédie indochinoise*, p. 285.
42. Viollis, *SOS Indochine,* pp. 56–7.
43. See Sarraut, *Grandeur et servitudes coloniales*, p. 117.
44. Roubaud, *Vietnam: la tragédie indochinoise*, p. 284.
45. This class-based criticism also perhaps reflects the negative feelings about a debased post-1918 France and its new modern classes.
46. See Challaye, *Souvenirs sur la colonisation*, pp. 187–207.
47. Ibid., p. 203.
48. Ibid.
49. Ibid., p. 18.

Conclusion to Part I

By the 1930s, France had evolved a colonial doctrine which revolved around a trinity of values or attributes: *devoir, responsabilité*, and *générosité*. This ethical basis for colonial action drew directly upon the Republican ideology and revolutionary heritage of the French nation. French colonial rule in Indochina was viewed as harmonising, liberatory and fraternal. The *mise en valeur* of Indochina, and the application of metropolitan values of progress, development and technological aid which were brought to bear, were perceived as acts of altruistic generosity and fraternal sharing. *La Plus Grande France* functioned both to protect and nurture Indochina, and to develop and complete Indochina. The strength of this belief in the value of French colonialism can be measured through the variety of sources which reiterated and disseminated these constant themes.

Faith in the value and humanitarian nature of the nation's *doctrine coloniale* was thus strong. Where one might finally have expected an insistent and consistent *remise en question* of the French colonial ideal in the early to mid-1930s, one finds instead a reiteration and commendation of these principles of colonialism. Elements of disquiet, unease or uncertainty about the current practice of colonialism had begun to emerge in the 1930s. These concerns remained consistently circumscribed, however, by the belief that French colonialism was of inherent value, and that any contemporary slippage from this ideal was simply attributable to the incompetence or inferiority of the incumbent administrations. Indeed, the mid-1930s witnessed the reassertion of notions of metropolitan superiority and control, the reiteration of discourses of hierarchy and differentiation.

Nonetheless, France's ideal of empire was riven with contradictions. The imperial and colonial ideal is undermined by unresolved tensions surrounding France's conception of itself as an imperial power. France's was an Empire without an emperor. The nation's Republican ideology and culture, and the legacy of the 1789 Revolution, conspired against the practice of empire to create an incoherence within the nation's own rhetoric of empire. This fundamental incoherence is exemplified by France's perception of her relationship with, and role in Indochina.

The ideal of French colonialism depicted both at home and in Indochina presented the French nation as a unificatory agent, rallying diverse and dispersed fragmented territories to its greater self. In keeping with the principles of 1789, imperial France was presented as the epitome of generosity and protective benevolence. The founding principles of French national identity under the Third

Republic, its Republican heritage and humanitarian *génie*, were perceived as being extended wholesale to its Empire. This consistent universalising discourse, epitomised in the French policy of assimilation, and perpetuated through many colonial practices under the guise of association, demonstrates a profound discomfort with diversity. The interplay in the colonial arena of notions of alterity and similitude, a concept which has underpinned much recent post-colonial criticism, led in the case of France and Indochina to an ambivalence which bisects their entire colonial relationship. Accorded a special status, yet simultaneously indistinguishable from France's other colonial possessions, valued yet debased, Indochina epitomises the metropole's colonial ambivalence.

Once the conquest and pacification had been accomplished, Indochina was to be remodelled as a French territory – *l'Indochine française* – through the rigorous exclusion of cultural and political influence from neighbouring Asian cultures, and the gallicisation of indigenous history, culture and political institutions. A hybrid territory made up of diverse regions, cultures and traditions, Indochina was perceived as being made a coherent whole through the homogenising and unificatory action of the French nation.

In both educative and official works, Indochina was consistently imagined as weak and chaotic in its pre-colonial state: a void space bereft of the light of knowledge and civilisation. Colonisation consisted of the deliverance of the colony from this state of nothingness. Colonial Indochina was thus presented as having gained stability and security, prosperity and progress, and increased its prestige and stature through association with imperial France. French colonialism in Indochina was presented as a mutually beneficial project, as opposed to one which France desired in order to shore up its prestige.

The innate superiority of the French nation and its colonial representatives in Indochina is clearly asserted throughout metropolitan discourses of colonialism, reinforcing the grandeur of the French nation. Thus although the French colonial presence in Indochina is perceived as generous and altruistic, and although the colonial ideal examined in a variety of cultural media asserts the liberatory and protective nature of French colonialism, it also reveals that in order for colonial rule to be maintained Indochina must remain in an inferior position vis-a-vis the metropole. *La Plus Grande France* is imposed upon Indochina in restricted cultural terms, but the equality which the term suggests remains shrouded in hierarchical discourses of French superiority. Colonial practices reveal that this extension of French civilisation is both severely limited in political terms, and authoritarian in character.

These discrepancies between colonial practice and imperial rhetoric are repeated in the ambiguous duality of metropolitan perceptions of Indochina. In spite of the proliferation of discourses which posited Indochina, alongside France's other colonial possessions, as backward, inferior and weak territories in need of metropolitan aid and guidance, Indochina was concomitantly accorded a special status, and a more elevated rank.

Indeed, if the Franco-Indochinese relationship can be summarised through a series of antitheses, then perceptions of Indochina appear equally paradoxical. France's colonial role in Indochina is imagined as generous yet self-seeking; liberatory yet authoritarian; modernising, yet encouraging the maintenance of Indochina in a 'primitive' or 'traditional' state. The relationship was simultaneously perceived as reciprocal and impositional, fostering development and yet a hindrance to autonomous cultural and political growth. Fraternal towards and respectful of Indochina, imperial France sought also to express its superiority and control over its colonised peoples. Indochina was France's 'pearl', advanced, worthy, accorded special status. Indochina was nonetheless chaotic and weak, inferior and needy. Indochina was a showcase of success, but also a site of disaster. Indochina was singled out and praised, but it was also denied specificity, both internally and in relation to France's other colonial possessions. Praised and held up as a shining example of the value of French colonialism, Indochina was simultaneously diminished, commodified and debased.

These dual narratives of success/disaster, value/ambivalence were manifest not only in the textual accounts of the relationship, but were most striking in the visual discourses of the *Exposition coloniale de Vincennes*. The exhibition demonstrated the importance of Indochina to the French nation and Empire. Indochina over-shadowed the nation's other colonial possessions, but more importantly, was seen to rival Britain's 'jewel in the crown'. Central to Indochina's 'special' status as *perle de l'Extrême-Orient* was Angkor Wat, a marvel unrivalled by the architectural features of any of France's other colonial possessions. A symbol of French ideals of protection and *mise en valeur*, Angkor Wat nevertheless also functioned as proof of metropolitan superiority over decadent and inferior native populations. Displayed to advantage and held up for admiration, Indochina was nonetheless debased and commodified, its populations simultaneously applauded and reprimanded.

On the eve of the Second World War belief in Empire was thus strong in metropolitan France. Official rhetoric, colonial policy and cultural interpretations of French colonialism all appeared to support the reinforcement of the accepted version of the colonial ideal, and the perpetuation of French colonial rule in Indochina. This faith in the enlightening and nurturing value of French colonialism was later to be demonstrated in the lengths to which the metropole went to sustain colonial rule in Indochina in spite of growing nationalist demands and agitation, a costly war, and growing distaste for colonialism, both at home and abroad.

Part II
Disturbing the Colonial Order

Introduction to Part II

A variety of colonial and governmental sources in France had thus combined to produce and construct an image of France as an imperial nation in South-East Asia, and of Indochina as the nation's showcase colony. Many images, perceptions and representations of Indochina in popular cultural media or elsewhere reinforced and/or mirrored this state-sanctioned 'official' version of the territories' identity which colonial France had constructed. Official discourses had attempted to contain, control and codify the colony and the colonial relationship: to justify, legitimise and perpetuate French rule in Indochina; and to create a coherent cultural image of France in Indochina.

Nonetheless, however rigourously the nation's policymakers, its colonial lobby and its colonial administrators may have thought they had defined, codified and fixed the identity of the colony and set the terms of the relationship between France and Indochina, Indochina always eluded those definitions, and undermined the conceptual foundation which had been constructed for it. This occurred either through the resistance or refusal to comply on the part of the colonised peoples; or through slippages – linguistic, cultural, and ideological. These took the form of counter-narratives which disturbed the colonial order or orthodoxy, and threatened to undermine that officially conceived identity. What emerges then, is a plethora of competing images of Indochina: some reiterative and stereotypical, others paradoxical and antithetical. Thus in spite of the widely disseminated pro-colonial propaganda, and a strong underlying commitment to the French colonial doctrine, counter-narratives and discourses which undermined or disturbed both the prevailing colonial orthodoxy and received ideas about Indochina were manifest.

The following three chapters are thus interested not so much in indigenous resistance to (or complicity in) the French colonial project in Indochina, nor in the overtly anti-colonial voices which were slow to (but did finally) emerge in metropolitan France in the post-war period. The interest of this part lies in the analysis of the discomfort, unease or dissent which occurred in seemingly pro-colonial texts; in the voices which provide a counterpoint, however hesitatingly, to the prevailing ideological hegemony. These voices reveal the instability or precarity of the colonial project; they are voices which point to an altogether less universal acceptance of France's colonial ideals, and which provide alternative discourses to the established myth of French colonial identity and the nation's role in Indochina.

There were early indications of an unease or dissatisfaction amongst French settlers and travellers to Indochina. These gnawing doubts gradually gather momentum, build, grow and extend to the extent that counter-narratives can be discerned, which coalesce around certain features such as gender issues, health and hygiene, the erosion of masculine power, and the transgression of boundaries.

6

Utopia or Dystopia? Colonial Disillusionment

Colonial propaganda had succeeded not only in drawing up and disseminating the image of the colony as a field for French civilising and constructive action, it had also constructed an ideal image of the settler: hardy, courageous, virile, and enterprising – an intrepid *broussard* or a talented engineer or businessman. Many were seduced by the colonial dream and the exotic charm of a life overseas. For those imbued with state's colonial ideology, the appeal, not to say challenge, of colonial emigration often stemmed from the idealistic goal of fulfilling France's mission overseas, and living up to that idealised image of the French settler abroad.

In Marguerite Duras' *Un barrage contre le Pacifique*, a retrospective portrayal of settler life in Indochina, the appeal and influence of the colonial 'dream' is evident. For a young, idealistic couple, Indochina presented an outlet for ambitions and energies which could not be fulfilled in the mainland:

> "Engagez-vous dans l'armée coloniale", "Jeunes, allez aux colonies, la fortune vous y attend". A l'ombre d'un bananier croulant sous les fruits, le couple colonial, tout de blanc vêtu, se balançit dans des rocking-chairs tandis que les indigènes s'affairaient en souriant autour d'eux. Elle se maria avec un instituteur qui, comme elle, se mourait d'impatience dans un village du Nord, victime comme elle des ténébreuses lectures de Pierre Loti. Peu après leur mariage, ils firent ensemble leur demande d'admission dans les cadres de l'enseignement colonial et ils furent nommés dans cette grande colonie que l'on appelait alors l'Indochine française.[1]

The glamour, charm and allure of Indochina, and of the trappings of settler life, both fed by the exoticism of writers such as Loti, and by colonial propaganda, create a compelling portrait of the colonial dream or ideal. This initial appeal, in both Duras' work, and also, as we shall see, in earlier narratives, is however rapidly displaced by feelings of disappointment, failure and impotence. The propagandist value of the colonial dream was often rapidly dissipated on contact with the colony. For belief in France's colonial ideal, and Indochina's status as France's colonial 'perle', the most precious and successful of the overseas possessions, were dealt perhaps the severest blow by tales of settler life in the colony.

Apart from the small colonial enclaves in the Pacific Ocean, Indochina was the farthest flung of France's overseas possessions, and this sense of distance is itself an important aspect of the metropolitan image of Indochina. Much popular literature was concerned with themes of exile and nostalgia for the homeland. Metropolitan settlers felt cut off from the homeland: boat journeys to Indochina took four weeks, and regular air transport to Indochina was not established until 1938.[2] Unlike many of the French overseas territories, particularly Algeria, Indochina was never a settlement colony. The metropolitan population was perhaps more isolated or insular in Indochina, as figures for French settlers never exceeded 42,000.[3] Whereas Algeria had a far larger metropolitan population, was geographically closer to the mainland, and enjoyed a political status which ensured that the territory was closely linked to France in the metropolitan imagination, Indochina remained distant both spatially and conceptually.

In much popular fiction concerning Indochina, distance from the mainland is repeatedly shown to have a disorienting and debilitating effect on the French settlers. This sometimes manifests itself as a form of counter-exoticism: it functions, unlike the Baudelairian desire for departure, or the impulse which propels the self towards *évasion* and the Other, not as an escape from *ennui* experienced in the mainland, but as the fear of departure. In Georges Groslier's *Le Retour à l'argile*, Raymonde Rollin's anxiety about her future colonial life commences before her departure for Indochina, where her husband had been nominated his firm's representative. Raymonde

> fut affolée aussitôt à l'idée d'abandonner sa vie mondaine et ses habitudes. Dans son appréhension de séjourner deux années sous les tropiques (. . .) elle imagina un affreux exil, se vit campée dans la brousse menaçante, loin de tout confort, épiée par des indigènes sournois, par la fièvre et les bêtes.[4]

Where colonial propaganda had emphasised the authority and superiority of the colonial settler, Raymonde imagines only threat and menace. Where colonial propaganda had emphasised the fortune awaiting settlers and held out the promise of a glamorous lifestyle, Raymonde imagines only loss and deprivation. Raymonde's is a partially self-fulfilling prophecy, for once in Indochina she does indeed 'vit mal, en proie à un ennui qu'entretiennent ses regrets de la France',[5] and remains convinced that she lives 'en pays ennemi'.[6] Whilst difference and alterity have often been viewed as constituting part of the appeal of colonial migration, here the different and the inhabitual are sources of anxiety. The move towards the Other embodied in exoticism, is here displaced by a strong sense of *repli sur soi*: an inward-turning and anxious response to difference and movement. Western imperialism's traditional desire to know is replaced by a fear of knowing. In spite of the widespread appeal of settler life conveyed through colonial propaganda, official discourses of colonialism could not entirely dissipate the anxieties provoked by emigration and colonial otherness.

Elsewhere, even if colonial propaganda has succeeded in its objective to popularise metropolitan emigration to the colonies, writers are quick to highlight the disjunction between the colonial ideal and the reality of settler life in Indochina. Once that unknown becomes known, and experienced at first-hand, the illusion or dream of Indochina recedes rapidly, resulting in nostalgia and *spleen*. In Jean Jacnal's "Dans la boue", the isolation suffered by the white settler in Indochina exacerbates the sense of *dépaysement* and culture shock:

> Il est dans ce pays des étranges silences,
> Où l'on sent mieux son coeur qui pleure dans l'exil,
> Pour les regrets cuisants fontaines de Jouvence,
> Où la pluie et l'ennui tombent fins et subtils.[7]

This isolation is often reflected in the novel titles themselves, such as Jean Dorsenne's *Loin des blancs*.[8] Similarly, in Pierre Loti's *Un Pèlerin d'Angkor*, his travel diary of his journey to Angkor Wat, the author emphasises the inward-turning and sorrowfully reflective response to the migratory experience: 'comment dire la tristesse, le recueillement songeur, pendant les nuits, de ces coins de la France, de ces semblants de patrie égarés au milieu de la grande brousse asiatique, isolés de tout, même de la mer'.[9] These portrayals of settler life in Indochina run counter to the traditional, confident view of the imperial nation's desire to dominate the colony, and to impose itself both physically and metaphorically upon the colonised territory. Loti's portrayal of those 'coins de la France', scattered throughout the vast, engulfing space of Indochina provides a counterpoint to the nation's self-affirming belief in its transformative enterprise in Indochina. The scope and implantation of *la plus grande France* is called into question, and the imperative of making Indochina French is undermined by doubt and lack of confidence when faced with this most daunting of prospects and the enormity of the task. These instances of doubt and uncertainty produce an altogether less confident portrayal of France's role in Indochina. Settlers are fearful of the challenge of colonialism, and fearful about the coloniser's ability to fulfil his functions: they display a less than unshakeable belief in the possibility of carrying out France's colonial mission.

Portrayals of nostalgia for the homeland amongst settlers in Indochina also bring to light the notion of time lost or wasted in Indochina. Of the French members of the expeditionary corps, Loti produces a sentimental view of nostalgia for the homeland and the comforts of France: 'pauvres garçons, que les mamans anxieuses attendent au foyer trop lointain, et qui vont consumer ici une ou deux des plus belles années de leur vie!'[10] This is mirrored in Jeanne Leuba's attempt to convey the settler's apprehension concerning time spent in Indochina to the metropolitan reader:

Je voudrais qu'il aperçut confusément un peu de cette existence qui est la nôtre, un peu de ce pays où nous vivons – où nous souffrons – l'exil volontaire où nous passons nos jeunes, nos fortes années à lutter contre le spleen, la chaleur, les maux physiques, les énervements, les incompréhensions, les hostilités de la nature et des hommes.[11]

The notion of time squandered or time misspent, with its particular emphasis on wasted youth, clearly runs counter to popular colonial propaganda in which the young, energetic and virile European found in the colony a worthy and rewarding outlet for his enthusiasm and energies. This very sense of waste implicitly calls into question the purpose and value of France's *mission civilisatrice*.

Indeed, not all representations of Indochina conformed to the positive view of the colony as a space for male action and adventure, a privileged site for development and improvement. Traditional rhetorical oppositions had construed France as an energetic European nation reinvigorating and improving a backward, impoverished and slothful Asia. While, as we have seen, the principle of *mise en valeur* was thought to embody this ideal version of French intervention in Indochina, many fictional or autobiographical representations of life in Indochina again showed that behavioural patterns amongst settlers ran counter to this model. Many fictional accounts of settler life in Indochina highlighted the way in which the alienation of the settler community militated against their potential to carry out their idealised functions. A sense of creeping passivity and lassitude often overwhelmed the European French in Indochina. Coupled with their sense of *déracinement* and gradual dislocation from Western life, and the attendant anxieties of living a life of exile in 'un pays étranger', the coloniser's authority, and his ability to function as an agent of the nation's principle of *mise en valeur,* were sapped and undermined.

Contact with the colony is shown to distort time, and seems to effect a physical and psychological disjunction in the French settler in Indochina. Indeed, in the novel *Raffin-Su-Su*, Jean Ajalbert's eponymous protagonist loses any sense of time once he arrives in Laos. Time becomes to him an alien concept: his life of exile in Indochina becomes 'un bail à long terme'.[12] His life lacks the routine and clock-driven patterning which had organised and comforted him in the mainland: 'le temps ne compte plus au Laos comme ailleurs. On ne le détaille pas. On ne le découpe pas en parcelles précieuses, minutées, sous globe, comme chez nous.'[13] Time and exile combine to produce a sense of alienation. More importantly however, the lack of sense of time produces a lassitude: a penchant for wasting time which overturns the ideal of the vigourous, constructive male coloniser. Raffin's initial energy and enthusiasm are frittered away by the intangible yet inexorable effect of the climate and atmosphere of Indochina:

A l'arrivée, il avait été surpris de la négligence de ses compagnons, dont pas un ne songeait à agencer, à orner tant soit peu son logis (. . .) Raffin, aussi, devait glisser peu à peu à l'emprise captieuse, malgré sa volonté de résistance.[14]

Whilst Raffin still felt a tangible contact with the mainland - here through his attempt to woo a Frenchwoman ('Madame Français'), who surely signifies also the impact upon Raffin of an idealised version of an imperial *mère-patrie* – he could motivate himself to fulfil his function as model settler:

Sous l'empire idéal de "Madame Français", Raffin se gardait actif et volontaire, avec mille projets de routes, de chemins de fer, de cultures, d'élevages, d'exploitations minières, forestières, d'assistance médicale, de relèvement physique, intellectuel et moral de l'indigène, – dont il apprenait la langue. La paresse ambiante souriait de tant de zèle, qui se calmerait.[15]

The narrator's ironic intervention at the end of the quotation undermines our faith in the transformative power of the male coloniser and of colonialism and calls into question the maintenance of the initial impetus of *mise en valeur*. Life in Indochina for Raffin is like a long siesta, where a carefree laziness – 'le-cheveu-dans-la-main' – takes over from the missionary vigour of building, exploring, developing and improving.[16]

The type of slothful, passive idleness to which Raffin succumbs is viewed as a harmful yet often inevitable feature of colonial life in Indochina. Thus far from underwriting the utopian vision of Indochina as an outlet for male creative energy, many portrayals present the reverse: the colony becomes not a utopian space, but a dystopic reality of exile and disillusionment.

The dissipation of the initial energy and committment to the French colonial project of the white European newly-embarked in Indochina partially constitutes what Marguerite Duras was later to call 'le vampirisme colonial'. Duras details the sapping of the psychological and physical resilience of the poor white settler; and charts the initial hope and expectation of idealistic parents, imbued with official France's missionary zeal, on their way to bring French civilisation to Indochina; and their gradual disappointment, loss of hope and despair as their projects fail.

In *L'Eden Cinéma*, the stage version of *Un Barrage*, the ideal of *mise en valeur* in its various manifestations is constantly invoked. The tenacity of this ideal, and its appeal to the *bonne foi* of the idealistic settler is reflected in the Mother's consistent refusal to lose faith in her project to build her 'barrages contre le Pacifique' and cultivate her land.

Si les enfants ne mourraient pas. Ni de la faim. Ni non plus du choléra. On aurait des médecins. Des institutrices comme jeune, elle, elle avait été . . . On construirait une longue route qui longerait les barrages et qui desservirait les terres libérées du sel. On serait heureux. D'un bonheur mérité.[17]

The Mother's idealism seems unshakeable; the colonial ideal of progress, development and *mise en valeur* is pursued without heed: 'Elle était sortie de la nuit de l'Eden ignorante de tout. Du grand vampirisme colonial. De l'injustice fondamentale qui règne sur les pauvres du monde.'[18] In *Barrage contre le Pacifique*, the death of the family's horse symbolises at once the good intentions and ideals of the European migrant to Indochina, and the failure of those ideals: 'Il essaya honnêtement de faire le travail qu'on lui demandait et qui était bien au-dessus de ses forces depuis longtemps, puis il creva.'[19] Like her horse, the Mother becomes a victim of the nation's colonial design: she fights to keep the colonial dream alive, struggles to realise a hopeless project, succumbs to a seemingly incontournable outcome: madness and death. The overarching despair of the settler, and the inevitability of the failure of both the Mother and colonialism, are mirrored in Duras' prematurely closed narrative: 'C'est là que nous avons été jeunes. Que la mère a vécu son espoir le plus grand. C'est là qu'elle est morte.'[20]

The colonial dream, however, is in part betrayed by the very sense of superiority and its attendant arrogance which the successful inculcation of France's colonial doctrine appears to have produced. The Mother consults no one about her project, nor makes any form of enquiry into the viability of her plan to erect the *barrages*. Furthermore, she persuades the local populations to take part in the enterprise.

Ecoutez: les paysans de la plaine, eux aussi, elle les avait convaincus. Depuis des milliers d'années que les marées de juillet envahissent la plaine. . .
Non . . . disait-elle. Non . . . Les enfants morts de faim, les récoltes brûlées par le sel, non ça pouvait aussi ne pas durer toujours. Ils l'avaient crue.[21]

The figure of the Mother – always referred to as *the* mother, *la mère*, generic and universal – can be viewed as a debased version of *la mère-patrie*. The Mother also embodies that Western arrogance which refuses to accept the untameability and inexorability of Nature. Although the ocean repeatedly pours through the barrages, destroying the crops, the Mother, imbued with colonialism's conquering spirit, battles on against inhospitable nature and an intractable land. The refrain in *L'Eden Cinéma*, which recalls the ocean's destruction of the barrages, emphasises the inexorability and aggression of nature, and its repetition is expressive also of the Mother's implacable struggle to fulfil the colonial ideal: 'La marée de juillet monta à l'assaut de la plaine et noya la récolte.'[22]

In Duras' retrospective counter-narrative to the ideal of *mise en valeur*, this portrait of abject colonial failure functions not only as a *mise en scène* of the psychological, individual, sexual and social impact of the failed colonial dream, but also as an indictment of the corruption of colonial administrations in Indochina. Duras' epithet of 'vampirisme colonial' thus also contains the notion of the settler's spirit and energy worn away by its consistent struggle against the *escroquerie* of a rotten colonialism: 'Pour avoir une concession fertile il fallait la payer deux fois. Une fois ouvertement, au gouvernement de la colonie. Une deuxième fois en sous-main, aux fonctionnaires chargés du lotissement.'[23] In *Eden Cinéma*, the Mother's monologue concerning her unsent letter of recrimination to the colonial authorities reveals her indignation at the position in which she finds herself.[24] Although it appears that the reader is intended to sympathise with her, and to condemn the colonial authorities for their 'vampirisme', the Mother too, is clearly guilty of a sort of 'vampirisme manqué'. The irony of her monologue (which might be read as a retrospective indictment of colonialism as a whole) is that she is unable to recognise how she is implicated in the 'crime' she accuses the colonial authorities of perpetrating. The Mother is indignant, I would argue, precisely because she has been prevented from gaining her share of the colonial spoils. The Mother envies the richer white settlers, and attempts to emulate them. The family's poverty creates distance between them and other white settlers, and instead creates a form of *rapprochment* with the natives: they are united in their poverty. Thus although the monologue stresses the harmful effect upon the natives of corrupt colonial practices, and reveals a well-intentioned colonialism on the part of the Mother, her bitterness is nonetheless rooted in her inability to secure and profit from the capital gains she implies are the due of the coloniser.

In this rather ambiguous portrayal of colonial failure and disillusionment, the only outcome for impoverished and unfortunate settlers is either madness, corruption or death. In Duras' work, the authority and confidence of the colonising nation is thus shown to be partial, precarious and based on individual responses and fortunes rather than on an inherent national superiority. The economy of capitalism which underpins colonialism militates against the universal success of the coloniser.

In earlier narratives, the latent doubts over the realisability or advisability of the colonial project manifest themselves in anxiety and fear, and in both physical and psychological debilitation. This gradual debilitation suffered by white settlers in Indochina, which might be likened to Duras' later portrayal of 'vampirisme colonial', is disclosed in several ways and is blamed on a variety of sources. Again, Indochina's climate and natural features are a prime source of anxiety amongst settlers. Colonialism is widely represented as a battle against the forces of nature and many novelists presented the metropolitan settlers' lives abroad as constituting a constant struggle against the maleficent forces of nature. Whereas in the case of Africa, it is the vastness of the territories which produce awe and fear in the metropolitan colonists, in the case of Indochina, the forest, and more particularly the Cambodian forest, embodied this struggle.[25] The image of the intractable forest serves as a metaphor for Indochina, and France's relationship with the colony:

Si familier que je croie être avec la forêt et ses aspects multiformes, il y en a, en elle, je ne sais quelle réserve de vie primordiale, dont la masse m'impressionne toujours, je ne sais quel air de bête feuillue, crochée au sol, tas obscur et moiré . . . de bête intuable . . . au point que je regarde avec admiration, à notre droite et à notre gauche, les deux bourrelets de chair écailleuse et brillante, qui ne demandent qu'à se refermer sur le dérisoire estafilade infligée par les ingénieurs du Siam-Cambodge.[26]

The forest emblematises the ambiguous hold that the metropole has over Indochina. However familiar the French settler might feel he has become with the country, there is a certain element of it which forever escapes his grasp or understanding, and which will forever be beyond that grasp. In these metaphorical portrayals, colonialism is not presented as a durable force, as Indochina is waiting to close in over the French presence, to become whole and thoroughly impenetrable once more. The forest functions as a symbol the impossibility of transformative colonial action: the magnificence of the forest dwarfs the derisory efforts of the French engineers to cut a swathe through its dense vegetation. Analogous to France's relationship with its indigenous subjects, this evocation of the forest recalls the series of antitheses which mark French colonial discourses concerning Indochina. It concretises a view in which Indochina is familiar yet unknowable, domesticised yet untameable, held in check but constantly threatening to break loose from metropolitan control.

In Boissière's short stories, the natural environment of Indochina is both deadly and magnificent: 'dans ce pays où regne, en souverain orgueilleux et absolu, le végétal', 'la meurtrière émanation du végétal'.[27] The organic omnipotence of Indochina's vegetation thus at once threatens and dethrones French control. Similarly, in Malraux's rather anachronistic *La Voie royale,* it is the insuperable organicism of the forest which signals the threat of decomposition of the self. Malraux's protagonists believe that only through the assertion of will can 'déchéance' or failure be avoided. The search for some form of action which will enable this escape from *déchéance* and submission is thwarted precisely by the sinister power of the Cambodian forest, which negates the will to overcome and dominate:

La forêt et la chaleur étaient pourtant plus fortes que l'inquiétude: Claude sombrait comme dans une maladie dans cette fermentation où les formes se gonflaient, s'allonge-aient, pourrissaient hors du monde dans lequel l'homme compte, qui le séparait de lui-même avec la force de l'obscurité (. . .) L'unité de la forêt, maintenant s'imposait; depuis six jours Claude avait renoncé à séparer les êtres des formes, la vie qui bouge de la vie qui suinte; une puissance inconnue liait aux arbres les fongosités, faisait grouiller toutes ces choses provisoires sur un sol semblable à l'écume des marais, dans ces bois fumants de commencement du monde.[28]

The pervasive formlessness of the decomposing vegetation seems to affect Claude Vannec both physically and psychologically. He is weakened, disgusted, yet dominated by the forest. It is beyond his control and threatens both his physical and mental integrity. It challenges his ideological precepts and saps his control.

> Quel acte humain, ici, avait un sens? Quelle volonté conservait sa force? Tout se ramifiait, s'amollissait, s'efforçait de s'accorder à ce monde ignoble et attirant à la fois comme le regard des idiots, et qui attaquait les nerfs avec la même puissance abjecte que ces araignées suspendues entre les branches, dont il avait eu d'abord tant de peine à détourner les yeux.[29]

Thus the forest attacks the European's mental faculties through his enfeebled bodily responses. The virility of the adventurer is challenged and his lucidity questioned. The pervasive decomposition of the forest and the excessiveness of the vegetation here have an almost infectious capacity: they threaten mental decay and idiocy. In Malraux's work, Cambodia and the forest are perhaps coincidental in that they serve simply as a backdrop to the *mise en scène* of the Nietszchean efforts of Claude Vannec and Perken. One might nonetheless argue that this portrayal encapsulates the anxious response of Western logic when faced with the disorder and untameability of the anarchic colony, thereby challenging perceived imperial certainties.

As in much colonial literature, and most particularly in the context of *fin-de-siècle* fears about European degeneration,[30] this battle against nature is also presented as a psychological struggle. It might be argued that the themes of sickness, mental disturbance and death are related to the psychological trauma experienced by those metropolitan individuals who constituted the early wave of departure to the colonies. It is as though colonial expansion was undermined from within by the repressed self-doubt which seemed insidiously to pervade the nineteenth-century unconscious.

Reflecting an almost unconscious unease with Empire and the colonial situation in Indochina, the psychological changes which occur in the characters of Henry Daguerches' novels, for instance, are always imputed to Indochina, and most often to its climate:

> L'âme et l'esprit s'anémient ici (. . .) Une nervosité veule, une sorte de halètement débile de la pensée trahissent l'édifice intérieur qui flageole.[31]

These fears mirror the concerns and anxieties expressed in contemporaneous health and hygiene manuals which also associated climate with mental and physical degeneracy. Indochina is here compared to a debilitating virus which gnaws away at the psychological stability and mental faculty of the European settlers.[32]

Enfeeblement, mental anaemia, and spinelessness work from the interior to weaken the psyche, and are evoked in physiognomical terms, as exterior signs of deterioration: sagging and spinelessness. Whilst fictional portrayals of Africa reflected fears of cannibalism, and possible capture and death by wild animals, in the case of Indochina, the notion of insidious disease appears to have constituted the most acutely felt anxiety.

The perceived insalubrity of Indochina is frequently evoked in fiction and memoirs. The exotic appeal of Indochina was at once seductive and debilitating. It was imagined metaphorically as a malignant life-draining organism. As is the case with many of France's overseas possessions, the first mass metropolitan experience of Indochina was almost inevitably that of war and conquest, thus adding to the association between Indochina and death. The first fictional metropolitan representations of Indochina appeared around the time of the pacification of Indochina. Later than the heroic accounts of the conquest, they take the form of autobiographical *récits*, journals and diaries and give highly subjective accounts of Indochina and its inhabitants, which are often coloured by the writer's own experience of war and suffering.

Loti, for instance, candidly documents his dislike of Indochina, and states quite clearly the personal origins of this consistent antipathy. Loti's elder brother was killed in 1865 while returning in ill health from Indochina, where he had been a naval officer. Arriving in Saigon, Loti notes: 'Une ville (. . .) dont le nom seul jadis me paraissait lugubre, parce que mon frère (. . .) était allé, comme tant d'autres de sa génération, y prendre les germes de la mort.'[33] This very personal experience of loss is echoed in *Pêcheur d'Islande*, where the hero dies on board the ship headed for France as a result of a tour of duty in Tonkin.[34] The ship for France becomes an 'hôpital mouvant', an 'étouffoir de malades'[35]:

> Depuis le départ d'Ha-Long, il en était mort plus d'un, qu'il avait fallu jeter dans l'eau profonde, sur ce grand chemin de France, beaucoup de ces petits lits s'étaient débarassés déjà de leur pauvre contenu.[36]

As noted above, while fear of sickness in any of the French overseas territories may have been a common theme in colonial literature, it is particularly noticeable in the case of Indochina, which is often evoked through allusions to insidious sickness leading to death. As Malleret has noted, these accounts were filled with disturbing detail about the

> expéditions meurtrières accomplies dans des pays d'épouvante où la vie humaine est à la merci des surprises des fauves, de la fièvre, de la forêt perfide et des exhalaisons malsaines qui montent de la terre mouvante des deltas.[37]

In Boissière's short stories, sickness and death were linked consciously to the natural environment: 'la terre qui est imprégné de toutes ces corruptions'.[38] His protagonists are prey to 'la fièvre des bois' and the threat of malaria, producing a sense that sickness in Indochina is again organic and omnipresent: 'bue dans l'eau des ruisseaux et respirée dans les brouillards du matin'.[39] Early literature thus often concentrated on the macabre – corpses, burials and cemeteries. Malleret puts this down to a contemporary taste for 'littérature d'horreur', and indeed, it does contain many of the aspects and images of traditional metropolitan 'histoires d'épouvante'.[40]

Heroic portrayals of the conquest were perhaps still popular, but these later images provide a counterpoint to the heroic vision of French expeditionary, exploratory and military prowess. The association of Indochina with death certainly originated in metropolitan France with the popularisation of literature which reported the exploration and conquest of the territories. This image was undoubtedly perpetuated by the parliamentary colonial debate of the late nineteenth century, which pitched convinced colonialists against those who deplored the sacrifice of 'l'or et le sang français' in foreign territories. As Malleret notes:

> Les souvenirs colportés par les soldats qui firent la rude expédition de Cochinchine et la pénible guerre du Tonkin, ont laissé jusqu'à nos jours une trace profonde dans les esprits. Incapable de s'affranchir de cette notion formée aux premiers jours de la pénétration coloniale, le public a confondu pendant longtemps, tous les pays indochinois dans un ensemble qui conservait, à ses yeux, la même signification sinistre.[41]

Clearly these initial portrayals of Indochina as a vast burial ground for young Frenchmen are important, yet the question remains as to why this 'first impression' was never truly replaced, even once Indochina had been 'sanitised' through metropolitan progress, with a less maleficent representation. The durability of the association between Indochina and death, between Indochina and disease and suffering, thus suggests a residual unease with the experience of colonial expatriation.

The hostility and threat of Indochina's environment is often coupled with acutely felt sense of living amongst a hostile population. Whilst most sources between the turn of the century and the early 1920s tended to confirm a view that French rule in Indochina was successful and that the Indochinese populations were peaceable and appreciative subjects, there nonetheless occurred rather less explicit indications of anxieties related to inter-cultural encounters. On the one hand, commentators seemed to agree that Indochina of the 1920s appeared as a model of Franco-indigenous collaboration and harmony. Paul Claudel, for example, visiting Indochina in 1921 as part of his duties as French Ambassador to Japan,[42] was full of praise for the colony:

Jamais en Indo-Chine la collaboration entre l'élément indigène et l'élément européen n'a été plus intime et plus pacifique. On assiste au mouvement d'un peuple entier dont le désir le plus profond semble n'être que d'adopter notre culture et notre langue elle-même.[43]

He demonstrates the view which had come to be accepted of the indigenous populations of Indochina as peacefully and gratefully collaborating with their French rulers:

L'Annamite n'est ni un sauvage, ni un fanatique, et il n'est pas notre ennemi. C'est un homme remarquablement intelligent, d'un amour-propre intense, avide de s'instruire et de s'élever. Il s'est rendu compte aujourd'hui que la culture chinoise ne répondait plus à ses besoins. Il s'en est complètement détourné et c'est à nous qu'il s'adresse pour la remplacer.[44]

Similarly, the visual representation of native Indochinese populations at the colonial exhibition of Vincennes had perpetuated this image of a docile peasant people: malleable *figurants* who actively sought the guidance of the superior imperial nation. Other, more anthropologically-minded texts often offset these positive attributes against a disparaging résumé of the natives less desirable and potentially menacing qualities. Writing a history of the French overseas possessions, Gaffarel states:

Les Annamites ont des qualités: ils sont gais, braves, entreprenants, polis, hospitaliers, dévoués à leur famille, avides d'instruction et passionnés pour le progrès: mais ils sont aussi malpropres, gloutons, disputeurs, inconstants, ingrats, cruels, voleurs, menteurs et débauchés. Ces défauts disparaîtront ou diminueront peut-être avec les progrès de l'instruction.[45]

Here, those negative qualities are seen as being held in check by French civilising action and education. The analysis leaves unspoken the potentially negative consequences for French rule in Indochina should that 'instruction' not be successfully accomplished.

Views and representations such as these reinforced the founding colonial premise of imperial superiority and authority over the subjugated colonised. On the other hand however, much colonial fiction and travel writing nonetheless revealed what might be construed as a far less firmly held belief in the innate authority of the coloniser. As we have seen, fictional responses to settler life tended to expose certain anxieties related to the experience of living as an ethnic minority in a dominated territory: these responses range from Raymonde Rollin's extreme fear of living in 'un pays ennemi', to less overt instances of tension and apprehension.

Contemporary commentators have noted that one of the ways in which colonial authority manifests itself is through the commanding gaze of the European. To be an observer is to re-enact the power hierarchy of the colonial relationship. The act of observing implies a position of authority, through which a sense of mastery over the unknown is conveyed. Natives are 'obligated to show themselves to view for the white men, but they themselves lack the privilege of the gaze; though looked at, they are forbidden from looking back (. . .) gazed upon, they are denied the power of the gaze'.[46] The colonial gaze becomes a means through which to control, and to enact disciplinary surveillance over subjugated populations. For the European in Indochina however, this economy of the colonial gaze often appears to be reversed: the European becomes the object of study, and is imprisoned by the gaze of the Other; the European is stripped of the authority and privilege traditionally preserved for the Western observer.

Fears concerning the potential hostility of the native Indochinese populations often reflect a discomfort which may stem from being allied with the conquering and ruling class. This is manifested psychologically through the projection onto the indigenous populations of a residual antipathy towards the European, which threatens at any moment to erupt into violence. The latent discomfort and disquiet of the conquering nation vis-à-vis its own role and actions are thus revealed through individual accounts of physical isolation and excessive visibility.

Anxiety is often provoked in crowd situations where the the disequilibrium of the minority/majority equation for the European becomes most tangible. The engulfing threat of the 'péril jaune' is discerned in the seemingly malignant fusion of the massed crowds of Indochinese. Viollis for example, notices 'la foule silencieuse, vêtue de noir et de blanc',[47] and experiences a 'singulière impression que celle de rouler entre les flots contenus de cette foule noire et blanche, absolument silencieuse, aux milliers de jaunes visages impassibles où guettent les prunelles aïgues'.[48] Faces are lost in crowds and individuality recedes to leave a homogenous and hostile mass. When visiting Hué, she and her companions feel a 'sensation d'être guettés par des centaines d'invisibles prunelles',[49] and the amassed crowd is described as a menacing throng of 'ombres'.[50] The experience of living or travelling as a minority group amongst the overwhelming numbers of the Other subverts the power of the European gaze. Experiencing the surveillance of a numerically superior population provokes doubt concerning the authority of the representative of the ruling colonial nation. In Duras' *L'Eden Cinéma*, the unbreachable distance between European and native populations confirms the impossibility of authentic complicity and fraternity within the hierarchical confines of the colonial relationship. The end of the text emphasises the inevitable distance between the two communities and denies the possibility of harmonious integration into the society of the colonised:

Blanche. Elle était blanche. Même si elle vous [les paysans indigènes] aimait. Même si son espoir était le vôtre et si elle a pleuré les enfants de la plaine, elle est restée une étrangère à votre pays ... Nous sommes restés des étrangers à votre pays. Elle sera enterrée dans le cimetière colonial de Saïgon. [51]

The disillusionment and disappointment unveiled in many accounts of Indochina thus provide a counterpoint to the quasi-utopic portrayals of French Indochina disseminated by official sources. Indeed, Indochina often represents the very antithesis of the official version of Indochina as the 'perle' of the Empire. Indochina becomes, on contact, a veritable dystopia: its defining features are disease, debilitation, threat and isolation. Thus although official portrayals of Indochina were perhaps the most widely disseminated sources of metropolitan knowledge about Indochina, there nonetheless existed a series of narratives which, although less concerted than the 'official' image of France in Indochina, strongly reflected colonial doubts and unease.

Notes

1. Duras, M., *Un Barrage contre le Pacifique* (Paris: Gallimard, 1950), p. 23.
2. Franchini, P., 'La Cité blanche', in Franchini, P. (ed.), *Saigon 1925–45: de la 'Belle Colonie' à l'éclosion révolutionnaire ou la fin des dieux blancs* (Paris: Editions Autrement, 1992), p. 69.
3. The metropolitan population in Algeria during the same period was estimated to be 946,000. For further statistics relating to the metropolitan settlement of the French colonies, see Pervillé, G., *De l'empire français à la décolonisation* (Paris: Hachette, 1993), pp. 53–5.
4. Groslier, *Le Retour à l'argile* (Paris: Emile Paul, 1928), (repr. Paris: Kailash, 1994), p. 15.
5. Ibid., p. 25.
6. Ibid., p. 26.
7. Jacnal, J., *Rêves d'Annam* (Paris: 1913), p. 112.
8. Dorsenne, J., *Loin des blancs* (Paris: 1933).
9. Loti, P., *Un Pèlerin d'Angkor* (Paris: Calmann-Lévy, 1912), (repr. Paris: Kailash, 1994), p. 15.
10. Ibid., pp. 15–16.
11. Leuba, J., *L'Aile du feu* (Paris: 1926), p. 242.
12. Ajalbert, J., *Raffin Su-su* (Paris: Publications littéraires et politiques, 1911), *Raffin Su-su suivi de Sao Van Di*, (Paris: Kailash, 1995), p. 7.

13. Ibid.
14. Ibid., p. 14.
15. Ibid., p. 17.
16. Ibid., pp. 25-6.
17. Duras, M., *L'Eden cinéma* (Paris: Mercure de France, 1977), pp. 25–6.
18. Ibid., p. 18.
19. Duras, *Un Barrage contre le Pacifique*, p. 13.
20. Duras, *L'Eden cinéma*, p. 30.
21. Ibid., p. 25.
22. Ibid., p. 19.
23. Ibid., pp. 21-2.
24. Ibid., pp. 127-33.
25. See for example Vigné d'Octon, *Au Pays des fétiches* (Paris: [n.p.], 1891): 'une indicible stupeur plane sur tout, et le morne, l'effrayant, l'incroyable silence africain prend possession de la terre et de l'onde', p. 38.
26. Daguerches, *Le Kilomètre 83* (Paris: Calmann-Lévy, 1913), (repr. Paris, Kailash, 1993), pp. 65–6.
27. Boissière, J., 'Dans la forêt' in *Fumeurs d'Opium* (Paris: Flammarion, 1895), (repr. Paris: Kailash, 1993), p. 9.
28. Malraux, A., *La Voie royale* (Paris: Grasset, 1930), pp. 65–7.
29. Ibid., p. 67.
30. Elsewhere these fears were also projected onto syphilis, prostitutes, Jews etc., in the context of the fin-de-siècle mentality, thereby imputing perceived degeneration to different forms of Otherness.
31. Daguerches, *Le Kilomètre 83*, p. 135.
32. Loutfi relates this type of representation to a generalised 'goût du morbide' in metropolitan literature; see Loutfi, M., *Littérature et colonialisme: l'expansion coloniale vue à travers la littérature romanesque française 1871–1914* (La Haye: Mouton, 1971), pp. 5–43.
33. Loti, *Un Pèlerin d'Angkor*, p. 10.
34. Loti, P., *Pêcheur d'Islande* (Paris: Calmann Levy, 1893), (repr. Paris: Bookking International/Classiques français, 1994), pp 125–71.
35. Ibid., p. 127.
36. Ibid.
37. Malleret, L., *L'Exotisme indochinois dans la littérature française depuis 1860* (Paris: Larose, 1934), p. 17.
38. Boissière, 'Dans la forêt', p. 10.
39. Ibid., p. 11.
40. Malleret, *L'Exotisme indochinois dans la littérature française depuis 1860*, p. 79.
41. Ibid., p. 12.

42. Claudel was first Ambassor to China (1895–1909), then to Japan (1921–27). He visited Indochina on a number of occasions, making six short trips, and three longer visits in 1903, 1921 and 1925. It was his 1921 trip which gave rise to written reflections on the colony, which appear as a combination of the *récit de voyage* with a *rapport de mission*. These first appeared in May 1922 in *La Revue du Pacifique*.

43. Claudel, P., *Oeuvres complètes de Paul Claudel: Tome 4, Extrême-Orient* (Paris: Gallimard, 1952), p. 333.

44. Ibid., pp. 337–9.

45. Gaffarel, P., *L'Algérie et les colonies françaises: lectures géographiques et historiques* (Paris: Garnier, 1888), pp. 582–3.

46. Spurr, D., *The Rhetoric of Empire: Colonial Discourse in Journalism, Travel Writing and Imperial Administration* (Durham: Duke University Press, 1994), p. 13.

47. Viollis, A., *SOS Indochine* (Paris: Gallimard, 1935), p. 41.

48. Ibid., p. 30.

49. Ibid., p. 50.

50. Ibid., p. 55.

51. Duras, *L'Eden cinéma*, p. 154.

−7−

Gender Anxieties: Feminisation and the Erosion of Male Control

As we have seen, colonialism was often figured as a gendered enterprise and was undertaken in gender specific ways, by gendered agents. The conquest and pacification of Indochina were undertaken by men; the first settlers were admirals of the French Navy, and soldiers stationed in Indochina as part of *the Corps expéditionnaire*. The government of Indochina required male *fonctionnaires*, and hardy *broussards* who were sent out into the remotest areas of the territory to ensure French control. The construction of Indochina required engineers, builders and planners; the figure of the *colon bâtisseur* epitomised the idealised image of the active, energetic male in Indochina.

The nation in whose name these settlers carried out their various functions was also gendered in colonial discourses. France's role, however, was not so unambiguously figured. France's gendering as *la mère-patrie* encapsulates the anithetical and ambiguous positioning of the nation in its imperial role: France is both masculined and feminised. Although the French nation and the Republic are usually associated with female icons, the gendering of France in relation to Indochina was more problematic and liable to change. France is most usually associated, within its own boundaries at least, with female icons and emblems: *Marianne*, *la Semeuse*, and *la Moissonneuse*. France is often perceived as the wife, the lover, or the widow. France's gender-nation identification appears, at first glance, to be reversed in relation to the colonies. However, the issue is further complicated by the alternate and sometimes concomitant interplay of gendered metaphors of France, first as protective mother figure towards 'her' adopted 'children', the colonies; and second as a patriarchal and authoritative father figure. This ambiguity is epitomised by the term *la mère-patrie*.

As we have seen, France's response to Indochina can be summarised through a series of antitheses. *La Plus Grande France* functioned as both protective and nurturing mother, and constructive and edifying father to its colonial offspring. France's colonial role in Indochina was imagined as generous yet self-seeking; liberatory yet authoritarian. Imperial France sought to express its superiority and control over its colonised peoples; but it also emphasised its more fraternal and respectful relationship with its 'pearl' of the Far East. These dual narratives of success/disaster, value/ambivalence were manifest in France's representations of Indochina, and in the nation's imperial role. They reveal France's inability to fully reconcile the nation's revolutionary heritage and principles with an imperial vocation; the antitheses they produce thus find expression in the oxymoronic term *la mère-patrie.*

The language in the official texts concerning the exhibition reflects these ambiguities through its tendency to speak of colonialism in gender-related terms. Whilst consciously, attempts were made to distance France from the language of domination and force by qualifying its role in relation to its colonies as that of a nurturing, protecting Motherland, it seems clear that France was still unconsciously viewed as an authoritative Fatherland. As we have seen, key concepts of this gendered discourse revolved around values or attributes which have traditionally been viewed as masculine: vitality, energy, action and virility. In official texts the (male) settler becomes the prime symbol of this virile fantasy: 'le colon est, *par excellence*, créateur d'énérgie [issu de cette] terre d'énérgie qui est la France'.[1] Similarly, Pierre Laval, *Premier Ministre* in 1931, noted that 'l'exposition donne à tous les enfants de France la plus virile des leçons'.[2] The heroic *colon* was no longer presented as an explorer or a conquistador, but as an engineer, a builder of roads and bridges. The notion of 'le colon bâtisseur', an image which as we have seen proliferated in colonial texts of the 1920s and 1930s, is a key concept of French colonialism, but one which raises contradictions. For these new, peaceful channels for action continue to be described in terms which draw on imagery suggestive of war and conquest: 'de pacifiques batailles', nature as 'forces mauvaises' to be overcome.

This paradoxical desire to present the colonial settler as both peaceful and combative, virile yet moderate, relates to the conflicting imperatives of France's colonial enterprise in the 1920s and 1930s. France wished its superiority and the legitimacy of its presence overseas to be readily accepted and innately obvious, but it was becoming increasingly necessary to sustain authority by countering nationalist agitation in the colonies (the Rif War 1925, the Yen Bay Uprising of 1930)[3] with a military show of strength. The representation of the peaceful yet potentially combative *colon* thus contained the veiled threat of violent retribution should France's authority be further challenged.

These ambiguously wrought identities were further complicated by the addition to the equation of a sexualised dimension. As many critics of colonialism have shown, the colony often functions symbolically as a female to be penetrated, and possessed.[4] Clearly, much imperial ideology – be it British, French or Dutch – centred around the perception and portrayal of the colony as an erotic playground, a virgin bride to be ravished and penetrated by the white European male. Peopled with obliging native women, the colony was imagined as a sexual utopia. Similarly, the conquest of the colony has been viewed as an assertion of phallic power through rituals expressing the European claim of possession, such as flag-planting.

Such sexualised portrayals of Indochina distorted the archetypal parental positioning of the imperial nation vis-à-vis the colonised territory. When the *Union indochinoise* was first formally designated, it was referred to as a marriage between France and Annam. This rhetorical device was often used to mask or to exonerate France of its bloody role in the conquest of Indochina. Admiral Bonard observed on the signing of the treaty of 1862 which accorded France territories in Cochinchina:

> La cession des provinces que le souverain d'Annam a faite à Sa Majesté Impériale est comme un mariage où la jeune fille accordée à son fiancé, tout en devant obéissance à celui-ci, ne renie pas pour cela son père. L'épouse bien traitée par celui qui la protège et veille à ses besoins perd bientôt toute appréhension et, sans oublier ses parents, finit par aimer son mari.[5]

Here, traditionalist views of marital roles serve to confine Indochina to a subservient position, yet the metaphor also implicitly invokes the marriage vows to suggest a reciprocal and mutually beneficial arrangement. The later independance of Indochina from metropolitan France is similarly described in marital terms: as Hue puts it, 'le divorce à Genève'.[6] In this Franco-Indochinese 'marriage', the metropole is clearly positioned in the male role, and Indochina once again takes on the female gender identification: the parent/child relationship is thus tranfigured and becomes a fraught male/female, and often voyeuristic, sexual union.

Fictional accounts of the Franco-Indochinese relationship further explore this sexualised dimension of the colonial imagination. In Farrère's *Les Civilisés*, chronologically nearer to the male-dominated 'adventure' stories of the nineteeth century portrayals, Indochina still retains the allure of a 'virgin' territory. Farrère's character, Fierce, is a sea-faring adventurer, but he is also a sexual adventurer, seeking new delights and sensations in the Indochinese capital, which is laid before him to be taken and ravished. The analogy between the conquest of a colonial territory and rape is alluded to in Fierce's violation of an indigenous woman while on a military mission. The further allusion to Saigon as a 'marché aux femmes',[7] emphasises that women were viewed as the 'booty' of the conqueror.

The use of analogies between the female body and the colony thus reinvented colonial conquest in an age where allusions to violent intervention abroad had been superceded by an emphasis on civilising and protective guidance. Similarly, where there is no longer a place in fiction for the heroic conqueror, a textual equivalent is sought in the sexual conqueror. In *Raffin Su-su*, Raffin is thus congratulated upon his bigamous marriage: 'Raffin [fut] accablé de félicitations sur sa vigoureuse façon de coloniser et de pénétrer l'indigène.'[8] Furthermore, in the same novel male fertility is presented as a form of personal colonisation. Raffin's two concubines become pregnant at the same time, and the narrator notes that Raffin 'revendiquait toujours l'honneur d'avoir fourni l'exemple de colonisation le plus énergique: deux le même jour, lui, le même jour (. . .) Vive Raffin . . . Vive la France.'[9] Conquest is thus replayed through the vector of the female native body; and France's virile role as conquering nation is replayed through the sexual prowess of a fictional settler.

However, in extending these metaphors, and bringing them to their logical conclusions, some writers foresaw the collapse of French colonialism in Indochina. In Henry Daguerches' portrayal of Indochina in *Le Kilomètre 83*, metropolitan France is first positioned in the rather more parental role of educator, bringing up the Indochinese child, ensuring 'her' development, and *épanouissement*. These concepts are all in keeping with the stated aim of *mise en valeur* enshrined in official French colonial discourse. The child however, is approaching adolescence, and thus beginning to elude the control of the parent country. In a conversation between M. de Sibaldi and Tourange, Saigon is referred to 'une belle fille qui grandit vit'.[10] Metropolitan France is positioned as a paternal figure, threatened by the blooming sexuality of this young woman:

> Et maintenant la voilà femme, avec tout son visage riant et chaleureux, et sa grande respiration tranquille, et son activité harmonieuse, et ses nonchalances énervées de ses siestes . . . La voilà femme, et qui surprend et déroute![11]

Saigon is portrayed as escaping the paternal grasp of her metropolitan parent and becoming independent. France, as parent, created Saigon, but now laments her coming of age:

> Et vous, vous qui, jour à jour, heure à heure, avez suivi la transformation, vous qui croyiez connaître le moindre de ses désirs, de ses besoins, de ses rêves, chaque soir, lorsqu'elle s'endort, vous frémissez, en la contemplant, devant un mystère qui vous dépasse . . . Et il ne vous reste qu'à vous redire, les dents serrées: c'est nous, nous, nous les hommes venus de France, qui avons fait cela tout de même! qui avons fait cela tout seuls![12]

This sexualised and feminised portrayal of Indochina is extended beyond the paternalistic view of a young woman reaching adulthood, as the country becomes analagous with a seductive temptress:

> N'est-ce pas qu'elle est belle? Ah! je me garde de convier à sa contemplation ces impuissants qui jugent d'une cité par ses monuments, comme d'une femme par le dénombrement de ses bijoux; dont le cerveau réclame pour s'émouvoir, les relents d'un passé fameux, la fascination d'un musée plus gorgé de souvenirs qu'un oeil de vieille courtisane.[13]

Saigon, the showcase city of France's 'perle de l'Extrême-orient', needs no decoration in order to seduce. This at first appears to be a criticism of the ways in which the metropole had attempted to 'adorn' Indochina with opulent buildings and impressive monuments. However, it is precisely the 'adolescence' of this city which is so exciting to these 'papas maladroits'.[14] Saigon is still virginal and wholesome, untainted, and all the more alluring for her naivety. If Indochina is conceived as a sexually alluring adolescent, then France, as a doting, yet sexually-threatening father, occupies a parasitic, voyeuristic role. This positioning is further reflected in the fear of losing possession of Indochina:

> – je sais que ce à quoi j'assiste n'est que l'éclatement, le rayonnement, l'épanchement de sa vie, à elle. Je sais qu'elle peut rire de ses vieux tuteurs, qui ne se demandent plus, eux, qu'un honneur: celui de mieux se souvenir de ce qu'il a fallu de soins autour de son berceau! Non, Monsieur, elle n'a plus besoin de nous, elle se défend toute seule.[15]

This final quotation articulates the regret, nostalgia and unease of an ageing, and increasingly impotent, paternal metropolitan position in Indochina. It foretells of an end to colonial rule and demonstrates an early, if timid, *mise en cause* of the French role in Indochina.

Gender issues and gendered positionings of France and Indochina were further complicated with the arrival of female settlers to Indochina. Women settlers were encouraged to emigrate as wives of *fonctionnaires* and by the 1920s made up a significant proportion of the settler population in Indochina. As early as 1897 the *Société française d'émigration des femmes* was founded by Joseph Chailley-Bert[16] and the Comte d'Haussonville. The *Société française d'émigration de femmes* functioned as a placement agency. Its role was to propose jobs in the colonies to unemployed women in France; and it provided financial aid to facilitate their departure. In reality it functioned largely as a marriage bureau. In 1897, the society received 500 requests from women to emigrate to the colonies. These women were schoolteachers, governesses, office workers, midwives, seamstresses, and cooks. More importantly for France, they were also wives and potential mothers.[17] From marriages between France's colonial officials abroad, economic prosperity would ensue in the colonies, fertility would rise; decency and dignity would reign in the colonies:

> La présence d'une seule femme européenne dans un poste, dans un coin de brousse, – si elle comprend bien son rôle, – peut être d'une importance considérable au point de vue de la moralité générale.[18]

Certainly, the perpetuation of the 'French race' was a priority for a demographically weakened France at the turn of the century. Peopling the colonies with French children born and brought up in the colonies would, it was hoped, ensure the perpetuation of colonial rule, and would create a pool of knowledgable colonial administrators. As Knibiehler and Goutalier note: 'les colonies ne sont plus seulement une source de richesse ou un substitut de la revanche. Elles deviennent un lieu d'utopie où la race française se régénéra dans une vertu et une fécondité retrouvées.'[19]

The notion of utopia in the above quotation sits ill with the notion of utopia suggested in the earlier chapters. Two visions of the French Empire thus emerge, alongside two different versions of France's colonial utopia. On the one hand, the nation's colonial possessions often fuctioned as a playground for male adventurers and explorers; Indochina was perceived as a male haven, a virgin territory awaiting action; colonialism was imagined as a homosocial pursuit. On the other hand, there were concerns to populate the colonies and extend French influence through the means of the family; to create a utopia based upon the notion of heterosocial generation and regeneration. This tension is articulated in contrasting perceptions of the French woman's role and status in Indochina.

Propaganda from the late 1920s urging women to emigrate to the colonies based its perception of a French woman's role in the colonies on a feminised form of *mise en valeur* which emphasised the nurturing and protective qualities which they could bring to bear:

> S'imagine-t-on d'ailleurs les services que peut rendre la femme française auprès des populations locales? Son mari commande un poste: elle passe dans les camps des femmes de tirailleurs, distribue de ci, de là quelques conseils concernant la propreté et la tenue des cases, les soins à donner aux nourrisons, l'hygiène du vêtement et de la nourriture. Les médicaments apportés et présentés par elle sont absorbés avec plus de régularité. La santé physique et moral de toute l'agglomération indigène y gagne.[20]

This feminised version of *mise en valeur* reminds us of the benevolent and protective role which had been imagined for *la mère-patrie*. French women in the colonies were also perceived as a catalyst for improvement and modernity; their presence would bring tangible material results: 'l'adduction d'eau', the creation of gardens, the use of electricity, 'les installations intérieures se perfectionnent',[21] and

> Là où n'existaient que des cases plantées pêle-mêle s'élèvent des avenues bordées de villas élégantes et confortables. Tous bénéficient de ces améliorations, y compris les indigènes qui ont toujours une tendance à imiter l'Européen.[22]

This 1927 publication of the Colonial Army further observed that the presence of European wives would play a considerable part in raising moral standards in the colony: European women saved men from debauchery, and the ignominy of creating a 'temporary marriage' with an indigenous woman; they furthermore reinstated in male minds the benefits of a stable home life. French women were thus viewed as having a potentially moral and modernising impact in the French Empire.

Conversely, however, it appears that, for many writers and commentators, the arrival of women and the consequent feminisation of the settler community in Indochina marked the beginnings of an artificial, consumerist society which spelled the ruin of the earlier, more authentic and creative masculine society. As I asserted earlier, Roubaud and Viollis were both highly critical of the social tension which the arrival of women in Indochina was thought to have engendered. Louis Roubaud's bitterly class-ridden analysis of the 'petites bourgeoises' who obtain in Indochina 'leurs nouveaux quartiers de noblesse coloniale', highlights a perceived lack of respect and tolerance perpetrated by the women arrived in Indochina: '[elles] ont importé ici le mépris de l'indigène sans distiction de classe ni de culture'.[23] Roubaud laments the artificiality of their newly acquired bourgeois lifestyle, regretting that class superiority is no longer inherent in the French community, but has to be proved through ostentation and overt displays of power. According to Roubaud these women exacerbate social conflict, create barriers between colonised and coloniser, and perpetuate the despised 'esprit colon'. The corruption of an idealised period of harmony, order and respect of the coloniser is thus posited with the arrival *en masse* of metropolitan French women to Indochina in the 1920s.

Andrée Viollis similarly regrets the unproductiveness and passivity of the women settlers she meets. They are not 'consciente[s] de [leurs] responsabilités'; they fail to tend adequately to the natives; they are not 'à la hauteur de leur tâche qui pourrait être si belle'.[24] Viollis regrets the fact that the French women she meets are unwilling or incapable of performing the duties required of a benevolent French matriarchy. Colonial society, she implicitly concludes, was being damaged due to the failure of women settlers to fulfil their prescribed role.

Fictional works found further things to be regretted in the arrival of women in Indochina. Georges Groslier's *Le Retour à l'argile* of 1928, just following the influx of European women to Indochina, and the consequent transformation of the settler community, places more emphasis than the previous novels on the reactions of his female characters to life in the colonies. Much of his main protagonist's attitude towards the female European community in Indochina is coloured by his own desire for acculturation and his increasingly exclusive affection for the indigenous populations. Rollin thus negatively contrasts the elegance and sophistication of European women with the simplicity of indigenous women. His descriptions of a colonial ball focus upon the clothes and make-up of the metropolitan women:

> Voyant tourner ces femmes excitées qui gâchaient leurs charmes par leurs trémousse-
> ments, ces faces défardées par la transpiration, il évoqua irréstiblement la mesure, la
> pudeur, la discrétion des belles indigènes qu'il connaissait, timides, concentrées et
> baissant leurs yeux de biches.[25]

This emphasis on the 'veiling' of the female body is clearly linked to Groslier's discourse of 'the natural'. Adornment is seen as undesirable and unnatural, symbolising the artificiality and inauthenticity of Western women.

Simone Bertrand on the other hand presents the reader with Groslier's idealised view of how a metropolitan woman should behave in the colonies. Simone ('Pomme') is lively, gay, practical and efficient. The uncomplaining, supportive wife of Pierre, Pomme Bertrand is a model of physical and moral support to her husband. Groslier thus delivers a prescriptive, masculine view of an idealised female role in Indochina which mirrors colonial propaganda aimed at women migrants. Simone is 'rieuse', 'très ordonnée et courageuse',[26]

> Elle conduisit sa maison d'une main solide, collaborait aux travaux de son mari, chassait
> en brousse et cent hectares nets de la plantation aussi bien tenus que les autres,
> dépendaient de sa seule autorité. Elle soignait elle-même les coolies malades, ou, de sa
> cravache, le dos du caporal indocile. Elle ne quittait le bal que morte de fatigue, mais
> n'employait à recevoir les gens en leur offrant des petits fours que le temps qu'elle
> voulait. N'oublions pas qu'en cinq ans, elle avait donné à Pierre deux garçons nourris
> par elle.[27]

Mme Bertrand adopts masculine pursuits and traits in order to be accepted into the masculinised economy which prevails in the colony. Pomme Bertrand disci-plines her workers, works on the plantation, moves with ease within the colonial society.[28] The defining mark of womanhood – her ability to give birth to children – is added almost as an afterthought in the narrator's descriptions of her, and is never again alluded to throughout the course of the novel. Regarded by her husband and his peers as an honorary male, Pomme Bertrand is unthreatening precisely because she is denied her femininity.

By way of contrast, Raymonde Rollin, unwilling and unable to adapt to her new life in the colony is clearly positioned as the 'bad wife', and the narrow-minded *colon*. Unlike Simone Bertrand, Mme Rollin attracts the disapproval and antagonsim of the male society partly as a result of her manifestly female characteristics: her clothes, make-up, social activities and thoughts. Like many of her fictional male predecessors, she becomes bored once in Indochina; and longs to return to France.

This type of European woman in Indochina appears, in this novel, to escape the control and authority of their male counterparts. Mme Rollin, in contrast with Mme Bertrand, refuses to participate in the economy of masculinised values which predominate in Indochina. She is therefore presented as disturbing the prevailing order of male colonial society in Indochina, and by extension, subverting France's imperial mission. In escaping the control of her husband (and hence male society as a whole), she endangers the position of male dominance in the colony, and must therefore be punished. Her punishment consists of sexual betrayal by her husband and banishment from the colony. Although her departure from Indochina is presented as a choice, it is nonetheless clear that Mme Bertrand can no more remain in the colony than she can regain the affections of her husband. Public humiliation (the revelation that her husband has left her for an indigenous woman), and the removal of her role in the colony (for what are metropolitan women allowed to do other than support their husbands?) force her to leave. It is interesting that the vehicle through which Mme Rollin is punished is an indigenous woman. Not only does this gesture commodify women but in this instance it draws into focus the importance of racial hierarchies. If Mme Rollin had lost her husband to a metropolitan woman, her public shame would have been far less acutely felt.

If Indochina is widely viewed as a feminised territory, and if metropolitan women are frequently viewed as escaping male control, by extension Indochina is equally in danger of escaping from the authority of the male European settler. Once the colony is sufficiently Europeanised, it is feared that the indigenous populations will assert themselves. This fear is articulated in the emphasis on male preferences for simplicity (the country, the *con gai*, the customs). Thus on the one hand, certain representations appear to call for the policing of women's behaviour in Indochina; on the other, it is as if the presence of women exerts some form of disciplinary repression on male settlers, thus eroding their status in the colony. This erosion of the male role and status is all the more distressing, in that it casts a shadow over the authority of the coloniser, and produces a subconscious fear concerning the future of French colonialism in Indochina.

Gender issues, and the gendered representations of France and Indochina thus added a further layer of complexity to the Franco-Indochinese relationship. Firstly, gender issues highlight the indeterminacy of France's own conception of its role abroad. The ambiguous and confused emphases are contained in the term *la mère-patrie*, and find expression in France's double mission to both nurture and subdue. Secondly, the gendered and sexualised positions variously attributed to Indochina sit uncomfortably alongside the more parental or familial configurations of the Franco-Indochinese relationship which coincide with the ideological imperatives of *mise en valeur* and the French colonial doctrine. The coexistence of sexualised and parental representations of France's relationship towards Indochina once again reflect a double vocation: to penetrate and dominate, yet also to protect and guide. Thirdly, the arrival en masse of women settlers and the consequent feminisation of settler society clearly conflicted with the initial conceptualisation of Indochina as a male utopia. Indochina as a sexual paradise free from restraint, and Indochina as the heroic adventurer's playground, were images which were both shattered by the influx of metropolitan women. The imperatives of the colonising nation and its representatives on the ground can thus be seen to be somewhat at odds. Whilst official France desired the further domestication of Indochina, and hoped to achieve this partly through the tacit moral arbitration of women, certain sections of the settler community resented this evolution, and desired instead a return to what was perceived as a more authentic and unadulterated society and relationship with Indochina.

Notes

1. Quoted by Coquery-Vidrovitch, in Thobie, J., Meynier, G., Coquery-Vidro-vitch, C., and Ageron, C.-R., *Histoire de la France coloniale 1914–1990* (Paris: Armand Colin, 1990), p. 217.
2. *Le Temps*, 16 September 1931.
3. For a general overview of nationalist agitation in the French colonies during this period see relevent chapters in Thobie et al, *Histoire de la France coloniale 1914–1990*.
4. See McClintock, A., *Imperial Leather: Race, Gender and Sexuality in the Colonial Contest* (London: Routledge, 1995).
5. Quoted in Franchini, P., *Les Guerres d'Indochine* (Paris: Pygmalion, 1988), pp. 86–7.
6. Hue, B., 'La Noce indochinoise', p. 13, in Hue, B., (ed.), *Indochine: reflets littéraires*, Pluriel 3, (Rennes: Presses universitaires de Rennes, Centre d'étude des littératures et civilisations francophones, 1992).
7. Farrère, C., *Les Civilisés* (Paris: Flammarion, 1905), (repr. Paris: Kailash, 1993), p. 21.
8. Ajalbert, J., *Raffin Su-su* (Paris: Publications littéraires et politiques, 1911), *Raffin Su-su suivi de Sao Van Di* (Paris: Kailash, 1995), p. 47.
9. Ibid., p. 57.
10. Daguerches, *Le Kilomètre 83* (Paris: Calmann-Lévy, 1913), (repr. Paris, Kailash, 1993), p. 113.
11. Ibid.
12. Ibid., pp. 113–14.
13. Ibid., p. 114.
14. Ibid., p. 116.
15. Ibid., p. 117.

16. Chailley-Bert was an active member of the *Union coloniale*, and the son-in-law of Paul Bert, former governor of Indochina.

17. On France's pro-natalist policies, and their impact throughout the Empire, see Horne, J., 'In Pursuit of Greater France: Visions of Empire among Musée social Reformers', in Clancy-Smith J., and Gouda, F., *Domesticating the Empire; Race, Gender and Family Life in French and Dutch Colonialism* (Charlottesville: University Press of Virginia, 1998), pp. 21–42.

18. *Le rôle et la situation de la famille française aux colonies* (Paris: Editions du journal des coloniaux et de l'Armée coloniale réunis, 1927), p. 8.

19. Knibiehler, Y., and Goutalier, R., *La Femme au temps des colonies* (Paris: Stock, 1985), p. 89. See also Conklin, A., 'Redefining "Frenchness": Citizenship, Race Regeneration and Imperial Motherhood in France and West Africa, 1914–40' in Clancy-Smith and Gouda, *Domesticating the Empire*, pp. 65–83.

20. *Le rôle et la situation de la famille française aux colonie,* pp. 8–9.

21. Ibid., p. 9.

22. Ibid.

23. Roubaud, L., *Vietnam: la tragédie indochinoise* (Paris: Valois, 1931), pp. 233–4.

24. Viollis, A., *SOS Indochine* (Paris: Gallimard, 1935), p. 35.

25. Groslier, G., *Le Retour à l'argile* (Paris: Emile Paul, 1928), (repr. Paris: Kailash, 1994), p. 154.

26. Ibid., pp. 20–1.

27. Ibid.

28. This image of the 'honorary male' female settler was reiterated in the androgynous figure of Eliane Devries in Régis Wargnier's 1991 film *Indochine*.

—8—

Boundary Anxieties

If Indochina's climatic and natural features were physically debilitating for the white European, the colony was perceived equally to have a potentially harmful effect upon the settler's moral character and integrity. If contact with Indochina caused the dissipation of metropolitan energy and will, then the moral fortitude and civilised status of the settler was also perceived to be under threat. Many of these concerns took the form of boundary anxieties: boundaries between natives and Europeans, and the difference between colonised and coloniser; boundaries between the civilised status of the European and the immoral, if not barbarous, character of the native populations; and the physical and biological integrity of the European.

The maintenance of colonial rule reposes upon the premise of a disequilibrium between coloniser and colonised. The coloniser must epitomise and display power, a high degree of 'civilisation', authority, and moral fortitude. The hierarchical configuration of the colonial relationship, and the erection of differentiating boundaries between colonised and coloniser, are necessary to the maintenance and perpetuation of colonial rule. Boundary anxieties, in their various manifestations, reveal deep-seated fears of *rapprochement*, indifferentiation, and of shortening the gap between the self and the Other. Where France and the nation's representatives should have demonstrated their innate difference from Indochina and the indigenous masses, settler life proved that social contact could effect a blurring or disintegration of boundaries.

Boundary anxieties often articulated concerns regarding the physical and biological integrity of the European settler. Thus the fears over the untameability or uncontrollability of Indochina, coupled with the perceived insalubrity of Indochina, resurfaced in relation to metropolitan anxieties over health and hygiene. These fears were articulated implicitly even in government-endorsed policies and programmes, such as the urban plans for the development of Indochina's cities, and the medical and scientific discourses of the colonial administration's *Services publics*.

In comparison with the confident rhetoric which emerged from the exhibition, France's *urbanistes* often revealed distinct anxieties with regard to colonialism: fears of contamination by association and proximity; anxieties over difference and the integrity of the colonial body. These concerns are revealed not only in

Figure 18. Dalat

building plans for Indochina's cities, but also in the popularity of colonial sanatoria, and in the rhetoric of urban planners themselves.[1]

In Indochina, Ernest Hébrard's work as the colony's appointed *urbaniste*, is revelatory of the ways in which political, biological, moral and physical anxieties combined. Dalat, the *station balnéaire d'altitude* on the east coast of Vietnam which was to double as a summer seat of government, was one of Ernest Hébrard's largest projects, but was never entirely completed due to financial constraints.[2] It is also an urban project which combines the abiding concerns over health and hygiene with colonial urbanism most readily. In addition, Dalat was at once a military outpost, a sanatorium and a seat of government, thus combining all the predominant features and concerns of French colonial rule in Indochina. (Figure 18)

Dalat had been the focus of speculation for some time, although it was not until Hébrard's appointment as *chef de l'urbanisme* that a concerted attempt was made to draw up coherent and extensive plans for the development of this polyfunctional city. Hébrard's designs envisaged a governmental quarter with residences for administrators and functionaries, an electricity plant and an improved water supply, new wider roads and avenues, an artificial lake, a casino, hotels, sports pitches, lycées, two hospitals and a museum. The total area of the city was to cover some 1,760 hectares, of which 500 were to be given over to administrative and public service buildings, 185 for military quarters, 173 for the government quarter, and 206 reserved for indigenous use. The remaining areas were to be put up for sale.

This grandiose plan was intended to respond to the perceived need for a 'station balnéaire ou d'altitude pour permettre aux fonctionnaires et colons, et à leur famille, de prendre du repos et reconstituer leur santé'.[3] The mountain health resort, with its temperate climate and high altitude, was conceived of as a place in which metropolitan health and governing powers could be restored and rejuvenated; the type of city

> où le capital européen se conserverait, grâce à un climat sain, bien choisi, et qui serait l'organisme d'où partirait, comme d'un immense cerveau, la pensée directrice et créatrice.[4]

Hébrard viewed the 'zoning' of the colonial city as extremely beneficial to urban environmental concerns, and essential in the case of Dalat, which was planned according to the following five 'zones': an administrative centre; residential districts; recreational spaces (parks, cultural centres); commercial areas; and industrial sectors. Thus different areas within the city would be set aside for different uses, and European quarters segregated from indigenous ones:

> La ville est divisée en: quartier de commerce genre européen et indigène; quartier d'habitations, européen et indigène; quartier des garages; quartier des chantiers, ateliers, petites industries et usines.[5]

This strict manipulation of urban topography was perceived as 'une sauvegarde contre les voisinages industriels, dont nous souffrons tant dans la métropole'.[6] Hébrard's zoning design was intended to serve several purposes. Firstly, using this system of spatial organisation, Hébrard intended to implement rationalised plans which would override the economic interests which had previously governed the expansion and growth of Indochinese cities. By implementing his zoning plans, and rejecting the irregular and uncontrolled autonomous expansion of the city, Hébrard was, in effect, inscribing order onto the landscape. As Wright and Rabinow have suggested, Hébrard's colonial cities, and particularly Dalat, reflected his 'idéal d'ordre, de propreté, de ségrégation spatiale et de hiérarchie'.[7]

Hébrard's modernising vision of the colonial city was thus additionally used as a tool through which to control colonial topography and indigenous itineries. In recent theories of the use of city space, the map has frequently been viewed as a totalising device.[8] As Harvey has observed, the map can be seen as a 'homogenisation and reification of the rich diversity of spatial itineries and spatial stories'.[9] This question of order and control is particularly relevant in the case of Indochina, as Asian crowds were an extremely prevalent and disturbing mythological element of French literature on Indochina. As we have seen, the 'grouillement de la foule' was viewed by many writers as one of the most disquieting elements of the 'Indochinese experience'. Hébrard's modernising vision of the colonial city can thus be viewed as a tool through which he hoped to contain and subdue the unruly natives. The zoning of city space, and the inscription of its ghettoising strategy upon official maps and plans, can be seen as an attempt to re-establish control over the multiplicitous and thus evasive character of the indigenous populations.

Urbanism can thus be viewed as a disciplinary service in that it uses its techniques and forms to ensure the ordering of human multiplicity. If, in Foucauldian terms, space is necessarily a receptacle of social power, then the reorganisation of space can be viewed as a reorganisation of the framework through which social power is expressed.[10] The reordering of urban topography which Hébrard hoped to accomplish in Indochina can be viewed in part as a form of exclusionary social control. By delimiting ethnic quarters and producing visibly distinguishable, if not rigorously enforced boundaries, Hébrard's zoning of city space created indigenous ghettos which were immediately recognisable.

This form of ethnic segregation also tends to use visibility as a means of oppression. This is achieved through the exhibiting of the people and their city so that they can be observed and understood from an external viewpoint. By segregating European and indigenous populations, colonial urbanism directed surveillance and the gaze of the agents of social order to the excluded, or spatially marginalised sections of the city population. Segregation and zoning can thus be viewed as an attempt to neutralise the effects of counterpower that spring from multiplicity: agitations, revolts, spontaneous organisations and gatherings, and coalitions. Hébrard's supposedly reformist vision of colonial urbanism thus functioned in much the same way as the militaristic designs which prevailed under the policy of assimilation. More importantly, however, these architectural concerns reveal a deeply-rooted desire to segregate and to reinforce boundaries between coloniser and colonised, and thereby prevent indifferentiation, social *métissage*, and *rapprochement*.

Secondly, as the above observations imply, Hébrard's 'zoning' plans clearly raise the issues of class and racial segregation. Hébrard's plans show that he intended to separate and juxtapose European and indigenous commercial and residential districts, mirroring the class segregation which operated in the metropole. Hébrard's assumption was that the greater majority of the indigenous population in cities was roughly equivalent to metropolitan 'lower' classes. In the following quotation, for example, he imagines the urban-dwelling indigenous populations of Indochina as a useful workforce whose proximity to European residential areas would provide necessary manual labour:

Dans certaines contrées, les centres indigènes existeront; dans d'autres, il faudra les créer à proximité de la nouvelle ville européennne; tout groupement européen ayant besoin d'une agglomération indigène pour vivre; soit afin de disposer d'une domesticité indispensable, soit pour le commerce, soit pour les travaux d'exploitation.[11]

The contact Hébrard envisages between European and indigenous populations is thus one in which rules of social hierarchy and class segregation prevailed. Although the Indochinese populations were viewed as capable of scaling metropolitan-defined class structures, of attaining a similar status as a bourgeois metropolitan family through the accumulation of capital, the vast majority of these populations were relegated to inferior status, and habitation.

Il ne faut pas oublier que les Européens ont absolument besoin des indigènes pour leur existence, et que ceux-ci s'établiront à proximité de l'agglomération européenne et formeront un centre commercial qui prendra une importance en rapport avec le développement du centre européen. Les domestiques vivent chez leurs maîtres, mais tous les jours vont au marché pour leurs achats, ou dans la ville indigène voir leurs familles et leurs amis. Il se forme autour de tout établissement européen une ou plusieurs agglomérations indigènes; celles-ci correspondent, en somme aux groupements de commerçants et ouvriers de nos villes modernes, qui sont, en vérité, séparés des habitations bourgeoises sans qu'une limite absolue soit tracée.[12]

Although Hébrard asserts that boundaries between zones are not impermeable, or absolute, that contact between the races was inevitable, he also envisages that contact was organised, rationalised and sanitised:

Il est souvent question de quartiers européens et de quartiers indigènes, et certains pourraient croire à une spécialisation absolue et penser que des zones devraient être rigoureusement tracées pour éviter tout contact pouvant, par le temps d'épidémies, devenir dangereux. En Indochine, les groupements sont distincts, mais si très rarement les Européens habitent les centres indigènes, par contre des indigènes aisés vivent souvent dans les centres européens.[13]

These concerns had passed into law even before the plans for Dalat were made clear, when, in a 1922 bill, the *conseil municipal de Saigon* decreed that in a large section of the city only European houses could be built. This bill was intended to isolate from the European part of the city the poorer Asian populations whose proximity was perceived to constitute a danger because of their ignorance of the most elemental rules of hygiene. Furthermore, Hébrard's design proposals for Dalat reveal that he intended strict racial and environmental controls to be exercised within the city: the Vietnamese needed permission to enter the city, and were housed beyond its northern hills.

Thus urbanism and concerns with hygiene were closely linked during this period. Hébrard's plans for Dalat reveal an obsession with health and hygiene which is present in much writing and thought on France's colonies. An abundance of health and hygiene manuals proliferated during this period, which was also marked in Indochina by the construction of several further sanatoria for the metropolitan and European populations (other main sanatoria: Bokkor in Cambodia, built 1925; Tam-Dao, built in 1905 in Tonkin; Chapa in Tonkin). Hébrard's texts and speeches also express an abiding concern with hygiene. He relates these concerns principally to climactic problems specific to Indochina. Indeed, as we have seen, Indochina's climate was widely viewed as nefarious to the health of Europeans: as much writing, both fictional and factual, about Indochina shows, descriptions of the countries' tropical climate was frequently linked to metaphors of disease and contamination.

However, with regard to colonial urbanism in Indochina, it was not simply the colony's climate and topography which constituted a health risk to Europeans. As several of the quotations from Hébrard's papers above show, the native populations of Indochina were also perceived as a danger to public hygiene. In a 1912 hygiene manual which is representative of the many which were published from the turn of the century onwards, Docteur Pavrel (*secrétaire adjoint de la Société des Etudes coloniales et maritimes*) makes the following observation on the location of European residences: 'La maison doit être bien située, c'est-à-dire à une certaine distance des agglomérations indigènes trop souvent infectées et malpropres.'[14]

This view is not simply one which reflects the concerns of early settlers to the colonies. It is a view which is reiterated throughout colonial discourses well into the 1930s. Dr Marcel Léger (a former director of the *Institut Pasteur* in Dakar), presenting a paper entitled, 'L'Habitation coloniale du point de vue médicale', at the *Congrès de l'urbanisme* in 1931, wrote in favour of racial segregation:

Pour éviter la contamination de ces locaux sommaires, les Européens agiront sagement en ne permettant que le moins possible aux indigènes de pénétrer chez eux, et en surveillant soigneusement à ne laisser aucun détritus d'aliments qui attire les bêtes, en particulier les rats. Les raisons d'ordre sanitaire qui militent en faveur de la ségrégation sont donc de première importance et indiscutables.[15]

Alongside vermin, debris and waste, the indigenous populations are viewed as vectors of disease and agents of contamination. (Figure 19) The indigenous individual is viewed as the intermediary between a malignant Nature and Civilisation. The bearer of disease, he represents the threat of rampant, uncontrollable, and pernicious forces of nature interposed against and threatening to the civilised metropolitan settler. As Léger continues:

Les indigènes sont, en effet, pour certaines maladies, des *réservoirs de virus* qu'il est bon d'éloigner. On connaît le rôle important qu'ils jouent dans le maintien de *l'endémicité paludéenne* [emphasis in the original].[16]

Figure 19. Traditional indigenous huts

Here, the human is conflated with the biological, forming a type of 'demographic pathology'[17] in which the role of a rapidly spreading malignant organism is imputed to the indigenous populations.

This notion of fear and loathing is a common feature of colonial discourse. As Spurr has noted,

> The obsessive debasement of the Other in colonial discourse arises not simply from fear and the recognition of difference but also, on another level, from a desire for and identification with the Other which must be resisted.[18]

One might be tempted to suppose that this fear and loathing be somewhat mitigated in the case of Indochina, for Indochina occupied a high status in imperial French racial hierarchies. The Indochinese were not comparable, as Félicien Challaye had noted, to 'n'importe quelle peuplade nègre du centre de l'Afrique'.[19] However, the medical experts quoted above drew frequent comparisons between Indochinese and African natives, rarely distinguishing between the housing and health situations of the two.[20] This type of blurring of colonial territories, their homogenisation into *les colonies* rather than separate and different areas is repeated in the title of Pavrel's document: *Hygiène colonial: comment vivre aux colonies*. This lack of distinction between the various overseas territories suggests a more profound malaise. Imperial France appears unable to accept diversity at some basic level.

While it was acceptable, if not advantageous, to distinguish between the colonies on grounds of relative cultural sophistication, in more fundamental questions such as health and hygiene, imperial France blurred all 'native populations' into one indistinguishable morass of disease and filth.

Segregation from the Indochinese populations was thus conceived of as an act of preservation, or self-preservation, against the danger of of collapse into indifferentiation. The notion of indigenous abjection, which is an important component of the discourses of catastrophism which served as a pretext for colonial intervention, is also consistently invoked as a means to reinforce difference between colonised and coloniser. Segregation thus functioned as a means by which to avoid contamination (both physical and moral). This fear of contamination, as Fanon's work has shown, is social and psychological as well as biological.[21]

Indeed, moral and social fears arise from the same discussions of physical health and the biological fear of disease. In a similar way to the imprecations of hygiene manuals concerning physical health, these discourses operate around notions of potential metropolitan degeneracy in the face of indigenous debilitation. The ostensible dirt, filth and moral degradation of the indigenous populations is viewed not simply in physical and medicinal terms, the insalubrity of the natives is also perceived as a threat to the moral order of European settlers. This link between the physical and the moral order is made explicit in the following extract from Pavrel's 1912 manual, in which he asserts that anyone enjoying good health can live in the colonies 'à condition de se plier aux lois d'hygiène de pays chauds, d'être sobre, économe de ses forces physiques et riche en énergie morale.'[22] Not only do Pavrel's hygiene imprecations appear to acquire legal status, he also predicates health upon moral character or 'energy'.

Concern for the moral character of Europeans settled in the colonies was an almost ubiquitous feature of fictional works on French Indochina, particularly the fiction of the first decades of the twentieth century. A privileged site of decadence and moral degradation, Indochina, and more particularly Saigon, was widely perceived as an amoral, or immoral society. Rife with the dangers of infestation and pollution, Saigon was therefore linked to the potential physical and moral degradation of the European populations. Seen from this perspective, the significance of Hébrard's plans for the mountain retreat of Dalat are highlighted: its remoteness from the dangers of Saigon and Indochina's other large cities, the idea of a 'cure', both physical and mental, and the emphasis on its 'elite' of residents, all reflect a desire to distance the European population from sites of contamination.

These issues of sanitation and segregation open up a further avenue of enquiry which revolves around questions of 'moral hygiene' and differentiation between colonised and coloniser. In his health manual, Pavrel, for example, moves almost imperceptibly from expressing a medicinal desire for segregation to a moral desire for segregation:

On a quelque tendance en pays tropical à se laisser aller aux douceurs du *farniente*, à prolonger outre-mesure la sieste, à fumer paresseusement sur de moelleux sofas à l'ombre des vérandas en s'intoxicant de nicotine, d'opium ou d'alcool; on en vient ainsi rapidement à un état déplorable de déchéance physique qui prépare la faillite de la volonté et de l'énergie. Là-bas on appelle cela *s'indigéniser*. C'est en effet descendre des hauteurs de la Civilisation pour tomber dans les abîmes de l'abrutissement négritien [emphasis in the original].[23]

As this quotation demonstrates, the principles of boundary, exclusion and difference which characterise discourses of abjection and debasement are intimately linked to notions of indifferentiation and the fear, or threat, of 'going native'. Reflected in this fear and in the exaggerated concerns with boundaries and frontiers, is a lack of confidence in France's imperial identity. Human bodies and colonial cities become metaphorical substitutes for one another, expressing a physical, moral and spatial anxiety over the integrity of imperial identity.

Indeed, Pavrel's disquiet over the moral conduct of the settler communities in the colonies reveals more profound misgivings concerning the stability or security of France's colonial project. The imperial identity of France, predicated on the perceived moral strength and rectitude of Western, and more particularly French, civilisation, is here perceived as easily threatened, and readily abandoned. The whole issue of health and segregation is connected explicitly with the perpetuation of France's Empire, and with its colonial aspirations. Health, hygiene and segregation come to assume the status of a pillar upon which rests the very possibility of the continuation of French rule.

Finally, it is the terms and terminology of France's *mission civilisatrice* which disguise these anxieties and reassert difference as a means of shoring up France's imperial identity and integrity. In his conclusion, Léger explicitly considers hygiene and health concerns in the same framework as that of France's *mission civilisatrice*. It is, in fact, the very modalities of this civilising ideal which allow for a metropolitan discourse of fear and loathing of the indigenous populations to be masked:

La tâche est rude, mais elle est bien française. Elle se résume ainsi: permettre à ceux qui s'expatrient de conserver la santé, de manière à augmenter au maximum nos échanges et notre production nationale; répandre nos idées parmi ceux que nous devons guider et protéger; imposer l'hygiène, non par la force, mais par la persuasion et par l'exemple; amener les indigènes à envier notre façon de procéder, en particulier, nos habitations, de manière à ce qu'ils nous imitent.[24]

It is a measure of official France's success in diffusing its ideal of colonialism, that it permeates both cultural, and here, scientific thought on the colonies. Not only does this last quotation draw upon all the fundamental principles of French colonialism, it also points to the contradictions inherent in those very discourses. Behind the French colonial discourse of generosity and protection lies a desire to reaffirm difference between colonised and coloniser, thereby asserting metropolitan superiority over more 'primitive' and backward populations.

Encongayement

If contact between the European and native populations could be controlled through urban planning and design, thus preventing contamination, personal relationships remained largely beyond the realm of state control. Whereas other imperial nations in Europe instituted (successfully or not) laws in order to regulate physical relations between colonised and coloniser, the French legal system seems not to have addressed the colonial situation in any coherent way. In 1864 local laws in Cochinchina were reformed by the conquering admirals, and a corps of native interpreters was dispatched to aid the French in the application of the Napoloeonic code. Later, as the imperatives of the policy of assimilation were brought to bear, the entire French legislative procedure was to apply to Annam and Tonkin (1879). Once association replaced assimilation as the *mot d'ordre* of native policy, the legal framework in Indochina became more complex and less coherent. On 2 April 1909, the Chamber of Deputies voted that it was essential to modify the economic and judicial regime in Indochina in line with the associative stance France was to take in native affairs.[25] Albert Sarraut reformed the penal codes, criminal procedure and many civil service statutes without departing too far from indigenous traditions. This meant that the *Code annamite*, dating from 1812, and the twelfth year of Gia-Long's reign, held sway through a large proportion of the territory.[26] The perhaps surprising lack of judicial intervention into the potentially fraught arena of inter-cultural relationships may well be explained by the legal pot-pourri which seemed to have existed in colonial Indochina.[27]

Physical relations with the indigenous populations nonetheless appear to have been a source of tensions amongst the settler community in Indochina. Anxieties over proximity between colonised and coloniser in Indochina focused notably on sexual relations between white males and native women, and on what in Indochinese parlance came to be known as 'encongayement'. The term derives from the Vietnamese term for the female concubine of a white male: the *con gaï*, which in turn finds its roots in the Vietnamese 'co', meaning girl.[28] The widespread practice of taking an indigenous lover thus gave rise to the gallicised expressions: 'encongayement', and 'encongayé' meaning a metropolitan male cohabiting with a native woman.[29] A frequent feature of metropolitan fiction, the *con gaï* represents an Indochinese version of the traditional and mythologised indigenous woman: the compliant sexual conquest of the dominant white male coloniser.[30] The stereotypical image of the *con gaï*, or 'Eve asiatique', is most fully and succinctly elaborated in a popular colonial song of the period, 'Petite Tonkinoise', which vulgarised the myth of the submissive and malleable Indochinese *con gaï*. Its third and fourth verses, reproduced here, dramatise the colonial cliché of 'loving and leaving' an indigenous mistress:

III
Très gentille
C'est la fille
D'un mandarin très fameux:
C'est pour ça qu' sur sa poitrine
Elle a deux p'tit's mandarines.
Peu gourmande,
Ell' ne d'mande
Quand nous mangeons tous les deux
Qu'un banan', c'est peu coûteux,
Moi, j'y en donne autant qu'ell' veut.

IV
Mais tout passe
Et tout casse,
En France je dus rentrer
J'avais l'coeur plein de tristesse
De quitter ma chè' maîtresse.
L'âme en peine,
Ma p'tit' reine
Etait v'nu' m'accompagner
Mais avant de nous séparer
Je lui dis dans un baiser:

Refrain
Ne pleur' pas si je te quitte,
Petite Anna, petite Anna, p'tite Annamite,
Tu m'as donné ta jeunesse
Ton amour et tes caresses.
Je t'appelais ma p'tit' bourgeoise,
Ma Tonkiki, ma Tonkiki, ma Tonkinoise.
Dans mon coeur j' garderai toujours
Le souv'nir de nos amours.[31]

The song demonstrates the facility with which metropolitan males 'acquired' their indigenous mistresses, and the value or worth they accorded them. Simple and inexpensive to keep, these women are abandoned as easily and rapidly as they were acquired.

Many colonial narratives follow this 'landing, loving, leaving' pattern, which forms the backbone of the plot and drives the narrative forward. A metropolitan male arrives in the colony, falls in love with an indigenous woman, then leaves her behind on his return to the metropole. Pierre Loti is generally regarded as the master of this type of thematic and structural stereotype. Amorous relationships between indigenous women and white metropolitan males are a significant feature of many fictional works concerning the colonies, and Indochina is no exception.[32] The early portrayal of tropical climes as territories in which the European male could experience free and abundant sexual relations with indigenous women proved an enduring fascination for metropolitan France. Diderot's Tahitian women established a literary topos which would be seized upon by many metropolitan writers fictionalising the colonial experience. This type of image was perpetuated by travel writing of the nineteenth century, and as Goutalier and Knibiehler note,

> l'Occidental pouvait donc croire que les pays d'outre-mer lui offriraient en abondance des femmes aimables, amoureuses, et toutes nues. Le mythe de la bonne sauvage transformait d'avance toutes les colonies en paradis du sexe.[33]

The theme became so popular, however, that it becomes difficult to distinguish between one colony and another in this type of work: 'l'exotisme y masque la diversité des cultures'.[34] The site itself becomes irrelevant to these writers, and the differentiation between nationalities of the female characters even more so.

The portrayal of a cross-cultural sexual liaison added an extra frisson to the fictionalisation of the metropolitan experience of the overseas possession.[35] The indigenous woman was portrayed as one of the prizes or rewards due to the colonising male: in a symbolic sense, she represented the possession of the conquered country. Nevertheless, fictional works tended to ignore the colonial dynamic of the relationship, as Knibiehler and Goutalier have noted:

> La femme indigène, lorsqu'elle accepte un partenaire occidental, est supposée céder ou consentir par amour, ou par vice, ou par vénalité. En réalité, dans la plupart des cas, elle n'a guère le choix, mais les contraintes qu'elle subit sont laissées dans l'ombre et le rapport des forces n'entre pas en ligne de compte.[36]

Indeed, many of these liaisons were discussed in terms of commodity/consumer relationship. Lefèvre notes of the metropolitan males who remained but a short period in Indochina: 'Le colon s'offrait une jeune "Annamite", moyennant des avantages matériels, argent et cadeaux.'[37] Even the least attractive, and lowliest of metropolitan males could be assured of 'getting' his indigenous lover. Here, Jean-Pierre, a character from Henry Casseville's novel *Sao, l'amoureuse tranquille*, reveals the supplementary advantages of the coloniser/colonised hierarchy to his love life:

Je sais que j'ai une sale gueule, on ne me l'a pas caché. Jamais chez nous une femme ne m'a montré de la tendresse, je ne parle pas d'amour! Si, une peut-être, celle qui m'a dépucelé, mais elle avait cinquante ans et je ne l'ai jamais revue. Alors voilà. Cette *con gaï* que je connais depuis deux jours, elle ne m'aime pas évidemment, mais elle a été tendre avec moi . . . Elle m'a donné du bonheur, comprends-tu, du bonheur! Est-ce que je retrouverai ça ailleurs?[38]

The indigenous woman is thus presented as an easy conquest: she is mythologised as more compliant, and less discerning than her European counterparts, more interested in the financial rewards of being associated with a metropolitan male than with questions of love. The presentation of the ease with which metropolitan males can engage in sexual liaisons with indigenous women completes the male fantasy of Indochina. A territory in which he is undisputed monarch (governmentally, administratively), a territory in which he can exercise his fantasies of heroism and adventure, a territory in which his sexual desires are easily satisfied, the colony becomes a male utopic fantasy.

Seduction plays a major part in the process of acculturation. 'Ah! ce pays me séduit,' exclaimes Rollin in Groslier's *Le Retour à l'argile*.[39] Cambodia's seductive qualities entail the gender positioning of the colony as female, and a substantial part of the country's seductive power resides in the charm of her native women. The indigenous women of these novels are regarded as 'initiatrices du héros', 'lui permettant de découvrir "l'âme" de leur pays'.[40] A crucial feature of many colonial narratives, the indigenous woman figures not only as one of the colony's seductive aspects, however, in many senses she represents the colony itself. The *con gaï*, the Indochinese incarnation of the stereotypical portrait of the indigenous woman can thus be seen to function as a cipher through which the metropolitan male possesses Indochina: she is a 'dictionnaire en peau', or a 'dictionnaire horizontal'.

Indeed, *encongayement* and indigenisation are presented in Groslier's novel as ways in which the male *colon* can know and possess the colony. When Pierre Bernard informs Rollin that there are rumours flying amongst the French circle in the city, Claude's response is to refer to the above concepts as a learning process:

Des mots nouveaux, mon cher, qui depuis plusieurs siècles que nous colonisons ne figurent pas dans nos dictionnaires. Eh oui ! Nous dispensons progrès et civilisation. Nous sommes, paraît-il, les bienfaiteurs de ces peuples, à jet continu. Ils ont tout à apprendre de notre Protectorat. Nous ne cessons pas d'être en chaire! Si l'un de nous, de temps en temps, tentait l'inverse? N'aurions-nous donc absolument rien à apprendre, par hasard?[41]

This romantic and sentimental notion obfuscates the colonised/coloniser relationship. Although Claude may learn from the indigenous civilisation which he temporarily inhabits, he is not himself colonised. Colonisation is romanticised as a mutually beneficial and rewarding relationship. Power hierarchies, economic plundering and political subjugation are all ignored. Claude is free to learn from the Cambodians, should he choose to do so. As Gidley has noted,

> members of the dominant group – no matter how intimate (. . .) their sense of their involvement with the people concerned, no matter how deep their professed interest in their subject – will represent nothing but the assumptions of their own kind.[42]

Groslier thus presents a utopic image of living amongst Cambodian society. His portrayal of European acculturation verges upon the paradisiacal. Although his evident personal love of, and interest in, the country encouraged early critics to view his portrayal of Indochina as unmitigatedly sympathetic, it is clear that Groslier's 'sympathy' is circumscribed by his belief in the innate metropolitan position of power in relation to the very populations he seeks to 'join'.

The battleground of colonial power is transplanted in Groslier's novel to the site of gender-based *dominateur/dominé* struggles. The authority of the white male *colon* is clearly duplicated in the less contentious (at the time) authority of the male spouse. If Indochina is so consistently represented as a sexualised and feminised entity, then the indigenous woman clearly becomes an emblem and signifier of that mythologising colonial gesture.

Nonetheless, even if the *con gaï* was expendable and replaceable, often controllable and usually subjugated, she could also function, alongside (as we have seen) Indochina's climate and natural features, to exhaust and deplete the white male, both physically and morally. The *con gaï*'s powers of 'envoûtement', her seductive charms, could enslave the white male, deprive him of his faculties, and drain away his energy. She could tempt him away from his own culture and lure him into the native way of life. Far from France, and dwelling morosely on his sense of exile and solitude, the French coloniser became an easy prey: Raffin 'sans perspective du retour, commença de se sentir loin, perdu, écrasé de solitude; il ne résista plus.'[43]

Colonial propaganda acknowledged the temptation embodied in the indigenous woman, and sought to prevent, or at least contain the frequency of mixed-race unions through encouraging the emigration of French women to the colonies. A 1927 publication encouraging female emigration observed:

> N'est-ce pas surtout vrai, pour l'homme qui se trouve à mille lieues de son village natal, qui ne reçoit de nouvelles du pays (. . .) que tous les deux ou trois mois. Sans distractions, il s'adonne fréquemment à la débauche; le mieux qu'il fasse est de conclure un mariage occasionnel, temporaire, avec quelque femme indigène, ce qui d'ailleurs ne le met pas toujours à l'abri des maladies vénériennes.[44]

Relations with the *con gaï* were perceived not simply as morally reprehensible, but also as physically risky. The bearer of disease, she was also a vector of moral turpitude. If she was a threat to the moral rectitude of the *colon,* by extension these mixed-race relationships constituted a threat to the status of France abroad. The potential sexual incontinence of the metropolitan male, faced with these alluring native women, also risked diluting the French race. However, the presence of metropolitan women was viewed as a stabilising force:

> Qu'il soit accompagné de sa famille, les conditions changent: il retrouve son 'home', les joies du foyer; son installation est plus stable, et comporte plus de confort et de bien-être.[45]

The presence of European women would mean that indigenous mistresses 'se font plus discrètes', but more importantly, 'la dignité de l'Européen se trouve ainsi rehaussée.'[46]

The risk, both sexual and moral, of becoming too close to the Other clearly had political ramifications. Firstly, although the colony was intended to provide an outlet for male energy, it is certain that the colonial authorities did not primarily understand Indochina's role as an outlet for French sexual energy. The dissipation of that colonial 'virilité' and energy through sexual adventures clearly distracted from the work ethic of *mise en valeur*. Secondly, the collapsing of boundaries separating civilised from uncivilised would shatter the framework of colonial hierarchies. If the representative of the superior power showed himself to be sexually and morally weak, then colonialism's objective to civilise was undermined. The attempt, through the means of propaganda, to extend colonial jurisdiction and interdiction to the private realm is revelatory of concerns over the commitment of colonialism's own agents to the nation's colonial enterprise. As we shall see, in a number of fictional portrayals, the French settler was shown to have clearly slipped beyond the control of the imperial nation. As a representative of France, his proximity to the native functions as a threat from within.

Going Native

Encongayement often featured as a constituent element of 'going native', otherwise known as 'indigenisation'. Indigenisation was the ultimate manifestation of acculturation, and pushes to the extreme one of the fundamental premises of exoticism – departure and rejection of the homeland. Indigenisation amounts to the extension and exacerbation of the dissatisfaction with the Western world, and a movement towards its Other.

Much of Georges Groslier's work is taken up with the themes of acculturation. His *Le Retour à l'argile* presents a sustained portrayal of the perennial problems of feeling either attraction to the country of 'exile', or an overbearing desire to return to the metropole. In his portrayal of the Rollin couple, Groslier depicts the extreme poles of these common metropolitan reactions: indigenisation and repulsion. In a classically 'exoticist' sense, Groslier's novel can be viewed as the philosophical critique of Western civilisation. The gradual identificatory process of the 'exiled' metropolitan with his newly-adopted country is presented through the character of Claude Rollin. As Laude has noted:

> Le personnage de Rollin prend, tout au long du roman, une conscience de plus en plus nette de la distance qui le sépare de sa société d'origine, incarnée par sa femme, et approfondit au contraire par sa communion avec la société traditionnelle cambodgienne.[47]

Rollin's need for contact with other Europeans slowly diminishes, and he severs more and more ties with the Western world. Rollin rids himself little by little of his 'European' possessions. He begins to display a critical attitude towards European customs:

> Au cours d'un grand bal officiel, ce recueillement, ce détachement se renforcèrent encore, car déjà ils avaient armé en lui une susceptibilité plus aiguë. Des toilettes prétentieuses collant à la peau en sueur, les contorsions de certains couples et d'impudiques contacts, l'afféterie ou le vide de la plupart des conversations, l'origine médiocre de quelques hauts bonnets, cette animation factice, les conventions impératives qui forçaient la plupart de ces gens à assister à ce bal – le stupéfaient.[48]

Here Rollin is beginning to view Western mores as superficial, and even artificial. Against the background of traditional Cambodian society, Rollin becomes more and more aware of what he perceives to be the 'méfaits' of modern Western civilisation, which denature man, and cut him off from his 'natural' environment. This process of acculturation begins with feelings of *déracinement*, and moves gradually by stages to full indigenisation:

> Parce qu'il voit autour de lui tant de fécondité, la paix du peuple, la bienveillance des doctrines, des moeurs simples, une civilisation immobile et satisfaite, il se demande dans une inquiétude progressive si notre progrès ne lui apparaîtrait pas, vu d'ici, comme une influence détestable; si ce n'est pas ce progrès, uniquement lui, qui par son confort, son luxe, ses perfectionnements, sa puissance désagrégante aurait dépouillé Raymonde de ses vertus féminines et de la confiance en l'avenir qui l'eussent conduite ici, vaillante. Il se demande si lui, les excès et la fièvre de ce progrès, ne l'auraient pas rendu avide d'isolement et de simplicité, au point de fausser son jugement et de lui faire prendre, en ces lieux, une immobilité misérable et de l'impuissance pour du calme et de la contemplation.[49]

The view which Groslier presents through Claude Rollin is a profoundly anti-modernist one. Indeed the emphasis on isolation, calm, contemplation and simplicity are reminiscent of Romantic narratives of the nineteenth century. Throughout the novel, metropolitan commercialism, and materialism are contrasted with indigenous simplicity and peace. Through the presentation of metropolitan modernisation in Cambodia as 'détestable', Groslier undermines the value *of mise en valeur* and questions the purpose of French colonialism in Indochina. His novel displays a nostalgia for pre-capitalist society which leads to an interrogation of the notion of 'progress' as a desirable goal: as Rollin says, 'Nous nous décivilisons en nous livrant au progrès.'[50]

The protagonist's rejection of his profession and of society are linked once more with a quest for the natural: 'Les premiers pas de notre progrès ont commencé à nous éloigner de la nature, contrairement à notre essence qui est de nous y mêler.'[51] Although, during the process of his acculturation, Rollin's criticisms of colonial society in Indochina remain circumscribed by the belief that colonialism has simply evolved in the 'wrong' direction, his realisations express a growing uncertainty or unease vis-à-vis one the principal tenets of the French colonial doctrine – the ideal of progress:

> Claude jugeait la société coloniale sans cohésion spirituelle. Elle ne se reconnaît pas de chefs, car le fonctionnarisme les lui impose. Les populations conquises qui l'entourent dans la servitude, la gonflent de vanité en lui servant de piédestal: un adjudant ou un douanier devient un haut seigneur entouré de mille coolies.[52]

While Groslier's portrait of indigenisation is largely sympathetic, even if it reveals a degree of metropolitan doubt, in many fictional representations of settler life the collapse of boundaries between colonised and coloniser clearly represents a site of great tension, and as a result indigenisation is viewed entirely negatively. In the following passage from Daguerches' *Le Kilomètre 83*, the narrator's disapproval of indigenisation is emblematised through the differences between metropolitan and indigenous ways of life and the use of a series of contrasts between women, gods, and architecture:

> C'est un ancien sous-officier d'infanterie colonial. Le soleil et les pluies d'Indochine ont repétri son argile, lui ont fait faire prise définitivement avec ce sol adoptif. Il a une épouse indigène, une trôlée de gnôs que, sur le seuil de sa case de bambous, emplissent de riz leurs ventres nus. Il a totalement oublié, j'en ai la conviction, l'ardoise fine de son clocher natal, quelque part là-bas, en Touraine ou en Picardie, et les filles aux yeux clairs penchées sur les javelles. Et je suis sûr que lui aussi, l'heure venue, saura mourir doucement dans le giron chaud de la forêt, tandis que les tam-tams charitables écarteront de sa tête les mauvais Génies et que là-haut, par-dessus les dernières palmes pâles, miroitera un ciel étrange, corail et soufre, comme ce soir.[53]

The indigenous wife and children are referred to dismissively, using a mixture of slang and gallicised Vietnamese. The contrast between the 'fine' spires of the officer's native France, and the poor bamboo of his Indochinese home, invokes a cultural hierarchy which further castigates the practice of inter-race relationships. Indeed, indigenisation or going native, is regarded with shame: '- O honte, hélas! Quelques-uns des nôtres, comment le nier? ont succombé à la tentation.'[54] Here, indigenisation is equated with renouncing one's racial superiority, abdicating one's duty, and succumbing to vice and lust:

> Ils ont abdiqué la maîtrise et la race . . . Ils se sont couchés aux pieds de l'Asie, de cette idole obèse et prometteuse de luxure. Cela c'est la pire ignominie.[55]

The racial and cultural boundaries separating colonised and coloniser have been transgressed and collapsed. Desire for the Other, and the temptation which the Other represents thus threaten to dismantle the differentiating boundaries which colonialism requires in order to remain stable and intact.

Besides the acquistion of an indigenous concubine and the lassitude which affects settlers, opium too features as a path towards indigenisation and as an undesirable transgression of the norms of metropolitan civilisation. The portrayal of opium dens had initially formed part of the exotic appeal of Indochina. It was a sign of difference and an exotic marker. Although China had long been linked with the theme of opium in literary works, the topos of the opium den, and the evocation of the heightened sensory states which opium produced were ubiquitous throughout early metropolitan fictional representations of Indochina. Benefitting no doubt from the vogue for *Chinoiseries*, and the interest in the association between South-East Asia and opium which had already developed, these early French works drew on the theme for the purposes of exoticism rather than making the theme specific to the French experience of Indochina. Variously described as a divinity, an idol, and a gift from heaven, opium was initially used as a short-hand to evoke this 'exotic' location, rather than as a way in which to differentiate Indochina from China.

Opium, as a primary theme, gradually died out after conquest and pacification, and was replaced by images and themes which constituted the new concerns of the metropolitan French in Indochina: France's role in Indochina, the administration and government of the colony. It might be argued that this theme died out precisely because the French government had 'domesticated' opium through the management and monopoly of the opium trade in Indochina. The exotic appeal of opium was thus lessened by the intervention of the State in this romanticised practice.

However in later fiction, although no longer a primary theme, opium still often figured as a 'rite of passage' for the newly-arrived settler to Indochina. Where it recurs intermittently nonetheless is in portrayals of physical and moral degeneracy.

Opium marks the erosion of status, decadence, and the disintegration of the self. Boissière's addicts intoxicate themselves in order to escape from the omnipresent sense of sickness and death. The 'absolu bonheur' obtained through opium thus displaces the dystopic vision of soldiers dying an agonising death: 'maigres et jaunes, ou bouffis de malegraisse et le teint creux'.[56] However, whilst opium may be 'la panacée qui sent bon', [57] coming under the addictive influence of 'la fée brune' entails the disintegration of individuality, the distancing of the 'moi', detachment and ultimate alienation: 'Je bâillais invinciblement, un larmoiement piquait et rougissait mes paupières, d'horribles crampes tordaient mon estomac, je tombais en défaillance.'[58] Opium satisfies a craving for inertia, it 'grandit l'indifférence et le dégoût d'agir', and creates an 'anéantissement', which prevents the addict from fulfilling his colonial functions.[59]

In Claude Farrère's *Les Civilisés*, opium becomes just one of many ways in which to signal the degeneracy and decadence seemingly encouraged in his main protagonists through their contact with Indochina's inhabitants and customs. In Henry Daguerches' and Groslier's novels, opium operates as a sign that a character has leaned too far towards the adoption of native customs and lifestyle: it functions as an indication of 'indigenisation', or 'going native'; as a sign of the disintegration not only of the self, but of the boundaries which separate self from Other.

Colonial administrations in Indochina were concerned of the ill effects of opium of the nation's representatives abroad. In 1907 a circular emanating from the Governor General in Indochina forbade 'à tous fonctionnaires et agents européens de tous services de fumer l'opium sous peine de sanctions disciplinaires les plus sévères'.[60] The dissolution and degeneracy which going native and *opiomanie* represented were suggestive of the decay of French civilisation once in contact with the Other.

Les Civilisés

What these representations show is that the integrity of the nation's colonial identity, and more worryingly, its civilisation, were perceived to be under threat, often from France's own agents' behaviour in Indochina. One of the most striking examples of this form of counter-narrative is Claude Farrère's *Les Civilisés*, which, perhaps somewhat surprisingly, won the *Prix Goncourt* in 1905.[61] Farrère's novel is cynical and disconcerting. It may be viewed in many ways as a sustained attack on the idealised values and principles of French colonialism. It shocked a significant proportion of its metropolitan readers, for whom his portrayal of Indochina seemed at odds with the offical version of Indochina as France's *perle de l'Extrême-Orient*. Ernest Babut went as far as to write a pamphlet denouncing Farrère's work, *Un Livre de diffamation indochinoise: Les Civilisés*,[62] in which he asserted that the novel was too 'anti-colonial'. Lebel voices the criticisms of many contemporary detractors, when he dismisses Farrère's work in a single sentence as unrepresentative of colonial life in Indochina: 'Ce n'est pas là une oeuvre d'observation et de vérité générale qui soit représentative de la colonie et des Français de Cochinchine.'[63]

Nonetheless, the renown of *Les Civilisés* ensured that Farrère's representation of Saigon, and the image of Indochina it produced, made an important contribution to the picture of Indochina building up in the metropolitan imagination by providing a counterpoint to the officially-sanctioned version of Indochina. Finally, Farrère's novel is also one which is replete with sub-textual references to veiled metropolitan concerns of this period: decadence and degeneration. These strands intertwine to create a complicated novel which aptly reflects the complex relationship which France was building with Indochina.

Farrère's novel provides an ironic intervention into the conception of the notion of civilisation, and settlers as bearers and agents of French civilisation. The novel's play on the notion of 'civilisation', which is present in the novel's very title, immediately recalls the nation's colonial *mission civilisatrice*. Farrère's 'civilisés' however, represent the antithesis of the 'civilising' values which imperial France hoped to both embody and to export to the colonies. Saigon, as the 'capitale civilisée' is portrayed as dissolute and therefore worthy of Farrère's protagonists, who view themselves as 'les civilisés'.

Farrère's novel presents the evolution of these three French 'civilisés' in Saigon. Stopping over in Saigon, Fierce, an officer with the *Marine française*, rejoins his two friends and fellow 'civilisés' – Mévil, doctor and dissolute *tombeur*, and the engineer Torral, who has renounced women in favour of young boys. The three friends view themselves as superior, subscribing to a philosophy of life which ignores all moral arbitration. They are sceptical and nihilistic. To be truly 'civilised', in their view, is to act with complete licence, eschewing all notion of 'good' and 'bad'.

The 'civilisés' operate within Saigon, which is perceived as befitting their philosophical stance, for Saigon is portrayed as a cosmopolitan city *par excellence*. According to Torral, Saigon is the 'capitale civilisée du monde, par la grâce de son climat propice et par la volonté inconsciente de toutes les races qui sont venus s'y rencontrer.'[64] Saigon's cosmopolitanism is not only due to the fact that the city is a melting-pot of diverse races; it derives also from the fact that the city, like the three protagonists, has renounced any moral or religious affiliation:

Chacune [each race] apportait sa loi, sa religion et sa pudeur; – et il n'y avait pas deux pudeurs pareilles, ni deux lois, ni deux religions. – Un jour les peuples s'en sont aperçus. Alors ils ont éclaté de rire à la face les uns des autres; et toutes les croyances ont sauté dans cet éclat. Après, libre de frein et de joug, ils se sont mis à vivre selon la bonne formule: minimum d'effort pour maximum de jouissance. Les respect humain ne les gênait pas, parce que chacun dans sa pensée s'estimait supérieur aux autres, à cause de sa peau différemment colorée, – et vivait comme s'il avait vécu seul. Pas de voyeurs: – licence universelle, et développement normal et logique de tous les instincts qu'une convention sociale aurait endigués, détournés ou supprimés. Bref, incroyable progrès de la civilisation, et possibilité unique pour tous les gens susdits, de parvenir, seuls sur terre, au bonheur. Ils n'ont pas pu, faute d'intelligence. Nous, vivant en marge d'eux, nous y arriverons, – nous y arrivons. Il ne s'agit que de faire à son gré, sans souci de rien ni de personne, – sans souci de ces chimères malfaisantes baptisées 'bien' et 'mal'.[65]

This perception of Indochina overturns the principal tenets of the French colonial doctrine. The notion of 'progress' within the colonial situation – the respect for others, and the pursuit of the common good embodied in the ideal of associationist colonial policy – disappear. In their place emerges a notion of progress in which an exagerrated individualism overrides the pursuit of a collective advantage. The racial hierarchies which underpin colonial rule have collapsed, but their disintegration does not promote a heightened sense of fraternity; instead, it exacerbates segregationist practices and worsens racial tensions. Here, the freedom offered by the empty space of the colony, does not necessarily offer a field for constructive action. The 'formule civilisée' in fact runs counter to the model of altruistic endowment in that it embraces the hedonistic formula of 'minimum d'effort pour maximum de jouissance'. Thus the ironic use of the 'formule civilisée' condones lawlessness, licence, debauchery, opiomanie, homosexuality, and prostitution.

Farrère's portrayal of this lawlessness provides an ambiguous image of the settler community in Saigon. Saigon's population is described by the narrator as a

prodigieux pêle-mêle d'honnêtes gens et de gens qui ne l'étaient pas, – ceux-ci plus nombreux: car les colonies françaises sont proprement un champ d'épandage pour tout ce que la métropole crache et expulse d'excréments et de pourritures. – Il y avait là une infinité d'hommes équivoques, que le code pénal, toile d'araignée trop lâche, n'avait pas su retenir dans ses mailles: des banqueroutiers, des aventuriers, des maîtres chanteurs, des maris habiles, et quelques espions; – il y avait une foule de femmes mieux que faciles, qui toutes savaient se débaucher copieusement, par cent moyens dont le plus vertueux était l'adultère. – Dans ce cloaque, les rares probités, les rares pudeurs faisaient tâche. – Et quoique cette honte fût connue, étalée, affichée, on l'acceptait; on l'accueillait. Les mains propres, sans dégoût, serraient les mains sales. – Loin de l'Europe, l'Européen, roi de toute la terre, aime à s'affirmer au-dessus des lois et des morales, et à les violer orgueilleusement. La vie secrète de Paris ou de Londres est peut-être plus répugnante que la vie de Saigon; mais elle est secrète; c'est une vie à volets clos. Les tares coloniales n'ont pas peur du soleil.[66]

This description of the settlers as 'excréments' and 'pourritures' provides an early avatar of critical views of the settler community which were to emerge in the 1930s. Here, it is the freedom from moral arbitration which the colony affords, which allows for such criminality and immorality to show its face. Furthermore while Farrère's fictional Governor General confirms the view that 'aux yeux unanimes de la nation française, les colonies ont la réputation d'être la dernière ressource et le suprême asile des déclassés de toutes les classes et des repris de toutes justices',[67] he nonetheless believes that from this 'fumier humain' a new 'civilisation' will be born:

> Sur des terres coloniales fraîchement retournées et labourées par le piétinement de toutes les races qui s'y heurtent, il vaut peut-être mieux qu'un fumier humain soit jeté, pour que, de la décomposition purulente des vieilles idées et des vieilles morales, naisse la maison des civilisations futures.[68]

From this cauldron of corruption, venality and degradation, Farrère's Governor asserts, will emerge a rejuvenated and superior 'civilisation': the formation of a new elite. The notion of a new civilisation springing from the 'fumier' of the mainland alludes at once to the decadence of *Belle-Epoque* France, and to the new hopes embodied in the French Empire. Nonetheless, this vision of a future, redeemed civilisation in Indochina undermines the precept of French civilising action. In Farrère's portrayal, the impact of France on Indochina is imagined through metaphors of decomposition and decay. France is the 'fumier' necessary to the refertilisation of the metaphorical colonial land; it is not, to extend the metaphor, the ripened fruit which official France imagined French civilisation to be.

Farrère's novel thus also constitutes a critique of mainland France and its perceived values through the cipher of Saigon. For Saigon is also *civilisée* in that the city is gallicised and cosmopolitan, a mirror of Paris, and the capital of France's *Perle de l'Extrême-Orient*. It was the epitome of *l'Asie française* – a gallicised version of an Asian city. It might be argued therefore, that Saigon represented immorality precisely because the city had become a replica of Paris, that renowned city-prostitute. In this sense, the location of the plot in Saigon functions as a displaced version of Paris. Similarly, Farrère's portrayal of Saigon's immorality and lawlessness can be read as a critique of the premise that French civilisation was inherently superior and a worthy export mainland. Given that Indochina was a constituent part of *la plus grande France,* and a mirror image of the *métropole*, this negative portrait implies a recognition of equally negative aspects of metropolitan culture. It might then be argued that the motivations of these characters reside in the concerns of a *Belle-Epoque* metropolitan mentality, rather than in an engagement with Asian culture.

Throughout the novel, however, Farrère plays down this comparison by contrasting the 'exotic' amorality of Saigon and the lives of his protagonists, with the hypocrisy and perceived prudery of Western mores:

La débauche parisienne n'a pas grand-chose à envier à la débauche exotique, quand au fond; mais elle s'embarrasse hypocritement de volets clos et de lampes baissées. Ailleurs, les gestes voluptueux n'ont point peur du soleil.[69]

Farrère thus presents Saigon society as embodying a kind of ontological authenticity. Saigon allows for a more overt adoption of habits which were covertly accepted but outwardly vilified in the metropole.

An implicit discussion of morality thus permeates the work. Farrère's novel has been viewed as an early parody of Loti's 'landing, loving, leaving' narrative model. Fierce falls in love, not with an indigenous woman, however, but with an aristocratic metropolitan woman. Sélysette's discovery of his debauched lifestyle leads to her breaking off their engagement. He dies in battle aboard his ship, with her name on his lips. This *dénouement*, coupled with the ignominious death of Mévil and the cowardice of Torral, has led critics to consider *Les Civilisés* as a moral tale.[70] Farrère, however, clearly views Indochina through the lens of *fin-de-siècle* preoccupations with decadence and degeneracy.

The novel reveals a morbid obsession with sexual proclivity and perceived sexual deviance as if to provoke the reader's prurient curiosity. Rape, homosexuality, prostitution, drug abuse, and alcoholism are all placed under the spotlight in this novel, which opens with a description of Mévil fondling the breasts of an indigenous concubine. Fierce, the marine officer, a sea-faring adventurer who has travelled widely, is also the sexual adventurer, seeking new carnal sensations and experiences in each new country he visits. Indochina, the metropole's most recently captured 'virgin' territory, is symbolised, for Fierce, in his possession of the body of a thirteen-year-old native girl. The analogy between the conquest of a colonial territory and sexual possession is reinforced when, towards the end of the novel, Fierce rapes a local woman whilst on military manoeuvres. This narratological voyeurism appeals strongly to the powers of interdiction and attraction. The fears and obsessions of the metropole are displaced onto Saigon, which acts as a repository for repressed sexual desires and fears. Farrère thus feeds a metropolitan *Belle-Epoque* desire to witness, but from a safe distance. The distancing effect produced is two-fold: both the narrator and the very distance of Indochina from the metropole are interposed between the metropolitan readership and the events and actions which are narrated in the novel.

The image Farrère thus presents of Saigon, and by extension Indochina, is one which combines prurient disapproval and fascination, interest and dismay, desire and disgust. Both a critique of bourgeois morality, and a tale in which its alternative, sexual and moral licence, visibly fails, Farrère's novel reflects the ambivalence of a metropolitan society attempting to define its moral position both at home, and in the new arena of the colony.

More importantly, however, Farrère's novel provides the most sustained narrative reversal of France's vision of itself as an imperial nation, of its colonial doctrine, and of its role in Indochina. In the context of Saigon's 'melting-pot', barriers between civilised and uncivilised, and distinctions between classes and races, good and bad, are torn down. The myth of colonial progress, and the ideal of French civilisation are demolished and replaced with a vision of moral regression and colonial venality.

Notes

1. As previously, a version of the present work on urbanism first appeared as an article in *French Cultural Studies*, and I am grateful for permission to reproduce it here. See Cooper, N., 'Urban Planning and Architecture in Colonial Indochina', *French Cultural Studies*, vol. 11, part 1, no. 31, February 2000, pp. 75–99.
2. See Pineau, L-G., 'Le Plan d'aménagement et d'extension de Dalat, in *La Vie Urbaine*, no. 49, 1939, pp. 29–49.
3. Pouyanne, A., *Les Travaux publics de l'Indochine* (Hanoi: Imprimerie de l'Extrême-Orient, 1926), p. 283.
4. Abbatucci, Dr, 'Aperçu sur les stations climatiques des colonies tropicales françaises', in Royer, J., *L'Urbanisme aux colonies: vol. 2* (Paris: Editions d'Urbanisme, 1935), pp. 12–16. Abatucci, quoting Governor General Doumer, p. 13.
5. Hébrard, E., 'L'Urbanisme en Indochine', pp. 278–89, in Royer, J., *L'Urbanisme aux colonies et dans les pays tropicaux*, vol. 1 (La Charité-sur-Loire, Delayance, 1932), p. 284.
6. Ibid.
7. Wright, G., and Rabinow, P., 'Savoir et pouvoir dans l'urbanisme moderne colonial d'Ernest Hébrard', *Cahiers de la recherche architecturale* (villes nouvelles, cités, satellites, colonies: de l'art urbain à l'urbanisme), no. 9, 1981, p. 38.
8. See for example, de Certeau, M., 'Parcours et cartes', pp. 175–80, in *L'Invention du quotidien 1: arts de faire* (Paris: Folio/essais, 1990).
9. Harvey, D., *The Condition of postmodernity: an Enquiry into the Origins of Cultural Change* (Oxford: Blackwell, 1989), p. 253.
10. Foucault, M., *Surveiller et punir* (Paris: Gallimard/Collection tel, 1975).
11. Hébrard, E., 'L'Urbanisme en Indochine', in Royer, *L'Urbanisme aux colonies et dans les pays tropicaux*, vol. 1, p. 279.

12. Ibid., p. 285.
13. Ibid.
14. Pavrel, G., *Hygiène colonial: comment on doit vivre aux colonies* (Paris: 'Colonia', 1912), p. 4.
15. Léger, M., 'L'Habitation colonial du point de vue médical', in Royer, *L'Urbanisme auc colonies et dans les pays tropicaux*, vol. 2, p. 39.
16. Ibid., p. 46.
17. Spurr, D., *The Rhetoric of Empire: Colonial Discourse in Journalism, Travel Writing and Imperial Administration* (Durham: Duke University Press, 1993), p. 89.
18. Ibid., p. 80.
19. Challaye, F., *Souvenirs sur la colonisation* (Paris: Picart, 1935), p. 20.
20. See for instance Léger, p. 41.
21. Fanon, F., *Peau noire: masques blancs* (Paris: Seuil, 1952).
22. Pavrel, *Hygiène colonial*, p. 2.
23. Ibid., p. 6.
24. Léger, 'L'Habitation colonial du point de vue médical', in Royer, *L'Urbanisme aux colonies et dans les pays tropicaux*, vol. 2, p. 46.
25. *Journal officiel*, 3 April 1909.
26. See Philastre, P., *Le Code annamite*, 2 vols. (Taipei: Ch'eng-Wn, 1967).
27. See Pederson, J., 'Special Customs: Paternity Suits and Citizenship in France and the Colonies 1870–1912', in Clancy-Smith J., and Gouda, F., *Domesticating the Empire; Race, Gender and Family Life in French and Dutch Colonialism* (Charlottesville: University Press of Virginia, 1998), pp. 43–64.
28. The Indochinese women who served as wives, mistresses and prostitutes to French soldiers and administrators were known in Vietnamese as 'me tay', which translates as 'French mothers'.
29. Lefèvre notes that the women destined to become *con gaï* were generally aged between 16 and 22. Orphans, widows or peasants whom poverty forced from the countryside to the towns, they were generally uneducated and unskilled. See Lefèvre, K., 'Eves jaunes et colons blancs', in Franchini, P. (ed.), *Saigon 1925–45: de la 'Belle Colonie' à l'éclosion révolutionnaire ou la fin des dieux blancs* (Paris: Les Editions Autrement/série mémoires, no. 17, 1992), pp. 111–19.
30. Nguyên Xuân Tuê discusses later representations of the *con gaï* from the late 1950s and 1960s, and particularly Jean Hougron's portrayals, in his article 'Congaï: une race de femmes annamites, produit de la colonisation', pp. 69–77, in Hue, B. (ed.), *Indochine: reflets littéraires*, Pluriel 3, (Rennes: Presses universitaires de Rennes, Centre d'étude des littératures et civilisations francophones, 1992).

31. 'Petite Tonkinoise', words by H. Christiné, music by V. Scotto (Odéon 36801 – XP 2744), 1906. This song, alongside many others has recently been reissued in a compilation album entitled *Chansons coloniales et exotiques* (Paris: EPM, 1995). This version is interpreted by Karl Ditan. Goutalier and Knibiehler quote a slightly different verision, see Knibiehler, Y., and Goutalier, R., *La Femme au temps des colonies* (Paris: Stock, 1985), pp. 44–5.

32. Moura suggests that Salomé might be the prototype for this sort of representation, and notes that the literary use of the sensual indigenous woman progressively became a stereotype from the early nineteenth century onwards, 'où elle constitue l'un des grands attraits du voyage en Orient'. See Moura, J-M., *Lire l'exotisme* (Paris: Dunod, 1992), p. 104.

33. Knibiehler and Goutalier, *La Femme au temps des colonies*, p. 29.

34. Ibid., p. 37.

35. Book covers reflect this voyeuristic tendency. See illustrations in Goutalier and Knibiehler, *La Femme au temps des colonies*.

36. Ibid., p. 37.

37. Lefèvre, K., 'Eves jaunes et colons blancs', p. 111.

38. Casseville, H., *Sao, l'Amoureuse tranquille* (Paris: G. Cres, 1928). Quoted by Lefèvre, p. 113.

39. Groslier, G., *Le Retour à l'argile* (Paris: Emile Paul, 1928), (repr. Paris: Kailash, 1994), p. 52.

40. Moura, *Lire l'Exotisme*, p. 104. Moura views this stereotype as originating with Loti.

41. Groslier, *Le Retour à l'argile*, p. 77.

42. Gidley, M., *Representing Others: White Views of Indigenous Peoples* (Exeter: University of Exeter Press, 1992), p. 3.

43. Ajalbert, J., *Raffin Su-su* (Paris: Publications littéraires et politiques, 1911), *Raffin Su-su suivi de Sao Van Di*, (Paris: Kailash, 1995), p. 42.

44. *Le rôle et la situation de la famille française aux colonies* (Paris: Editions du journal des coloniaux et de l'Armée coloniale réunis, 1927), p. 7.

45. Ibid., pp. 7–8.

46. Ibid., p. 8.

47. Laude, P., *Exotisme indochinois et poésie* (Paris: Sudestasie, 1990), p. 79.

48. Groslier, *Le Retour à l'argile*, pp. 153–4.

49. Ibid., pp. 50–1.

50. Ibid., p. 199.

51. Ibid., p. 200.

52. Ibid., p. 156.

53. Daguerches, H., *Le Kilomètre 83* (Paris: Calmann-Lévy, 1913), (repr. Paris: Kailash, 1993), p. 140.

54. Ibid., p. 125.

55. Ibid.
56. Boissière, 'La Prise de Lang-Xi', in *Fumeurs d'Opium* (Paris: Flammarion, 1895), (repr. Paris: Kailash, 1993), p. 24.
57. Ibid., p. 22.
58. Ibid., pp. 27–8.
59. Ibid., p. 34.
60. See Meyer, C., *Les Français en Indochine* (Paris: Hachette, 1985), p. 263.
61. Farrère, C., *Les Civilisés* (Paris: Flammarion, 1905), (repr. Paris: Kailash, 1993). Claude Farrère (1876 1957) is the pen-name of Charles Bargone, who spent two years in Indochina between 1897 and 1899, as an officer with the French Navy. Farrère was elected to the *Académie française* in 1935 ahead of Claudel. Other works by Farrère include: *Fumée d'opium* (1904), a collection of short stories; *La Promenade en Extrême-orient* (1924), and *Une Jeune fille voyagea* (1925), both novels set in Indochina. *La Bataille* (1907) was set in Japan, whilst *Florence de Cao Bang* (1960), which was published posthumously, tells the tale of a Eurasian woman raised clandestinely in France.
62. Babut, E., *Un Livre de diffamation indochinoise: Les Civilisés* (Hanoi: [n.p.], 1907).
63. Lebel, R., *Histoire de la littérature coloniale en France* (Paris: Larose, 1931), p. 170.
64. Farrère, *Les Civilisés*, p. 22.
65. Ibid.
66. Ibid., p. 126.
67. Ibid., p. 62.
68. Ibid., pp. 63–4.
69. Ibid., p. 39.
70. See Siary, G., 'Immoralités comparées, l'Indochine dans *Les Civilisés* et *La Bataille* de Claude Farrère', in Hue, *Indochine: reflets littéraires*, pp. 97–110.

Conclusion to Part II

Although official France had attempted to produce its own truths about Indochina, and to articulate indisputable forms of knowledge about Indochina, it was ultimately unable to marshal all discourses on Indochina to a homogeneous, uniform and monolithic colonial image of French imperial identity as expressed through discourses of what French Indochina signified. Although official French discourses achieved a relatively high degree of internal consistency, divergent discourses emerged in a variety of sources, thus destroying the monolithic and essentialising desire of what Said has termed 'orientalism.'

These divergent discourses manifested themselves in multifarious ways, and embodied, for the most part, concerns and fears which arose from the often anxious response to colonisation on the part of settlers and colonial agents. Although they may not necessarily have challenged the premises of colonialism, the narratives which deviated from the received ideal of Indochina and of French identity nonetheless disturbed and undermined many of colonialism's orthodoxies. They violated the norms of the official discourse of French rule in Indochina. Indochina thus remained uncontainable and unknowable, in spite of efforts to understand and define it, and to fix and codify its colonial identity.

Of course, no matter how absolute a system of domination aspires to be, there will always be areas it cannot control. Thus the colonial production and domination of Indochina was often challenged unconsciously from within French colonialism's own ranks. The counter-narratives under discussion here reveal a complex and unstable web of responses to empire in South-East Asia, many of which called into question the fundamental principles of colonial rule: the superiority of the colonising nation and its agents; the difference between coloniser and colonised; and the binary oppositions between Western civilisation and Eastern barbarity. Some of the themes expressed through these counter-narratives might be read as early, and tentative, avatars of the ideas and issues which were to swell and amplify to form the basis of anti-colonial thought in France.

Part III
End of Empire?

Introduction to Part III

These concluding chapters take the form of a series of case studies, all of which examine the end of France's Empire in South-East Asia and its aftermath. The first section deals literally with the end of empire through an examination of the representation of the loss of Indochina on the battlefield of Dien Bien Phu. The second and third sections approach the notion of 'end of empire' in a more open-ended sense, in order to examine the repercussions of colonial rule in Indochina for contemporary France. Here, the question 'end of empire?' should indeed be posed, for I will argue that what might be perceived as a residual colonial mentality appears to resurface sporadically in relation to Indochina, and that both policies towards Vietnamese migrants, and contemporary representations of the period of colonial rule in Indochina appear to lay claim to the colonial legacy in more or less overt ways.

From the Second World War to War in Indochina

On the eve of the Second World War, a residual belief in the rectitude of colonial rule remained widespread. The French, it seemed, were not yet ready to contemplate either autonomy or independence as a serious alternative to colonial rule. There persisted a deeply-rooted and widely-held belief in the enlightening and humanitarian effect of French colonialism. Following the agitation of the early 1930s and the critical views of colonial management in Indochina, the accession to power of the Popular Front, and its reformist approach to the colonial 'question' renewed hope in the humanitarian character of the nation's civilising mission. However, France's experience of occupation during the Second World War, the growth and growing coherence of indigenous nationalist movements, and the nation's reliance on empire once more to save *la patrie* in its time of greatest need, all combined to toll the death knell of the French Empire.

This is not to say that France suddenly became resolutely anti-colonial. Many hsitorians have taken France's post-war intellectuals to task over their tardy espousal of the nationalist causes in the colonies. Most critical views of colonialism did not yet seek to denounce the project as an anti-humanitarian, anti-libertarian and anti-democratic practice. Raymond Aron for instance, who was prominent as a critic of empire during and after the War, based his anti-colonialism around a view of France's prestige and status. He argued that the economic burden of the Empire lay too heavily on the shoulders of a France already weakened by war and occupation.[1]

Aron was perhaps something of a lone voice at this point, given de Gaulle's professed, enacted and widely supported, faith in the Empire. In many ways these two opposing views replay the debate of the 1880s in which two visions of French grandeur and prestige vied for ascendency: the inward-looking *receuillement,* in which the nation should concentrate on domestic issues; and the outward-looking expansive vision which saw in the acquisition of empire the sole means of regaining international prestige after defeat by Germany in 1870.

During the Second World War, empire had been presented by the *parti colonial* as a source of strength and prestige. The Empire made good the weaknesses of the Motherland, and images of the strength and loyalty of the empire's manpower were used to offset France's chronic military inferiority to Germany. Both Daladier and Reynaud had seized upon the *parti colonial*'s slogans as a means of reassuring the public that the Empire's human resources would hold Germany at bay: 'La France de 110 millions d'habitants fait face à l'Allemagne.'[2]

If Algeria played the hero's role in the fight for Free France, then Indochina was a collaborator. The military defeat of France left Indochina cut off from the mainland and open to Japanese aggression. Indochina had only a small colonial army and limited supplies. The Governor General in power in Indochina at the fall of France was Catroux. He initially himself declared in favour of de Gaulle and Free France but was put under immense pressure from both the Japanese and from the Pétain government in the mainland. The Japanese government sought assurances that there would be no transport of arms or supplies to China through Indochina. Catroux sought the support of other generals throughout the Empire, hoping for reinforcements and munitions to enable him to withstand the Japanese. Neither were forthcoming. In June 1940, Catroux was forced to cede to Japanese demands and closed railway lines which were being used to transport arms to the Chinese front. The Japanese pushed for further concessions, demanding the right to send out control missions to check that Indochina's frontiers were closed. Catroux was then replaced in Indochina by Decoux, a Vichyite. The Japanese continued to pressurise the new Governor General, who yielded to their demands to the right to occupy airfields and to circulate freely throughout Indochina. The Japanese recognised French sovereignty in Indochina and the territorial integrity of the area. In return however, France recognised the Japanese interest in the area, agreed to discuss economic conventions, and to grant military facilities in Indochina to Japan.[3]

The Japanese seemed content to leave the framework of French control in place in Indochina, but at a price. After the attack on Pearl Harbour, the Japanese infiltrated Hanoi and took up key positions throughout the city. The Mikado issued an ultimatum to the French, demanding assurances that Indochina would do nothing to hinder the activities of the Japanese forces. If Decoux were to supply these assurances, his government would be left intact. If he refused, Japan threatened to take over Indochina. An agreement was reached on 9 December 1941. French sovereignty was confirmed. The French were still in control of their own army, and the administration of Indochina. Japanese forces were free to fight the war against the Allies from Indochinese soil.

Governor General Decoux modelled his government in Indochina on Pétain's Vichy regime.[4] He ruthlessly applied the laws of Vichy against Gaullists, liberals, freemasons and Jews. In other ways, his regime was, paradoxically, perhaps more liberal than some of the preceeding administrations. The French and Japanese fought a propaganda war for the hearts and minds of the Indochinese people. However, as war in the Pacific was drawing to a close, the Japanese moved suddenly to disarm the French and seize sovereignty of Indochina on 9 March 1945. On 11 March they set in place a puppet regime under the Emperor Bao Dai, who declared Vietnam independent of France. The French response was to reassert their authority immediately. On 24 March 1945, de Gaulle announced the creation of the *Fédération indochinoise*, which was to have a new status within the recently conceived *Union française*. Before the French could act however, an indigenous group led by Ho Chi Minh came to power in Tonkin. On 2 September 1945, Ho and his guerillas proclaimed the birth of the Democratic Republic of Vietnam. Bao Dai renounced his imperial title, and became part of Ho Chi Minh's new government.[5]

In response to this rather confused state of affairs, France set about what was essentially a war of reconquest in Indochina. This decision was embodied by the choice of General Leclerc, liberator of Paris, to head the expeditionary forces to Indochina. France thus initially replayed its narrative of protection in presenting the reconquest of Indochina as a liberatory gesture: designed to free the Indochinese populations from the Japanese, the acquistice intentions of the British Army overseeing the capitulation of the Japanese troops, or again from the influence of China and Russia. There ensued a protracted war, which has been amply documented elsewhere.[6] What concerns me here, is the press representation of the end of empire on the battlefield of Dien Bien Phu.

Notes

1. On metropolitan anticolonialism after the Second World War, see Sorum, P., *Intellectuals and Decolonization in France* (Chapel Hill: University of North Carolina Press, 1977).

2. On popular opinion and empire on the eve of the Second World War, see Ageron, C-R., 'Les Colonies devant l'opinion publique française 1919–1939', *Revue française histoire d'outre-mer*, no. 77, 1990.

3. On Indochina during the second World War, see relevant chapters in de Folin, J., *Indochine 1940–1955* (Paris: Perrin, 1993); Hammer, E., *The Struggle for Indochina* (Stanford: Stanford University Press, 1954); Isoart, P., *L'Indochine française 1940–45* (Paris: PUF, 1982); Kolko, G., *Vietnam: Anatomy of a War 1940–75* (London: Allen and Unwin, 1986).

4. Decoux, *A la barre de l'Indochine: histoire de mon Gouvernement général* (Paris: Plon, 1949).

5. See Shipway, M., *The Road to war: France and Vietnam 1944–1947* (Oxford: Berghahn, 1996).

6. See Ruscio, A., *Dien Bien Phu: la fin d'une illusion* (Paris: L'Harmattan, 1986); Ruscio, A., *La Guerre française d'Indochine 1945–54* (Bruxelles: Editions complexe, 1992); Dalloz, J., *La Guerre d'Indochine 1945–1954* (Paris: Seuil, 1987); de Boisanger, C., *On Pouvait éviter la guerre d'Indochine* (Paris: Maisonneuve, 1977); Lancaster, D., *The Emancipation of French Indo-China* (London: OUP, 1961); O'Ballance, E., *The Indo-China War 1945–54* (London: Faber, 1964).

−9−

Dien Bien Phu[1]

It was in Indochina then, that France's Fourth Republic experienced and lost its first colonial war. If Algeria has been commonly perceived as 'la guerre sans nom',[2] then the Indochinese conflict might well be termed *la guerre occultée*. Situated chronologically between two wars which were to mark the French national *conscience*, *imaginaire* and *mémoire* profoundly, and overshadowed by the traumatic American experience in Vietnam which followed it,[3] the Franco-Indochinese War was one which was conducted amidst profound metropolitan indifference.[4]

The Indochinese War was unlike other wars in which France had been involved in the twentieth century. The Franco-Indochinese War was neither a struggle for national sovereignty and territory (as in the case of the two World Wars), nor was it a war which involved conscription to the French Army. Neither did it provoke the same domestic tensions as the Algerian War which followed closely on its heels. It was a hybrid war, a war of changing focus and purpose; a national war of international dimensions.

The end of the colonial relationship, played out upon the battleground of Dien Bien Phu, is of interest as it is a period in which French imperial discourses of earlier decades are put to the test and finally reiterated, if in a somewhat diluted form. The front covers of *Paris Match*, which will be the principal focus of this chapter, depict the French retreat from its Indochinese Empire and provide an ambiguous conclusion to the period of French colonisation in Indochina. Whilst the anti-colonial metropolitan voice, so marked in its absence from the views of the Franco-Indochinese relationship of the 1920s and 1930s had been swelling during the nine years of war between France and Indochina, the 'fin du rêve indochinois' was nevertheless marked by visual and textual discourses which alluded frequently to the tenets of colonialism which had sustained French rule in Indochina for some ninety years.

Although contemporary domestic preoccupations with questions of national security (the fear of German rearmament most notably) inevitably drew attention away from this distant colonial conflict, it is the consistent ambivalence of the Franco-Indochinese relationship that appears to figure as the principal reason why this war was, and continues to be, largely overlooked in France. Whereas less than a decade later, the Algerian War would become an acutely felt domestic as well as colonial problem, the popular response to the Indochinese War, one essentially of well-documented indifference, is a measure of the metropole's tenuous affective link with Indochina.

This question of Indochina's status, and its place within the French Empire, can be linked, with the onset of war, to the perception of the French Army's role and duty. In previous conflicts of the twentieth century, war had been perceived as a glorious duty. The Third Republic had, through its preoccupation with civil, moral and military education, prepared generations of male citizens for whom their first duty was to *la patrie*, and for whom death in the name of *la patrie* was a glorious honour: blood shed in order to save the nation. The goals of these previous wars were (superficially at least) clearly defined: the Motherland was threatened, national independence was at stake. The Indochinese War on the other hand, had ill-defined goals, and an often 'invisible' enemy.

In its representation of its actions in 1945/6, official France drew on the same myths and discourses which had characterised its initial justification of the conquest of Indochina, in its attempt to square its actions in Asia with both the international community, and the home population. Thus, although in 1945/6 the Indochinese conflict seems clearly to be a war of reconquest, it was, however, perceived successively as a 'liberation' from Japanese control, protection from the potentially acquisitive desires of the British troops who oversaw the capitulation of the Japanese in Indochina, and from the increasing menace of Chinese and Russian intervention. This myth of liberation is embodied in the choice of General Leclerc, liberator of Paris, as the first commanding officer to oversee the expeditionary French forces in Indochina.

When, towards the end of the war, General de Castries observed the 'distance profonde' which separated what was at stake for the Viet Minh and what was at stake for the French forces: 'entre une armée nationale se battant sur son sol et pour l'indépendance de sa patrie, et une armée de métier faisant honneur à son contrat',[5] he could just as well have been talking about the differences between the previous wars France had fought in the twentieth century, and the conflict in which it was now embroiled. The *patrie* was not in danger; there seemed little connection between domestic concerns and this distant conflict. Confusion as to the role of the Army, or indeed the role and interests of France in South-East Asia seemed to have come full circle. Just as in the 1880s, Indochina was perceived as wasteful of 'l'or et le sang de la France'.[6]

The encampment at Dien Bien Phu was created on the orders of General Navarre in November 1953, and situated at the extreme west of Tonkin, on the border with Laos. It was constructed in response to rumours that Giap's forces were heading towards Laos. The decision was therefore taken to create a 'verrou', a 'bolt' which would ensure the control of the sole main road to Laos thus preventing passage from Tonkin to Laos. Mirroring French representations of the mainland's role in

Indochina since the conquest, Dien Bien Phu was envisaged as a protective and reactive gesture. Sixteen kilometres in length, the military camp was constructed inside a huge basin, surrounded by fortified hillsides. Inside the basin a runway was built to ensure supply routes to the camp. Hundreds of troops were parachuted in to secure the camp, which totalled 11,000 men.

It had been calculated that Giap would need from five to seven months to arm and supply himself sufficiently to mount an attack on the camp. French Command believed that Giap had insufficient troops to deploy in the area, his main bases were far away, and French firepower significantly outweighed Vietnamese artillery and firepower. Moreover, Giap would have to mobilise a significant section of the local population to ensure that supplies and arms were transported to Dien Bien Phu, by a stream of lorries, bicycles, and coolies on foot. No one believed the Vietnamese would dare to attack such a seemingly impregnable and unassailable fortress. By December 1953, however, the camp had been encircled by Giap's troops. On 13 March 1954 Giap's troops attacked. After heavy shelling, two of the advance hilltop positions were immediately taken: Béatrice and Gabrielle. By 17 March, the runway had been so severely damaged as to be impracticable, and a further post, Anne-Marie, had been lost. Dien Bien Phu was in fact a monumental miscalculation. As a response to a humiliating defeat, the mythology of Dien Bien Phu now commenced in earnest, and, as I hope to suggest, underwent a series of shifts and refocusings, as the French nation attempted to come to terms with news of events at Dien Bien Phu, and ultimately, the loss of this first colonial war.

Despite the seizure of important strategic locations around the basin at Dien Bien Phu, the French press initially remained buoyant. This confidence is reflected in the emphasis which was placed on the historical significance of the battle of Dien Bien Phu. The press was full of references to textualising and contextualising narratives of glory and success:

Ils écrivent une page de gloire dans le ciel de Dien Bien Phu.[7]

Les héroiques défenseurs de Dien Bien Phu écrivent un magnifique chapitre de l'histoire militaire française.[8]

The media consistently invoked a sense of history, and historical continuity around the battle, inventing a tradition of military glory for metropolitan France, and thereby adding weight, significance and depth to a conflict which scarcely interested the majority of the metropolitan public.

The need for a worthy point of comparison was found in the mythology of the First World War: Dien Bien Phu became 'Le Verdun tropical',[9] 'le Verdun de la brousse',[10] 'le Verdun de la jungle',[11] 'le Verdun tonkinois'.[12] Certain physical conditions at Dien Bien Phu bore some resemblance to the conditions at Verdun:

the proximity of the two sides, the violence, the existence of trenches, the huge bomb craters, the ubiquitous mud. But more importantly, Verdun was of course an idealised battle, embodying, in Poincaré's words, 'ce qu'il y a de plus beau, de plus pur et de meilleur dans l'âme française. Il est devenu synonyme synthétique de patriotisme, de bravoure et de générosité'.[13] Dien Bien Phu was thus initially envisaged as occupying a glorious place in the annals of French military history, a successor to Verdun, and also as embodying perceived national values, principles and attributes: patriotism, courage and generosity, all of which had permeated colonial discourses throughout the 1920s and 1930s.

As it became clearer that the French forces were losing their grip in Indochina, and defeat became probable as opposed to possible, press reporting gave rise to two thematic topoi : the representation of French defeats, through a slippage of language, as 'foudroyantes contre-attaques'[14]; and the hystericisation of the Viet Minh in the French media, drawing on colonial and racist discourses: 'innombrables masses jaunes', 'vagues hurlantes',[15] 'masses fanatisés',[16] 'soldats endoctrinés':[17] savage drunken masses who fired upon Red Cross vehicles and refused to allow French casualties to be evacuated fron Dien Bien Phu.

These are both standard rhetorical devices employed to 'explain away', and to deflect attention from military setbacks. They were used to discredit and devalorise the enemy as inhuman, fanatical, merciless, and in turn allowed for a further shift in press representation. For if the heroes of the French Army were not fighting an enemy who adhered to the 'rules of the game', international military convention, then the war itself was not being fairly fought, nor fairly won by the Viet Minh. The French heroes became martyrs, their defeat *un calvaire*.[18] The arrogant tone of the first months of 1954 was thus gradually abandoned in favour of a new theme: heroic martyrdom.

This evolution of representation was played out most visibly in *Paris Match* through the magazine's extensive use of photography. *L'Aurore* of 24 March published the first photographs of the battle, but it was *Paris Match* which became the specialist of war photography. From 20 March to 15 May it published 144 photos of the battle, of which five were front covers.

Although the series of photographs which *Paris Match* published inside its covers would be a fertile ground for analysis, the front covers themselves are perhaps more interesting as they attempt to convey, in a single image, the essence of Dien Bien Phu to the readership. Whilst the numerous shots of the battlefield, the parachutists, the HQ, and the trenches, which appeared inside the magazine, present a teleological vision of the war, a progression, albeit a progression which moves from possible victory to potential defeat, the front covers on the other hand, attempt to distil an exemplary image, to create an archetype, to formulate what we would term a myth of the French Army.

If, as Barthes noted of the African colonial soldier saluting the *tricolore* in a later *Paris Match* front cover, 'il est la présence même de l'impérialité française',[19] then what these photographs signify is perhaps 'la présence d'une impérialité française souffrante', but I would add, 'pas encore mourante'. The myth of Dien Bien Phu was accompanied by the headlines: 'la tragédie des blessés',[20] 'le calvaire et la gloire du Général de Castries',[21] 'l'épopée de Dien Bien Phu'.[22] Tragedy and suffering are thus offset by the glory, and the epic quality of the battle. French colonialism is undergoing severe pressure, but its principles remain untarnished, undiminished.

However, these new representations demonstrate the difficulty and the discomfort produced by the attempt simultaneously to represent heroism, or undiminished national grandeur, alongside defeat. In his mythical capacity, the warrior is valour, energy, idealism, and masculinity at its zenith. He is fearsome and venerable; a man of exceptional courage, valour and steadfastness, who is given to acts of bravery. In these photographs the warrior is agonised, despairing, exhausted, mutilated, the protected rather than the protector. The hero in these photographs has been transmuted into heroism's close but significantly more vulnerable partner: the martyr.

In the arena of war heroism and martyrdom have often become blurred in this way, and the hero has often been embodied by common man, elevated by sacrifice to the status of hero or martyr: the *poilu* of the First World War being the most enduring model of this traditional paradigm. His passage to heroism is marked by resistance in the face of overwhelming odds, his resilience when overwhelmed by appalling physical conditions. His glory and his heroism are achieved through the transgression of the limits of human condition, which in defeat or death marks his ultimate passage to martyrdom. This heroism of the common man can be translated as dogged determination to carry out one's perceived duty to a higher good, usually the good of the nation. It is 'not deserting', 'not leaving ones post' – it is 'ils ont tenu', rather than 'ils ont vaincu'.

Certainly, the soldiers at Dien Bien Phu 'ont tenu'. Both photographs and journalism of the period bear witness to the fortitude and steadfastness of the beleagured French Army: bomb craters, wounded men remaining at their posts in the trenches. As Jean-Marie Garraud reported in the *Figaro* of 5 April:

Depuis 120 heures, accrochés à leurs pointes d'appui, au milieu de la poussière et de la fumée des incendies, dans le fracas des explosions, ces hommes résistent magnifique-ment aux furieux assauts d'un ennemi cinq fois supérieur en nombre. Malgré la fatigue, l'insomnie, la chaleur, ils tiennent dans leurs tranchées, aux créneaux de leurs postes, les mains crispés sur leurs armes.

However, and to return to a point I made briefly at the beginning of this chapter, the French forces in Indochina were comprised solely of professional soldiers. In the case of the Indochinese conflict, the myth of the heroic common man can no longer apply. These myths of soldierly heroism are surely diminished and devalued when the men in question are professional soldiers, *engagés*. To recall de Castries, these men 'faisaient honneur à leur contrat'.

Neither does the image of the French forces presented by *Paris Match* accurately reflect their composition in reality. In 1952 the composition of the French forces in Indochina was as follows: 54,000 French; 30,000 North Africans; 18,000 Africans; 20,000 Légionnaires; 53,000 Natives; 50,000 members of the Vietnamese National Army; 15,000 members of the Laotian Army; 10,000 members of the Cambodian Army.[23]

While at a later date it was useful to represent French colonial interests by the association of a uniformed negro with the national flag, here the Army is very clearly portrayed as white and Western. A portrayal which is clearly at odds with the reality. Whilst the *ralliement* of troops of colonial origin to the aid of the Motherland in the First World War had been publicised and lauded, the Indochinese War appears to be represented, in spite of the Army's reliance on colonial troops, as an exclusively metropolitan affair. In the face of defeat by a colonised people, the French press redrew the battle lines along racial grounds. The French Army was depicted as just that. A *French* Army.

Additionally, the Indochinese War was, more than any other war involving twentieth-century France, a conflict which came to be represented from within a framework of French aristocratic dimensions. The two figures who feature prominently on these *Paris Match* covers are General de Castries, and Geneviève de Galard. Their names themselves indicators of an aristocratic descent.

As we have seen, much colonial thought of the 1920s and 1930s focuses on aristocratic values, and what I have termed the myth of 'autrefois': an unspecified period, or 'golden age' of French colonialism. The dynamic of this myth of 'autrefois' nostalgically imagines French Indochina as the last outpost in which aristocratic values have survived. The *colon*, innately superior by birth, nationality and class, commands immediate respect from his underlings through his very bearing and demeanour. The front cover depicting General de Castries, a former *cavalier*, signals the final death of the aristocratic colonial tradition in Indochina, and perhaps the aristocratic tradition of the French Army itself. For it was during this post Second World War period that the Army underwent a 'dégagement des cadres', which effectively reduced the numbers of senior officers in the Army by up to 45 per cent. Graduates from the military schools became a minority, and thus those of a bourgeois or aristocratic background became far less numerous, and increasingly officers rose from within the ranks of the regular army.[24] Thus in the immediate post-war period, the forces underwent a form of enforced democrati-

Figure 20. *Paris Match*, front cover, no. 268, 15–22 May 1954.

sation, which was at odds with its traditionally perceived image of the French national army.

Seen from the context of the Indochinese War, however, de Castries' portrait (Figure 20) signals the hopelessness of the French position. His is not the imperious gaze of a commanding officer confident of his troops. Bereft of his dress uniform, de Castries is allied not with his class, his ancestors and his political superiors at home: he is very firmly placed alongside his troops, he is 'one of them'. His photograph foretells of the rift whose seeds were sown in Indochina, but only came to bear fruit in Algeria, between the 'men on the ground', the serving soldiers, and the General Staff, the politicians at home. Castries is portrayed on the side of the heroic combatants against the traitors at home.

Geneviève de Galard, both aristocratic and a heroine, captured popular French imagination and became the darling of the French press. Galard was rapidly nicknamed by the popular press – 'l'ange de Dien Bien Phu' – and enjoyed several weeks of great celebrity, figuring on the front page of *Paris Match*, *France Soir* and *Le Figaro*. It was exceptional that a woman remain, right until the end, at the entrenched camp.[25] But this is not simply the portrait of a courageous nurse from *la France profonde*. De Galard becomes an icon because she is *de Galard*, a woman of aristocratic background. She is an appropriate and worthy figure to tend to the wounded French troops.

It is, at first glance, and discounting the 'human interest' angle, somewhat surprising that the press should have seized upon Geneviève de Galard to epitomise the French experience at Dien Bien Phu. Although it has become a standard reflex to observe that war exorcises the feminine, that war is a masculinised *domain par excellence*, a homosocial institution, it is nevertheless striking that media attention attached itself so firmly to a female figure at this point in the Franco-Indochinese War, for the feminine had been rigourously excluded from representations of Indochina until this point. Women, and more particularly female metropolitan settlers, had been marginalised and vilified in metropolitan literature on Indochina. In both popular and official texts, Indochina had been imagined as a male haven; a domain for male action, permeated with qualities such as virility, energy and courage.

De Galard's role was undoubtedly sentimentalised and therefore diminished by the press: *Le Figaro* of 6 May revealed that the French soldiers had nicknamed her 'Bécassine', 'à cause de son visage rond presque celui d'un bébé, [qui] garde, quelles que soient les circonstances, un calme extraordinaire et ne trahit aucune émotion'. Similarly, *Paris Match* of 1 May noted: 'la seule douceur des blessés: le sourire de Geneviève'. But de Galard is also the epitome of what metropolitan France imagined the woman settler in Indochina should be: useful, dutiful, practical. She embodies activity rather than passivity.

The portrait of de Galard (Figure 21), shows her in her nurse's uniform, looking straight at the lens. It is an accessible, open expression; she is a cheerful, capable figure. In another cover photograph, (Figure 22), de Galard is caught in action, loading a wounded soldier onto a truck. Here she appears as a comrade in battle. Directing the men around her, she is clearly in charge. The woman striding across the runway in the last photo (Figure 23) is purposeful, businesslike and from the expression, serenely confident despite being the focus of much attention from the group behind.

Indeed, this photograph represents her as a somewhat androgynous figure, dressed in combat uniform, she is viewed and observed, sexualised, but respected

Figure 21. *Paris Match*, front cover, no. 267, 8–15 May 1954.

Figure 22. *Paris Match*, front cover, no. 269, 22–29 May 1954.

Figure 23. *Paris Match*, front cover, no. 271, 5–12 June 1954.

at the same time. Photographed from both front and behind as she walks, and clearly the object of male sexual attention (note the stance of the bare-chested male figures in the background), her gaze is nonetheless directed at the soldier to the right of the picture who stands to attention as she passes.

These almost paradoxical significations surrounding de Galard might be related to the type of fantasy of the female on the battlefield popularised by the novel/ film *For Whom the Bell Tolls*, in which Hemingway's heroine represents the warrior's ideal mate: equally good with a gun or inside a sleeping bag. The woman in uniform (either nurse's or combat) is both slightly dishevelled and sexually inviting. Her sleeves rolled up in anticipation of action, de Galard nonetheless remains impeccably coiffured.

It is tempting to interpret these photographic images as yet another representation of the gendered and familial configuration of the Franco-Indochinese relationship, and even more tempting to see the Franco-Indochinese relationship as having come full circle: the infantilised colony rejects the parental control of France; the protective Motherland arrives at the moment of defeat to tend to her biological as opposed to her adopted children. But Geneviève de Galard also takes on something of a mythical status at Dien Bien Phu. Her name recalls Geneviève, the patron saint of Paris and protector of the capital. De Galard can, perhaps more convincingly, be viewed as a Marianne figure, the embodiment of the protective Motherland but also a symbolic substitute for the emasculated Republic: a defeated France, unable to regain authority in the colony, and unable to defeat the previously derided enemy of *petits jaunes*.

These images convey the confusion with which the French press viewed events in Indochina. Dien Bien Phu represented 'la tragédie des blessés', but was not 'une blessure tragique'. Dien Bien Phu was presented as an epic battle, but one with a vanquished hero. The reality of Dien Bien Phu was clearly humiliating – for the French Army, and for the France as an imperial nation. This humiliation was mitigated, however, through an attempt to demonstrate that although France had lost control of Indochina, the nation's imperial principles, the values of 'la mission civilisatrice' – generosity, protection and an innate sense of national and racial 'aristocracy' – remained undiminished. They were epitomised by the steadfastness of the French troops, the courage of Geneviève de Galard, and the torment of de Castries. One might wish to suggest that it was the very persistence and durability of these myths which led to the devastating and protracted trauma of Algeria.

Dien Bien Phu, and the Geneva Accords thus signalled the end of France's dominion in Indochina. Indochina was to slip from the headlines of the French press, and to emerge some few years later as Vietnam, and more specifically as America's Vietnam. The chronological gap between the French war in Indochina, and the American war in Vietnam was to play a crucial role in France's future relationship with its former colonised territories. Vietnam and Indochina became, in the French imagination, two quite separate entities. This connotative difference was to emerge in revealing ways during the next encounter between France and Vietnam: migration.

Notes

1. This chapter first appeared in Kelly, D., and Holman, V., *France at War in the Twentieth Century: Myth, Metaphor, Propaganda* (Oxford: Berghahn, 2000). I am grateful for permission to reproduce it here.
2. This epithet was coined by Bertrand Tavernier, in his film of the same name, which appeared in 1992.
3. See Ramirez, F., and Rolot, C., "D'Une Indochine à l'autre", *Cinémathèque*, 2, November 1992, pp. 40–55: "Le Viêt-nam et sa guerre ont, contre toute analyse et même contre tout bon sens, isolé l'Indochine dans un temps mythique et reculé. L'Indochine dans cet imaginaire-là, est désormais séparée du Viêt-nam un peu comme la Perse l'est de l'Iran. Elle est autre, coloniale et exotique, prête pour les regrets et les idéalisations", p. 42.
4. See Alain Ruscio's work on the Franco-Indochinese War and public opinion: Ruscio, A., *La Guerre française d'Indochine* (Brussels: Editions complexe, 1992); and 'French Public Opinion and the War in Indochina: 1945–54', in Scriven, M. and Wagstaff, P. (eds), *War and Society in Twentieth Century France* (Berg: 1991). See also Dalloz, J., *Dien Bien Phu* (Paris: La Documentation française, 1991); Delpey, R., *Dien Bien Phu: l'Affaire* (Paris: Editions de la pensée moderne, 1974).
5. Quoted in Rocolle, P., Colonel, *Pourquoi Dien Bien Phu?* (Paris: Flammarion, 1968), p. 407.
6. This metaphor was first used in relation to Indochina during the period of conquest and pacification, and became one of the principle arguments of the anti-expansionists in the parliamentary debates on colonialism of the 1880s.
7. *Paris Match*, 3 April 1954.
8. John Foster Dulles, quoted in *L'Aurore*, 24 March 1954.
9. *Le Figaro*, 15 April 1954.
10. *Paris Match*, 10 April 1954.
11. *L'Aurore*, 6 May 1954.
12. *Progrès de Lyon*, 2 April 1954.
13. Quoted in Prost, A., 'Verdun', in Nora, P., *Les Lieux de mémoire: La Nation III* (Paris: Gallimard, 1986).
14. *France-Soir*, 30 March 1954, carried as its headline: 'Foudroyante contre-offensive française à Dien Bien Phu'.
15. *Le Populaire*, 1 April 1954.
16. *France-Soir*, 1 April 1954.
17. *Le Figaro*, 23 January 1954.
18. This term was in fact used as a headline in one of *Paris Match*'s front covers.
19. Barthes, R., *Mythologies* (Paris, Seuil, 1957/1970), p. 214.
20. *Paris Match*, 22 May 1954.

21. *Paris Match*, 13 May 1954.
22. *Paris Match*, 8 May 1954.
23. Figures from de la Gorge, P-M., *The French Army: a military-political history* (London: Weidenfeld and Nicolson, 1963), translated by K. Douglas.
24. Statistics from de la Gorge, *The French Army*.
25. In fact Geneviève de Galard was not the sole woman remaining in the French camp. There were several prostitutes, sent from Hanoi, of whom certain were killed during the bombings. Some of them acted as nurses, although no mention of them was to be found in the press at the time.

−10−

From *indigène* to *immigré*: The Indochinese Migrant Experience in France

Of contemporary France's relationships with its non-European migrant populations, the Franco-Indochinese relationship has appeared the least contentious. Social, political and academic discourses, in both francophone and anglophone circles, regularly ignore the Asian dimension of the immigration 'question', to focus exclusively on Maghrebi populations, and to a lesser extent black populations in France. More recent discursive formulations of the relationship between France and its Others – such as the modish appellation *Black-Blanc-Beur* – specifically exclude South-East Asian migrants from the equation. Seemingly largely invisible, individuals of Vietnamese, Cambodian or Laotian origin in France rarely feature as participants in the immigration debate within France, or as subjects of that debate. Connotatively, it seems, 'immigrant' has long signified Maghrebi.

Reliable figures on the numbers of former Indochinese now living in France are difficult to establish. They have variously been said to represent between 3 and 8 per cent of the total 'foreign' population of France. The 1990 census of the population placed individuals of Vietnamese, Cambodian and Laotian nationality at 106,000, although clearly this does not include naturalised Asians.[1] Although their numbers are relatively small in comparison with figures for the Maghrebi populations, this fact alone does not entirely explain why this community has remained at the periphery of what has often been such a heated polemic in contemporary France. Here I will address this seeming anomaly within the framework of what has often been perceived as France's dichotomous response to its migrant populations: that is to say, France's separation of migrant communities into 'ses bons et ses mauvais immigrés'. For if the Maghrebi populations are often perceived as France's 'mauvais immigrés', are the Indochinese on the other hand part of France's 'couche noble de l'immigration'?

If France's Indochinese community has remained exterior to the immigration debate, it is perhaps because they are viewed as a far less 'problematic' section of the migrant populations. Their migration to France has not tended to provoke anxious responses from the mainland, and their integration into French society has been viewed as less fraught and ultimately more desirable than that of other migrant populations. The reasons for this are various and numerous. Firstly however, the legacy of colonial rule in Indochina may well offer some insights into the perplexing question of disparities between the status and perception of different migrant communities within the French nation. Residual images, ideas or memories of formerly colonised peoples may inform contemporary responses to immigrant populations. It is thus important to consider to what extent perceptions of migrants have been informed and shaped by earlier perceptions which find their roots in colonial images and stereotypes, and in the residual memory of the colonial relationship.

As we have seen, the most widely promoted image of the Indochinese during the colonial period was that of a docile, placid, peaceful, peasant population. The ubiquitous *nha que*, a peasant, wearing the equally ubiquitous conical hat, formed the principal visual image of the Indochinese. Fictional works, travel writing, colonial exhibitions and propaganda all drew upon pastoral images of a peaceful and backward peasant society, whose lack of modernisation required continued French colonial intervention. These representations reiterated the notion that these indigenous peoples were grateful for French intervention, and willingly collaborated in the French colonial project. The complicity between French and Vietnamese was often held up as exemplary.

Those Vietnamese nationalists whose revolt and agitation throughout the 1930s threatened to upset this comforting version of the Franco-Indochinese relationship were dismissed as troublesome minority, whose dissatisfaction could be assuaged by a reinforcement of the enlightening and fraternal principles of the French colonial doctrine. This representation of marginal forces of opposition was later actively propagated by a French colonial army about to lose its first colonial war on the battlefield of Dien Bien Phu: here, as we have seen, an insurgent minority was portrayed as savage, cruel, dishonourable and drunken, deranged fanatics and automatons, as opposed to the grateful majority who rallied to the French struggle against this aggressive nationalism.

This division of the Indochinese populations in the collective imagination between eager francophiles on the one hand, and hysterical communist-indoctrinated nationalists on the other, pitches a peaceful majority against an insurgent minority. Not only does France have its good and bad immigrants, but it appears the nation also has its good and bad Indochinese. The memory of this dichotomy between sections of the indigenous population may provide our first clue as to why Vietnamese, Cambodians and Laotians living in France have been generally well-accepted. For this is a memory which was reactivated during the wave of mass migration to France which occurred as a result of what became known as the Vietnamese Boat People crisis of the 1970s.

Indeed, the vast majority of Vietnamese migrants to France arrived after 1975, although there had been interspersed periods of minor Indochinese migration to France at certain key periods: recruitment to war industries during the First and

Second World Wars; repatriations and migrations after the Second World War and the Franco-Indochinese War. Little attention was paid to the movement of individuals from Indochina to France. Press, media and public interest in Vietnamese migrants, however, was aroused and exercised principally by the Boat People crisis of mid-1979 and by the subsequent arrival in France of Vietnamese on a large scale.

Although significant numbers of Vietnamese had fled their homeland in the aftermath of the American war and communist victory, the exodus was exacerbated by the blanket nationalisation of the private sector in 1978. The gradual global realisation of the extent of the crisis, and the lengths to which some Vietnamese went to flee their homeland clearly demanded an international humanitarian response. In France, the generally accepted version of a tyrannical Hanoi government provoking the flight of the Vietnamese masses, readily lent itself to comparisons with past views of a divided Vietnamese society. It allowed France to recuperate the image of the peaceful masses pitched against a tyrannical nationalism. As one respondent observed in a survey of attitudes to various migrant communities in France : 'les indochinois sont merveilleux (. . .) Ils ont fui le communisme.'[2]

It was all the more important at this period to appeal to a residual memory of the former Franco-Indochinese colonial relationship, and to that image of a peaceful people in need of protection, for it was also a period when the French government was asking France to distinguish quite literally between worthy and unworthy immigrant inhabitants of France. For the Boat People crisis is of interest not only as it represents a mass migration, and mediatisation of Vietnamese migrants, but also as it occurred at the same time that France was itself re-evaluating the status of immigrants within the nation, notably through debate on the Stoléru *projet de loi* on immigrant workers. As the government system of voluntary repatriation (*l'aide au retour*) had enjoyed little success, in collaboration with Christian Bonnet (Minister of Interior), Lionel Stoléru (Minister of State for Immigrant Workers) had devised a scheme whereby immigrant workers and their families would be forcibly repatriated if deemed surplus to labour requirements.[3] Debate on these legislative proposals to facilitate mass expulsions (1979-80) coincided with the Vietnamese Boat People crisis.

The juxtaposition of France's response to a global refugee crisis, and its internal polemic over a national immigration 'problem', is revealing of the seemingly irreconcilable split in France between the nation's tradition of *accueil* and *asile*, and its inclusion of certain immigrants within the fabric of the nation. For whilst on the one hand the French government were attempting to regulate and reduce the numbers of immigrants workers in French society (through proposed mass expulsion measures), at the very same time on the global stage, France's government was deploying the traditional rhetoric of *France terre d'accueil* with regard to Vietnamese, and later Cambodian, refugees. Once again, this infelicitous coincidence points up sharply the dichotomy which seems to exist in France between its 'bons et mauvais immigrés'.

It is significant that the plight of Vietnamese refugees had become a global concern. The seemingly paradoxical governmental response to different migrant communities (expulsion/incorporation) was side-stepped by the very invocation of the *tradition d'accueil*. Under attack from critics of the Stoléru proposals, the French government found in the refugee crisis an opportunity to offset its hard-line stance on immigrant workers against a highly visible and mediatised display of generosity towards the Vietnamese refugees. Critics of what was deemed to be a slow governmental response to the crisis also made use of this traditional discourse to plead the case of the Vietnamese refugees. As one commentator noted, clearly conscious of France's international reputation, in not accepting more refugees 'l'honneur de notre pays risque d'être gravement atteint'.[4]

Practising a form of international one-up-manship, the government sought to deflect this type of criticism through its boasts about the numbers of Vietnamese accepted into France, demonstrating the need for France to be seen to be doing humanitarian good on the global stage. A presidential declaration of 18 June centred around France's rank as premier asylum granter: 'La France a déjà accueilli entre le 15 mai 1975 et le 10 juin 1979 51,515 réfugiés en provenance de ces Etats. Cet effort, qui représente un pour mille de sa population est, avec celui des Etat-Unis et de l'Australie, le plus élevé du monde.'[5] Similarly, at a meeting of the Ministers for Foreign Affairs of the members of the European Community, François Poncet remarked that 'La France est le premier pays de la Communauté européenne pour le nombre des réfugiés indochinois recueillis.'[6]

In spite of such governmental boasts, intellectuals and politicians of the left lobbied the government to increase the numbers of Vietnamese granted refugee status. Mobilised under the banner of France's noble tradition of granting asylum were intellectuals such as Jean-Paul Sartre,[7] Michel Foucault, and Raymond Aron, who formed a campaign group known as 'Un bateau pour le Vietnam', which met with President Giscard d'Estaing to enjoin him to increase numbers of refugees accepted and to establish a regular air route to bring in refugees to France. The committee chartered a boat, an initiative spearheaded by the intrepid Bernard Kouchner. The rather tellingly named *Ile-de-Lumière*, which was stationed off Malaysia, was intended to provide medical aid for refugees in camps on the island of Bi Dong. A plethora of political, humanitarian, and religious associations and organisations appealed to public generosity, collected funds and distributed aid. By 27 June, the government had announced it would accept a further 5,000 refugees. Politicians of all persuasions jumped on the media bandwagon. As a Communist party commentator noted cynically, 'A chacun son réfugié.'[8] Veritable welcoming committees appeared at Parisian airports to greet 'their' refugees. Both

Chirac and Mitterrand got in on this appropriative act: in the name of the City of Paris, Chirac chartered a boat to aid refugees, and a plane to transport 'his' refugees to Roissy; not to be outdone, Mitterrand turned up at Roissy but a few days later to welcome 'his' refugees 'au nom du parti socialiste'.[9]

The government's greatest and most vociferous critics were the Parti Communiste. Indeed, the PCF was the only group in France to make a direct reference to France's own hand in the drama now unfolding. Pierre Juquin observed: 'Désigner ces émigrés vietnamiens comme des victimes du communisme, c'est vraiment mettre l'histoire sur la tête. A qui la faute de ce drame sinon à ces gouvernements de droite ou socialistes, qui il y a vingt ou trente ans, ont conduit contre le Vietnam une guerre coloniale atroce?' He further noted that 'La responsabilité du drame incombe au colonialisme français et à l'agression américaine qui en a pris le relais après Dien Bien Phu.'[10] PCF commentators were also among the few in France to point out the seeming paradox in the government's responses to immigrants. *L'Humanité* noted that

> Les propositions d'accueil des Vietnamiens par les municipalités coïncident avec la décision prise par M. Stoléru et le gouvernement d'expulser un million de travailleurs immigrés dans les cinq prochaines années. Elles coïncident avec les expulsions effectuées par la police dans les foyers de SONACOTRA. Quel cynisme il faut avoir pour lancer à la fois une campagne d'accueil aux Vietnamiens et la politique d'expulsion des immigrés![11]

However, the communist group of the *Conseil de Paris* also regretted that all the Vietnamese refugees were not being dispersed around the capital, but regrouped in *centres d'hébergement* which were 'tous situés dans des quartiers populaires de la capitale où la densité de la population immigrée a déjà atteint la cote d'alerte au point de constituer de vrais ghettos'.[12] That is to say, placed in communist-run *arrondissements* of the capital.

This political and intellectual mobilisation was accompanied by a relatively short yet intense period of press coverage, which began in June, and started to peter out by the end of July, particularly after the Geneva conference on refugees had ended on 20 July. The Vietnamese refugees occupied the front pages for well over a month. They were 'les malheureux', and, recalling Fanon, 'les damnés de la mer'.[13] Appealing to a sense of historical precedent and the need for an international humanitarian response press headlines associated 'le drame' and 'la tragédie des réfugiés' with the plight of Jews fleeing Hitler, and made frequent allusions to the Holocaust: 'Chaque boatman qui se noie est un gazé de plus à Auschwitz.'[14] In response to this pressure, by the close of the international Geneva Conference on 20 July 1979 it was announced that France would take yet another 5,000 refugees, nonetheless with the qualifying clause, 'en fonction des possibilités d'hébergement'.

While most headlines referred to the dramatic and horrific plight of *Vietnamese* refugees, in press reports and articles calling for France's acceptance of further refugees, columnists invariably preferred the term *Indochinese*. This seemingly slight semantic difference is in fact revealing of how, and under what circumstances, memories of the former Franco-Indochinese relationship resurfaced. The name Vietnam is indelibly associated with the American war, and its use effectively distances France from any associations with this area of South-East Asia, and from the causes of the present crisis. The French government was obviously reluctant to draw attention to France's hand in Western imperialism in South-East Asia (in fact it was only the PCF who made such associations), or to the fact that American intervention in Vietnam had grown out of France's requests for American financial and military aid during the Franco-Indochinese war. Indeed, the interposition between French involvement in Indochina and mass Vietnamese migration to France, and the American war in Vietnam, is crucial to French responses to Vietnamese migrants. For conversely, the use of the term Indochina – here used only with reference to the acceptance of refugees and not to the crisis itself – reinstates a proximity between France and Vietnam, and recalls the former colonial relationship as a means of persuasion. The seeming American monopoly on Vietnam allows for a vision of an exculpated French Indochina, which can be represented nostalgically as a better time and place. In this way, France can better position itself in an international humanitarian role as opposed to a post-colonial national role.

By the time of the Boat People crisis in 1979, a largely collective amnesia seems to have set in: an amnesia which forgets the negative and exploitative aspects of France's own imperial venture in Indochina, and forgets the violence of the French war in Indochina. It is an amnesia which precludes any association between French imperialism and subsequent American imperialism in South-East Asia. The chronological gap between the end of French colonial rule in Indochina and the end of American imperial aggression in Vietnam, a gap of some twenty years, thus seems to produce a memory lapse on the part of the French nation. Vietnamese anti-colonialism, and the French war in Indochina are obliterated in order to make way for a selective memory of the former colonial relationship – a memory which seeks nostalgically to rehabilitate the erstwhile image of Franco-Vietnamese complicity.

This amnesia was no so complete, however, as to forget the former colonial relationship with Indochina when it came to the governmental policy of selection of the Vietnamese refugees to whom entry to France was to be granted. Governmental policy was as follows:

Sont admis en priorité en France les Indochinois qui parlent français ou qui possèdent des éléments de langue française et ceux qui ont déjà de la famille en France, ou qui ont rendu dans le passé des services à la France ou aux Français.[15]

These criteria, it was argued, would greatly facilitate the insertion of the refugees in France. Here past Franco-Indochinese complicity under colonial rule is actively recalled into the present; the image of the compliant, collaborative and grateful *indigène* willingly serving *la mère-patrie* is not only remembered, but its rehabilitation is required. These notions are reinforced by other commentators: 'le courage, la volonté et la capacité de travailler, et la faculté d'assimilation de ces réfugiés (. . .) permettent d'affirmer que notre pays peut les absorber en assez grand nombre sans difficultés économiques et sociales majeures'.[16] Here emphasis is quite clearly placed upon the usefulness to France of the refugees, and on their assimilatory potential or capabilities. Unlike France's *mauvais immigrés*, these refugees possess desirable qualities, and, as under colonial rule, they will constitute a pliant workforce, and are likely to conform.

This conformity, and undemanding acceptance is also linked to a perceived humility amongst the Vietnamese populations:

> La qualité des réfugiés en compte aussi dans la réussite de la réinsertion: souvent de pauvres gens, beaucoup d'enfants et de personnes agées, mais tous désireux de s'intégrer dans la société en acceptant de travailler sans mettre en avant leur rang social antérieur.[17]

Not only are the Vietnamese eager to integrate and willing to work (unlike those immigrants Stoléru proposed to expel from France), but they are also willing to adopt a lower social status, thereby posing no competition to the European French. Similarly, by the beginning of July, when the press started to focus on the 'human interest' angle, and the arrival of Vietnamese boat people in France, further qualifications as to the desirability of the Vietnamese came to light. They were perceived as 'sages' and 'discrets', 'industrieux', and 'travailleurs'. These examples of a resurfacing paternalism and the seeming revalorisation of the hierarchical nature of the colonial relationship, require that France's *bons immigrés*, like their former colonised selves, know their place.

It is this colonial, and now post-colonial, stereotype which appears to have allowed for a less fraught integration of Vietnamese migrants into the French nation. A young member of the *Union des Jeunes Vietnamiens*,[18] a large cultural association, whose goals are to promote Franco-Vietnamese cultural exchange and understanding, spoke in 1985 of the status of Vietnamese in France in the following terms:

> Notre communauté forme une minorité paisible dans la population immigrée (. . .) Notre image, véhiculée par les médias, est positive. Nous faisons moins de bruit, on nous remarque moins que les jeunes Arabes, mais surtout, nous ne poursuivons pas les mêmes buts. Ils veulent être reconnus et courent après leur identité. Ils ont la tête politique. Nous ne souhaitons qu'une chose: réussir notre parcours dans la société française. Notre objectif est purement économique.[19]

The Vietnamese community in France is described as peaceful, apolitical, discreet, undemanding, not causing any fuss, industriously pursuing economic objectives, and slipping quietly unnoticed into the background. The overlap between this last quotation and descriptions of the quiet, untroublesome, discreet, and compliant Vietnamese from both the colonial period and the 1970s is striking. By investing in these stereotypes, playing the part and adopting the persona desired and required by France, populations of Vietnamese origin have thus invented a strategy through which they may avoid excessive visibility, persecution and racism. A rejuvenated French paternalism, reminiscent of the nation's colonial attitude to indigenous Vietnamese, thus sets the terms for migrant inclusion to the ranks of France's *bons immigrés*. Continued submission is required.

Notes

1. See Cheam, F., 'L'Insertion en France des communautés asiatiques: fidélité au pays d'origine et inclusion des diasporas dans le monde', in *Migrations Etudes*, no. 80, avril-mai 1998; Costa-Lascoux, J., and Yu-Sion, L., *Paris XIIIème; Lumières d'Asie* (Paris: Autrement, 1995); Le Huu Khoa, *L'Immigration asiatique: espaces économiques communautaires et stratégies d'ascension professionnelle* (Paris: Direction de la Population et des Migrations, 1994); Le Huu Khoa, *Les Vietnamiens en France: Insertion et identité* (Paris: L'Harmattan, 1985). Simon-Barouh, I., *Rapatriés d'Indochine: Deuxième génération – les enfants d'origine indochinoise à Noyant-d'Allier* (Paris: L'Harmattan, 1981).
2. *Le Nouvel Observateur*, 1984.
3. See Hargreaves, A., *Immigration, 'Race' and Ethnicity in Contemporary France* (London: Routledge, 1995), pp. 19–20.
4. Pierre Marcilhacy (sénateur non-inscrit, la Charente), *Le Monde*, 27 June 1979.
5. Giscard d'Estaing, quoted in *Le Monde*, 18 June 1979.
6. *Le Monde*, 20 June 1979.
7. Amusingly, Sartre is reported to have responded to the crisis by noting: 'Il faudra sans doute organiser une manifestation', *Le Monde*, 22 June 1979.
8. *Le Monde*, 10 July 1979.
9. *Le Monde*, 12 July 1979.
10. *L'Humanité*, 30 June 1979.
11. *L'Humanité*, 30 June 1979.
12. *Le Monde*, 12 July 1979.

13. *Le Monde*, 17/18 June 1979.

14. *Le Monde*, 17/18 June 1979.

15. *Le Monde*, 14 July 1979.

16. Rémy Prudhomme, quoted in *Le Monde*, 20 July 1979.

17. René Lenoir (former Secretary of State for *action sociale*) quoted in *Le Monde*, 2 July 1979.

18. The web page of *l'Union des Jeunes Vietnamiens de France* can be viewed at http://multimania.com/ujvf/. There are many active Vietnamese cultural asscoiations in France. See for example, *l'Union générale des Vietnamiens en France* at http://www.chez.com/ugvf/; *l'Amicale Franco-Asiatique Paris-Sud* at http://www.mediaport.net/Expo/Hue2002/afaps.fr.html; *l'Amicale des Vietnamiens de Lyon* at http://www.vietfrance.com/avl/indexfr.htm; *l'Association des artistes vietnamiens à Toulouse* at http://www.multimania.com/nah/introaavt.html.

19. Quoted in Moulin, J-P., *Enquête sur la France multiraciale* (Paris: Calmann-Lévy, 1985), p. 221.

–11–

Revisiting Indochina: Colonial Nostalgia in Contemporary France

Beyond the nation's response to the migration of formerly Indochinese populations, what resonances, if any, does Indochina have for today's France? How is the nation's colonial past in South-East Asia viewed now, at the beginning of the twenty-first century? In this concluding chapter it seems apt to pose these questions and to ask whether the colonial image of Indochina, and the perception of France's role in South-East Asia has been re-examined, challenged, reiterated or reworked; and to ascertain whether the current environment in France, which has been reassessing the nation's colonial past in relation to North Africa, has extended its critical gaze to Indochina.

Since the opening up of Vietnam in the post cold war era, France's former colonial territories have been viewed once again as a site for development – this time as a site for the development of France's capitalist and commercial outlets. Vietnam, as a country where the French language was once taught and disseminated as a means of bringing the Indochinese within France's cultural sphere and political control, now provides a target for the neo-colonial policies of *francophonie*:[1] Vietnam numbers 160,000 francophones, has been a member of the *Agence intergouvernementale de la francophonie* since 1970, and has taken an active part in the *francophonie* summits since 1986. The conference on *francophonie* was held in Hanoi on 14–16 November 1997. Indochina has also reappeared as a tourist destination. Yet it is not always marketed as Vietnam, and travel agents eager to cash in on France's former colonial relationship have been known to produce glossy brochures tempting the French to revisit the now defunct territory of Indochina. There is even a continued interest in what became that great symbol of Indochina – Angkor Wat, ever the prime feature of colonial exhibitions of the past, and the basis upon which Indochina was judged to be the 'perle' of the French Empire to rival Britain's 'jewel in the crown'. As recently as 1996, an extremely well-attended exhibition was held in Paris' Grand Palais which once more brought to the French mainland sculpture and architecture from Angkor, demonstrating the enduring appeal of this Indochinese signifier.

The popularity of 1980s pop phenomenon 'Indochine' probably did little to dispel the stereotypical images of Indochina which had circulated for so long.

Album titles such as *Le Péril jaune*, containing songs such as *La Sécheresse du Mékong*, and lyrics such as the following have wholeheartedly seized upon older stereotypes of Indochina for commercial gain:[2]

> Partis pour explorer
> Une forêt vierge
> La région inconnue
> Des rizières Kao-Bang
> Truffées de fauves féroces
> Et d'anthropophages . . .
> Durant la sécheresse du Mékong
> Ils restèrent dix jours isolés du monde
> Durant la sécheresse du Mékong
> Soudain c'est l'embuscade
> Par des sauvages
> Brutes sans foi ni loi
> Qui les enfermèrent
> Dans ces cages en bois
> La sombre prison
> Durant la sécheresse du Mékong
> Ils restèrent dix jours isolés du monde
> Durant la sécheresse du Mékong
> D'escale à Saigon
> Des hommes vaillants
> Partis pour les délivrer
> Des cannibales
> Dans un combat sanglant
> Les rescapèrent.[3]

Not only are the images of a virgin, unexplored territory revisited in this 1983 pop lyric, the added exotic feature of cannibalism is added to the colonial melting pot. This type of uncritical adoption of tropes which constituted the fixing of the colony in general, and of Indochina in particular, as backward and savage, may well have helped to create in the minds of a generation of young music fans, with little knowledge of France's colonial past, an association between primitivism and Indochina.

There are thus many ways in which France has renewed, or sought to reinstate aspects of its former ties with Vietnam in particular. Through travel, migration, the policies of *francophonie*, and through representational accounts of the colonial past, France of the 1990s has been reminded of the past relationship with Indochina, and has, at times, sought to rekindle that perceived closeness and complicity between colonised and coloniser upon which a benevolent French colonialism was believed to be predicated.

Certainly then, France's relationship with Indochina seems altogether less problematic than the nation's relationship with Algeria. Indochina is certainly not the open sore that Algeria appears to be in contemporary France. Nonetheless, imperial France fought and lost bloody colonial wars in both Indochina and Algeria; and where the memorial to the wars in Indochina was inaugurated by François Mitterrand on 16 February 1993 in Fréjus, it was not until 1999 that the Franco-Algerian 'conflict' was even recognised formally as a war. The contemporary repercussions of the former colonial order in Algeria continue to exercise France in ways which Indochina does not.

In these renewed interests in Indochina, contemporary France thus appears to be forging an entirely different style of relationship than in its other former colonial territories. Why should this be so? What form does this new relationship take? In order to analyse these questions, this concluding chapter will consider the most recent representations of Indochina in French culture – the cinematic *mise en scène* of the colonial relationship with Indochina. The focalising questions of this examination will be: to what extent has France re-evaluated its colonial past in relation to Indochina? What status is accorded to memories of the former colonial relationship, and have these memories produced a critique and therefore reshaping and reworking of that relationship which is more appropriate to the post-colonial environment?

Nostalgia in a (post-)colonial context may seem unimaginable in a France which is slowly and painfully coming to terms with the legacy of its colonial past in Algeria. For a variety of reasons, however, Indochina seems to have lent itself more readily than France's other former colonial possessions to a nostalgic, complacent, backward-looking and exoticising view. Indeed the term Indochina seems still to function largely as it did previously in the French imaginary. That is to say, as a signifier for an exotic Other; a utopian and ahistorical space onto which are projected collective fantasies and longings. Today, time past and incomplete memory conspire to create again that void in which desires and regrets entwine.

The early 1990s appeared to offer an opportunity for re-examination, with the release of three films which, perhaps for the first time in the history French cinema, focused entirely upon Indochina: Jean-Jacques Annaud's *The Lover*, Pierre Schoendoerffer's, *Dien Bien Phu*, and Régis Wargnier's, *Indochine*.[4] However, each film is replete with colonial nostalgia, and provides a romanticised image of Indochina which owes more to the tenacity of the colonial ideal than it does to the current environment of post-colonial critique. Indeed, these films reveal the extent to which the myths and images of both French colonialism and of Indochina which prevailed during the period of colonial rule still have currency today.

In these films Indochina is being remembered, reconstructed as it was thought to have been in memory, replicated, and rearticulated. Rather than the amnesia which, it has been suggested, occurs in relation to contemporary responses to

Algeria, Indochina, on the contrary, is being actively memorialised. However, it is the content and status of the memories which require closer scrutiny. For an analysis of the films of the 1990s seem to present an exemplary case of selective memory. In these films, Indochina is remembered sentimentally and then reconstructed romantically. These films represent the idealisation of a moment in the past, a distorted and sentimentalised vision of a lost era. They are thus not only examples of selective memory, but a nostalgic and imaginative reconstruction of an idealised past.

As Benjamin has observed, 'to articulate the past historically does not mean to recognise it the way it really was. It means to seize hold of a memory as it flashes up.'[5] However, a vagueness in recollection or memory often inspires the idealisation of the past. Indochina, as the least well-known and least represented of the French possessions seems indeed to be the object of widespread vagueness or approximative understanding. In these instances, the imagination is encouraged to gloss over forgetfulness in order to fashion a more aesthetically complete and satisfying recollection of what is longed for. Nostalgia thus summons the imagination to supplement memory. Such a glossing over of forgetfulness thus casts a nostalgic image that has been purified, clarified and simplified in order to supplant, through aesthetic intervention, the vagueness of the imperfect recollection.

To illustrate how this process might have allowed for a nostalgic vision of Indochina, I would firstly like to quote Régis Wargnier from an interview about his film *Indochine*:

> la motivation de départ, pour moi, c'était le mot 'Indochine' qui avait envahi mon enfance parce que mon père, qui était militaire, y faisait la guerre et que j'entendais répéter comme un leitmotiv: 'il faut garder l'Indochine' . . . Alors lorsqu'un producteur m'a proposé d'aller là-bas, j'ai tout de suite eu envie de voir ce trésor qu'il ne fallait surtout pas perdre.[6]

Here the aesthetic appeal to the *cinéaste* of this lost treasure, coupled with an incomplete memory of its significance, appears to allow that past image or impression to pass unexplored and unquestioned into the present, thus paving the way for a nostalgic contemporary vision of Indochina. Similarly, a commentator noted of film-makers returning to Vietnam, that they found 'dans ce retour à l'Indochine un formidable réservoir de rêves et d'aventures, une époque aussi où n'importe qui ou presque pouvait faire de sa vie une grand destin'.[7] Any analysis of Indochina is glossed over in order simply to repeat and reiterate earlier colonial stereotypes of Indochina (adventure, heroism, reservoir for development) which posit the territory as that *ailleurs rêvé* which satisfies some contemporary yearning for the unexplored. As an article on the films in *L'Evénement du jeudi* heralded, with no hint of irony, these films constituted 'La Reconquête de l'Indochine'.[8]

Following the logic of the definition and uses of nostalgia quoted above, both the vagueness of recollection of what Indochina was and represented, and also the distance, both spatial and temporal between France and Indochina, can be seen to have encouraged this contemporary cinematic exoticisation and aetheticisation. The evocative power of the very name Indochina, as Wargnier's words imply, conjures up a territory distanced geographically, distanced in time, and distanced through its name from the seeming American monopoly on Vietnam. Indochina is cinematically foreign. These films can perhaps be viewed as an attempt to wrest the cinematic construction of this corner of South-East Asia from the US, to recuperate *French* Indochina, for a French audience. Thus these films tend to depict Indochina as a 'better time and place' than the Vietnam we are used to seeing on Hollywood screens.

However, and particularly in the 1990s, a definition of nostalgia which implies that the loss of the object incurs pain and yearning is more problematic. What is at stake here, it seems, is the desire to reconstruct a rehabilitated and exculpated vision of Empire at its apogee. It is as if the aftermath of decolonisation has been swept aside in an attempt to relive an imagined version of Empire at its height, free from past and present repercussions of the former colonial order. Thus it is not such the depicted loss of Empire which is regretted, it is the possibility of looking back to that era with an untainted sense of national glory. These films attempt to repossess an ahistorical French Indochina, one unburdened by the niceties of post-colonial critique.

This observation is exemplified by the way in which the spectator is encouraged to view the characters depicted. Whilst it has been observed of British heritage films treating colonialism, that the British ideal appears to be the 'good sort', exemplified perhaps by the character of Daphne Manners in *The Jewel in the Crown* – pragmatic, honourable and distinctly unsexy[9] – the French ideal is, as one might expect, somewhat different: dangerous, passionate, adventurous, hedonistic. The films enjoin the spectator to appreciate and regret the social and political circumstances of colonialism which allowed these characteristics to flourish. This is suggestive of the resurgence of a certain idea of French national identity: a strong France, confident and authoritative.

These observations are most applicable to what is perhaps the most striking adaptation of the French colonial *doctrine* to the contemporary screen: Wargnier's *Indochine*. In it, Catherine Deneuve plays the role of Eliane Devries, a wealthy plantation owner who has adopted an orphaned child of royal indigenous friends. Clearly it could only have been Deneuve – Marianne incarnate – who played this part. Since Deneuve signals most overtly the female incarnation of the Republic in the collective imagination in France, it does not seem too far-fetched to understand the portrayal of Eliane Devries and an allegory of France's colonial role in Indochina.

The character of Eliane embodies the qualities and roles of colonial France towards Indochina: she is the adoptive and protective French mother, the narrator, teacher and guide; the authoritative *civilisée*, the exploitative consumer; the Republic; colonial France. Camille, the adopted daughter, represents Indochina, *la fille adoptée de la France*: an indigenous orphan, she is the subject of narration, and the object of metropolitan desire; her disorderly behaviour warrants control and guidance; the innocent and endangered student, she needs protection and nurture.

However, Eliane Devries is also a somewhat androgynous character, reflecting perhaps the ambiguous gendering of the imperial nation – *la mère-patrie* – and reminiscent of France's own confusion over its identity as an imperial power, and its colonial role in Indochina. For although Eliane nurtures the orphaned child, she has also has taken over the running of the rubber plantation from her father, she disciplines her workers, states her dream was 'être un garçon', refuses to marry the local head of police to remain resolutely single, and takes on male pursuits in the film: she frequents opium dens, and runs a sort of *garçonnière* for her casual affairs. She is a woman who takes on masculine qualities and characteristics at certain points in the film, whilst at others she functions as a stereotypical lovelorn woman: needy of protection and attention, a clinging desperate figure, she becomes 'une femme suppléante' in her affair with Jean-Baptiste. This double gender-identification is most clearly expressed in her coolie's response to her punishment of him: 'tu es mon père et ma mère'.

This portrayal of Eliane Devries raises the question of matriarchy and patriarchy within the colonial relationship, and to my mind suggests the antitheses and paradoxes of France's own perception of imperial identity. Guy Austin contends that *Indochine* presents 'the decline of the French Empire as a tragic, matriarchal narrative', as opposed to the 'patriarchal genealogy of imperialist power'[10] discernible in yet another film starring Deneuve: *Fort Saganne*.[11] However, as we have seen, France's sense of its own role as an imperial nation was never so clearly demarcated. While certain key concepts remained consistent, France's imperial identity was subject to many shifts and changes – both in relation to external events and in relation to France's evolving role and position in Indochina. *La Plus Grande France* functioned as both protective and nurturing mother, and authoritative and edifying father to its colonial offspring. These paradoxes and antitheses are replicated in the allegorical role of Eliane Devries. *Indochine* thus presents a disturbed matriarchy, shifting and protean, masculinised at times, exaggerated in its stereotypical weak femininity at others. Rather than reworking the imperial role as a 'tragic matriarchy', as Austin would have it, *Indochine* faithfully reproduces what might be termed a feminised patriarchy.

Received colonial ideas which seem more appropriate to the 1920s and 1930s resurface in other areas of the film. The sumptuousness of *Indochine*'s photography

signals a return to notions of exoticism and *évasion*. Of the Vietnamse landscape, Wargnier himself says:

> Le premier choc, c'est Hanoi, une ville figée par le communisme. Rien n'a bougé. On dirait une ville d'eaux française des années 40. Mais la grande émotion, c'est tout le nord du pays qui n'a pas été touché par la guerre. Nous avons traversé des régions immenses où jamais un cinéaste occidental n'avait pu filmer. Le plus beau de tout, c'est la baie d'Halong. On monte sur un sampan, on part à la dérive, on croit être en pleine mer et on découvre des dizaines d'îles au ras de l'eau sur lesquelles vivent des pêcheurs. C'est le Moyen-Age, c'est absolument bouleversant.[12]

Not only does Wargnier resurrect and reactivate the colonial stereotype of the fixed, primitive subject nation in contrast to the progressive, modern mainland, he also replays the myth of colonial discovery and conquest. The new conquistador, Wargnier goes where no *cinéaste* has been before. Filmed as a *produit publicitaire*, the colonial world enters connotatively into the sphere of the desirable: the lush vegetation; the luxurious colonial villas and the glamorous hotels and bars of the settler community; the spectacle of Vietnamese tradition, from the opening funeral cortège, to the imperial palace at Hué. Wargnier's film offers the spectator a chance to view and experience a world which died with the Geneva accords, a vision of *la France lointaine*.

This aestheticisation and reification of the Vietnamese landscape, and Wargnier's own appreciation of his role as cinematic conqueror, might well be perceived as a neo-colonialist project: to repossess the colony in imagination through the visual recapture or reconquest of its former glory. Here nostalgia appears to offer a compensation for that lost proximity by supplanting forgetfulness and invigorating memory. These 'invigorated memories' also resurface in the rehabilitation of the plethora of colonial stereotypes which had currency during the height of colonial rule in Indochina: the geographical markers which have long signalled Indochina, such as the rubber plantation and attendant coolies, the Bay of Ha-Long, the island prison of Poulo Condore, the Hôtel Continental, the French missionary school, the Royal Palace at Hué, the opium den. The stereotypical characters, reminiscent of the fictional protrayals of Indochina from the 1920s and 1930s: Monsieur Devries and his indigenous *con gaï*, the officers of the *marine française*, *le tout Saigon* attending a regatta, *le chef de la sûrêté*. Finally, the figurative topoi which permeated representations of Indochina: the debilitating (physical and moral) impact of Indochina, the fragility of the white European, mixed-race relationships, opium, *Asie éternelle*, going native. It is as if we are being enjoined actively to remember perceived moments of complicity and closeness between France and Indochina. It is as if Indochina had been seduced rather than subjugated by France.

The film thus conspires to give the spectator a rapid overview of these Indochinese signifiers within the first five minutes of the film, alongside a rather heavy-handed reiteration of the principal familial and hierarchical configuration of the Franco-Indochinese relationship. The sorrowful narrative voice, clearly looking back to the narrated time with a sense of regret and nostalgia, evokes that very sense of idealised complicity and closeness between France and Indochina:

> C'est peut-être ça la jeunesse, croire que le monde est fait de choses inséparables: les hommes et les femmes, les montagnes et les plaines; les humains et les Dieux, Indochine et la France.

This series of oppositions, which appears right at the beginning of the film, thus clearly reactivates the hierarchical status of the Franco-Indochinese relationship.

The narrative structure of the film also imbricates colonial stereotypes with former colonial projects or imperatives. Catherine Deneuve's voice-off is present throughout, providing a backbone and continuous thread to the plot, and binding the various subplots together. The narrative voice represents omniscience, omni-presence, and omnipotence – she narrates the various stories and histories of the film, whether she was present or not. Eliane Devries' voice-off provides the central axis around which the other characters turn, and other narrative voices are excluded from the film. This is very much the narrative of the white European ruler. Although half of the film is given over to Camille's story – her disobedience, disappearance, and consequent learning curve as she travels through her own country – it is the voice of Eliane Devries which informs the spectator of Camille's journey and escapades. In the later stages of the film, Camille is masculinised, her clothes change, her role changes, she becomes the 'Red Princess', a Marxist revolutionary, an unnatural mother who abandons her *métis* child to the hands of her white Western adoptive mother, and then Camille disappears from the narrative.

This deeply paternalistic and authoritarian narrative device should leave the spectator in no doubt as to the film's ideological stance. Midway through the film, between Eliane's story and Camille's story, the spectator is transported to the neutrality of Switzerland in 1954. The narrating subject (an older Deneuve) appears with the intended recipient of the narration – Etienne, the son of Jean-Baptiste and Camille. Once again the child has become Eliane's adopted child. At the end of the film, Etienne attempts to meet up with his estranged mother, now part of the Vietnamese delegation at Geneva. Although he catches a glimpse of Camille, he prefers not to approach, and returns to Eliane with the words: 'Ma mère c'est toi.' Controlling all aspects of narration and silencing the indigenous voice, the metropolitan desire is also to integrate the offspring of the mixed-race relationship into the society of the former coloniser. The pattern of control has come full circle.

This feature of *Indochine*'s narrative raises questions concerning cultural identity and the spectacle of miscegenation. While contemporary France often seems to have immense difficulty coming to terms with its visible population of various Others once present in the very fabric of the nation, the product of the mixed-race relationship is here unthreatening and desirable. Etienne functions as a symbol of continued metropolitan intimacy with, yet ultimate discipline over (former) colonial subjects. The intimate intermingling of the two cultures, epitomised not only in the relationship between Camille and Jean-Baptiste, but also in the ambivalent cultural belonging of Eliane (who says 'Je suis Asiate, une mangue'), and Camille (who becomes 'Jeanne d'Arc d'Indochine') suggest a crossing of boundaries which belies the reality of colonial spatial and corporeal anxieties. While 'going native' had been viewed as a treacherous betrayal of one's class and culture, but also a dangerous *rapprochement* between an inferior and superior, this type of portrayal turns that anxiety into a spectacle designed to re-excite the contemporary viewer's desire for the 'forbidden Other'. The spatial and temporal distance between the contemporary spectator and the narrated subject mitigates these former concerns and instead presents a softened and sentimentalised vision of colonial complicity and cultural polyvalency. The symbol of the desired union (or marriage) between France and Indochina – the Eurasian *métis*, Etienne – functions as the past thrust into the present, the intimacy of the relationship made carnate, and eternal. However, as his name suggests, and as the film leaves us in no doubt, this product of miscegenation is contained and controllable, made French, and assimilated.

The integration of Etienne into the sphere of metropolitan culture and history is mirrored in the reinscription of Indochinese history into a metropolitan framework. Blame for the increasing social agitation and rebellion in Indochina of the 1930s is placed at the feet of the Vietnamese mandarins, and the hierarchical social system which had flourished in pre-colonial Indochina. The depiction of the unrest provoked by the increasingly severe problem of famine thus masks the history of colonial mismanagement, abuse and fraud. Rather than opt for a nuanced and critical view of colonial government and administration, instead of having the rioting natives identify the root of the famine problem (as happened during the Yen Bay uprising), Wargnier decides to relieve post-colonial France of a sense of colonial guilt in scenes which show natives shooting and burning mandarins alive with cries of 'Death to landrobbers who have starved us.'

Not content with rewriting these uncomfortable and problematic aspects of the colonial relationship, Wargnier also attempts to appropriate for metropolitan France the ideological impetus behind the indigenous uprising. The scene in which Tanh, (Camille's fiancé, and later husband, who becomes a leader of the Communist Party) is exhorted to kneel in obedience before the altar of his ancestors allows Wargnier at once to deprecate Vietnamese tradition, and also to claim, in retrospect, some kind of historical moral high ground for France: 'Obedience has made us

slaves!' 'The French taught me the words "freedom", "equality", I'll fight with them.'[13] This exultation of French myths of freedom and equality in relation to the colonies suggests that it still remains for contemporary France to resolve the tension between the colonial project with the revolutionary ideals of 1789: the paradoxes of liberty and imposition, of equality and fraternity, hierarchy and control.

In Wargnier's film, Camille finally breaks from the control of both her physical and metaphorical adoptive mothers: Eliane and France. The question remains however, whether the France of the post-colonial era can finally break loose from this romanticised view of Indochina and of Empire which remains mired in the grip of a tenacious and pervasive nostalgia for the nation's *doctrine coloniale*.

Indochine leaves something of a pregnant gap in its narrative – entirely 'glossing over' the Franco-Indochinese War. This omission was felicitously overcome through the release, the following year, of Pierre Schoendoerffer's *Dien Bien Phu*. Focusing as it does on the loss and retreat from Empire, one might have expected Schoendoerffer to have eschewed the *passéiste,* nostalgic and unproblematic vision of French Indochina which was peddled in the other two films. However, as he remarked of his own film: 'Le film a été une affaire d'amour parce que la bataille aussi avait été une histoire d'amour.'[14] Recalling the stereotypical figuring of the Franco-Indochinese relationship as a marriage or love affair (leading to the 'divorce à Genève') this somewhat remarkable perception of the battle of Dien Bien Phu emphasises the extent to which these nostalgic views of Empire pervade attitudes and representations today. For Schoendoerffer goes on to add, quoting de Lattre midway:

> Nous étions avec les Vietnamiens, partie prenante dans une guerre civile (. . .). C'est de Lattre qui a dit: 'Mon fils n'est pas mort pour la France, il est mort pour le Vietnam'. Cette guerre n'est pas une guerre coloniale. (. . .) La France et l'Indochine, c'était une longue histoire commune, et c'est si vrai que, même lorsqu'ils nous faisaient la guerre, les Vietnamiens ne rejetaient pas la culture française.[15]

Concluding that 'la fin de notre temps en Indochine a été tragique', Schoendoerffer reactivates another tenacious colonial myth: that of Franco-Indochinese fraternity, and indigenous gratitude. In so doing, he also recalls the opposition of two different 'types' of Vietnamese: an insurgent minority of indoctrinated, hystericised and communist-inspired automatons is pitched against a peaceable, complicit section of loyal Vietnamese who remain eager francophiles.

While Wargnier's and Annaud's films were very conspicuously fictions – *The Lover* being an adaptation of Duras' *L'Amant*, and *Indochine* a fictional and melodramatic panorama spanning some thirty years, *Dien Bien Phu* is more problematic in terms of classification and genre. Described variously in the media as docudrama, 'film-vérité',[16] and 'fresque historique',[17] Schoendoerffer himself

declared: 'Ce film n'est pas un documentaire historique, ni un essai politique, ni une mise en cause des choix stratégiques et tactiques de l'état-major.' Instead, he claimed that, 'Je veux seulement porter témoignage sur ce qui a été vécu au jour le jour par mes camarades et sur l'esprit de ces combats.'[18] Nonetheless, Schoendoerffer's film hovers perilously between genres: autobiographical, historical, documentary, fiction, spectacle. While some critics have contended that Schoendoerffer attempts to erase the film/documentary dividing line, the man himself asserts that: 'J'avais un devoir de fidélité envers la mémoire de ceux qui sont morts là-bas et une mission d'espérence par rapport à l'avenir.'[19]

Where then, can we place Shoendoerffer's film? It appears to function as a commemoration or filmic memorial, a vehicle for testimony and homage. Indeed, if we are to take Schoendoerffer at his word, his film is an example of oral tradition preserved by memory. Schoendoerffer's status as an *ancien d'Indo* is in fact a omnipresent feature of his work. Having volunteered to go to Indochina, Schoendoerffer served as a cameraman with the French Army until his capture at Dien Bien Phu. In 1963, he published *La 317ème Section*, a novel based on his experiences in Indochina, which he himself filmed the following year.[20] Over a decade later he repeated the same pattern, producing first the novel, and then the film version of *Le Crabe tambour*.[21] Schoendoerffer's final 'homage' to Indochina was at last realised, after years of struggling to finance his films, in the big-budget production which became *Dien Bien Phu*.[22]

His own presence in the film is presented in two different ways. Firstly, the film is shot largely from the point of the French soldiers who took part in the battle, including an army cameraman who evokes the director himself. Secondly, and more importantly, Schoendoerffer himself provides the voice-over to the film throughout. His vocal and unifying presence is not made immediately clear to the spectator, however, as it is not until the end of the film, as the screen fades to black and the commentary passes into the present, that the unidentified narrator becomes 'I' and speaks of the shattering experience of returning to Dien Bien Phu after forty years in order to shoot the film. The tone of the film is portentous: as the camera slowly pans round the basin of Dien Bien Phu, the narrative voice, detailing place and time in a monotone, begins the regular countdown to the end of Empire. Schoendoerffer creates a semblance of suspense in the colonial stereotype of gambling joint, where everyone waits, expects, wonders and bets on the ineluctable end.

Schoendoerffer's film aspires to 'reality'. Like the growing number of documentary archive films commercially available in France on the subject of the Franco-Indochinese war, *Dien Bien Phu* aims to 'tell it like it was'. This poses several problems. Firstly, the overlap and interplay between reality and fiction, and the representational dilemma which this entails. Secondly, it poses the problem of point of view.

Firstly, why did Schoendoerffer create a fiction film rather than a documentary? For, in spite of the director's personal narrative intervention, the film's aspirations to 'vérité', or as Schoendoerffer put it, 'fidélité à la mémoire', and the autobiographical quality of the filmed sequences, the film also deliberately employs theatrical devices to frame and intersect this narrative. The opening sequence shows an orchestra warming up, then the lights going up on a stage set for a concert in Hanoi by French violinist Béatrice Vergnes (Ludmila Mikael) against a backdrop of the *tricolore* and of Marianne. The frame is closed at the end of the film as the concert finishes and the lights dim, the end of the concert mirroring the end of Empire.

The theatrical frame functions in several different ways as a distancing device. An explicit comparison is made between the stages of the battle and the timescale of the concert: 'c'était le début du deuxième acte'. Through juxtaposing shots, applause for the violinist becomes applause for the officer who refuses to obey 'les ordres imbéciles'. Thus not simply an opening and closing frame, but also a structuring metaphor and an integral part of the film, the mournful music from the concert appears as the sound-track over shots of the soon-to-be-lost vision of Hanoi, and as a dramatic accompaniment to the nocturnal bombardment of Dien Bien Phu. Here Schoendoerffer creates an elaborate and spectacular *mise-en-scène,* complete with appropriate musical effects. The artificiality of this representation is staged, emphasised, pointed up, and ultimately distances the spectator.

Firstly, the theatricality of the film distances the battle from events in Hanoi. The battle is portrayed in distinct contrast with settler life in Indochina. Schoendoerffer employs filmic crosscuts between *le camp retranché* at Dien Bien Phu, and scenes of the daily life of a colonial bourgeoisie. The explicit contrasts between the mirrored images of a mass at the Gothic cathedral of Hanoi and an improvised mass on the hilltops interrupted by sporadic gunfire, suggest that even at the time, the significance of the French experience at Dien Bien Phu was the exclusive domain of the soldiers fighting the battle.

Secondly, it distances the spectator from the reality of war. The use of slow-motion, and soundless shots of brightly lit shellfire across the night sky, and of the silhouette of a soldier against barbed wire create a balletic and aestheticised portrayal of war. Schoendoerffer produces a series of quasi-poetic images which seem to aspire to the sublime pity and terror of the First World War. This deflection of attention from the harsh truth of combat might well be perceived as another way in which to guard the spectator from encroaching upon the experience that only the *ancien* could possibly know.

Thirdly, the device distances the audience from Dien Bien Phu and Indochina in that it removes events from reality to a theatrical and fictional realm. Although it might at first appear inconsistent with the observation that *Dien Bien Phu* relies on the (here) unquestioned value and veracity of *témoignage*, the film encourages a view of the battle as legendary. At the time of the battle itself, as a previous chapter suggested, the French media consistently invoked a similar sense of history, and historical continuity around the battle, inventing a tradition of military glory for metropolitan France, and thereby adding weight, significance and depth to a conflict which scarcely interested the majority of the metropolitan public. Likewise, rather than focusing upon the humiliation of a first-world nation and army defeated by *les petits jaunes*, Schoendoerffer encourages a view in which Dien Bien Phu nonetheless becomes the stuff of legends: a worthy chapter in the annals of French military history.

Finally, this theatrical frame appears to function in yet another important way: with its clear intention of closure, the spectator is given to understand that the battle is contained, a visible whole, unified and therefore understandable, but only in the terms that Schoendoerffer has set out. This closure is undoubtedly the most significant failing of the film. Like many of the archive documentaries on the Franco-Indochinese conflict, it forecloses debate and precludes dissension. It homogenises a vision of French colonial rule in Indochina, and fixes the narrative of the war. Schoendoerffer's film never questions the logic behind the French presence in Indochina. He never wonders what *Indochine française* signified in 1950s mainland France. The film never asks what the French were fighting for. It does not seek to determine why the French underestimated the Vietnamese forces. Nor does it allow the Vietnamese a voice. On the contrary, the film panders, as I have already stated, to a nostalgic vision of Franco-Indochinese complicity and fraternity.

Indeed, discourses on the Franco-Indochinese War are essentially circular. The realm of the personal and the subjective is raised up and privileged to create a univocal and homogenising vision of war. The *témoignage*, the personal, subjective quality of the 'story' of the war which remains rooted in just one side of the lived experience of Dien Bien Phu alone, is unquestionable, certainly uncontested, but more significantly, impermeable to other narratives. It is a totalising vision, oral history backed up with pictures, positing a homogeneity: the testimony of the *ancien* is the only valid narrative of this conflict.

Furthermore, in terms of reception, the narrative is again circular: as in the documentary archive films, the narrator (*un ancien*) narrates his tale for the audience (*des anciens*). This over-reliance on the (French military) first-hand witness brings into focus the problem of point of view, for this approach also ignores the ideological position of the *ancien*: members of the *Corps expéditionnaire* in Indochina were conscripted soldiers, *des engagés*, and therefore, almost invariably saw themselves as guardians of the Empire, the agents of colonial rule, and the bearers of the French Army's values and traditions. To base a view of the loss of French Indochina on their testimony alone is not only to put forward an imperialist view of history, but also to espouse a neo-imperialist approach to history: to recreate a historical perspective which replicates that of the colonial era – where France writes Vietnam's history.

In Schoendoerffer's film then, the *récit* never escapes from this circle. The narrative of the conflict remains fixed and unchanging, forever trapped in its initial telling. No new lines of enquiry have been forged, no different representations, no heterogeneous panoramas of a complex and irreducible series of events. These 'docu' films display the traumatic experience of the veterans – and play out that experience over and over again. The Franco-Indochinese War thus remains repetition, there is no evolution, no progression, and therefore no deeper understanding. The war remains circumscribed by the words which characterise the memory and testimony of those who fought: *désarroi, calvaire, honneur, héroïsme, amertume, deuil, abandon, oubli.*

The place of Indochina in the French imagination is far from resolved. In refusing to look beyond a nostalgic and romanticised image of the colonial relationship both *Indochine* and *Dien Bien Phu* sustain and reinforce founding myths of the French colonial presence in Indochina, thus precluding any serious historical interrogation of the nation's colonial past in South-East Asia. Both films seem symptomatic of a culture which is still reluctant to fully embrace a post-colonial identity and thereby relinquish its control over the history and culture of its Asian Other.

These films, which constitute the most popular and most widely disseminated post-colonial representations of the Franco-Indochinese relationship, thus tend to rearticulate colonial myths of the past. They are largely uncritical of the nation's former colonial past in Indochina; they eulogise empire at its height; and they imagine a more equal and fraternal relationship between French and Indochinese than the colonial hierarchy could ever permit. Although some very vocal criticisms of American involvement in Vietnam emerged in intellectual circles, the nation nonetheless seems incapable of casting an equally critical eye over its own imperial legacy in Indochina. Indochina thus remains that better time and place than the Vietnam of the Americans.

Notes

1. See Daniel, V., *La Francophonie au Vietnam* (Paris: L'Harmattan, 1992).
2. Indochine, *Le Péril Jaune* (Clémence Melody: 1983).
3. 'La Sécheresse du Mékong', 1983, from *Le Péril Jaune*.

4. Wargnier, R., *Indochine* (1991); Annaud, J-J., *L'Amant* (1992); Schoendoerffer, P., *Dien Bien Phu* (1992). For comments on the release of these films, see Andreu, A., 'Pierre Schoendoerffer: "Oui, cette bataille a été une histoire d'amour!"', *L'Evénement du jeudi*, 27 February – 4 March 1992; Andreu, A., 'Cinéma français: reconquête de l'Indochine', *L'Evénement du jeudi*, 16–22 April, 1992; Ramirez, F., and Rolot, C., 'D'une Indochine à l'autre', *Cinémathèque*, 2, November 1992. I have chosen not to comment here on the film *L'Amant*, just as in a previous chapter I chose not to comment on Duras' novel of the same name, and its reworked version *L'Amant de la Chine du Nord*. The reason for this seeming lacuna is that I believe both the novel and the film offer very little in the way of insights into the representation of Indochina. For an analysis of *L'Amant* see Tarr, C., The Lover's Guide to Indochina', *Contemporary French Civilisation*, vol. 19, no. 1, Winter-Spring 1995, pp. 85–98.

5. Benjamin, W., *Illuminations* (London: Cape, 1970), p. 257. See also Ang, I., 'Hegemony in Trouble: Nostalgia and the Ideology of the Impossible in European Cinema', in Petrie, P. (ed.), *Screening Europe* (London: BFI, 1992), pp. 21–31; Rosaldo, R., 'Imperialist Nostalgia', in *Representations*, 26, Spring 1989, pp. 107–22.

6. Andreu, A., 'Pierre Schoendoerffer: "Oui, cette bataille a été une histoire d'amour!"', *L'Evénement du jeudi*.

7. Andreu, A., 'Cinéma français: reconquête de l'Indochine', *L'Evénement du jeudi*, 16–22 April, 1992.

8. Ibid.

9. See Wollen, T., 'Over our Shoulders: Nostalgic Screen Fictions for the 1980s', in Corner, J., and Harvey, S., *Enterprise and Heritage: Cross-currents of National Culture* (London: Routledge, 1991), pp. 178–93.

10. See Austin, G., *Contemporary French Cinema: An Introduction* (Manchester: MUP, 1996), p. 150.

11. Alain Courneau dir. *Fort Saganne*, (France, 1984).

12. Andreu, A., 'Pierre Schoendoerffer: "Oui, cette bataille a été une histoire d'amour!"', *L'Evénement du jeudi*.

13. In the film, these words are spoken in Vietnamese. I have quoted the subtitles as they appear on the version for anglophone audiences.

14. Andreu, A., 'Pierre Schoendoerffer: "Oui, cette bataille a été une histoire d'amour!"', *L'Evénement du jeudi*.

15. Ibid.

16. Macia, J-L., 'Dien Bien Phu: notre "Apocalypse Now"', *La Croix l'Evénement*, 6, March 1992, p. 2.

17. Siclier, J., 'Indochine: ton nom est femme', *Le Monde*, 17 April 1992.

18. Andreu, A., 'Pierre Schoendoerffer: "Oui, cette bataille a été une histoire d'amour!"', *L'Evénement du jeudi*.

19. Ibid.
20. Schoendoerffer, P., dir. *La 317ème section* (France, 1965).
21. Schoendoerffer, P., dir. *Le Crabe-tambour* (France, 1977).
22. The film cost 25 million dolars to make and included a cast of thousands. See Katharine Thornton's work on Schoendoerffer: Thornton, K., 'Selected Memories of the French War of Decolonisation in Indochina', in Aldrich, R., and Merle, I., *France Abroad: Indochina, New Caledonia, Wallis and Futuna, Mayotte* (Sydney: University of Sydney Press, 1996), pp. 1–17.

Conclusion to Part III

There are still very few voices emerging in contemporary France which are critical of the nation's colonial past in Indochina. If one cannot expect critical voices to emerge, then one might expect at least a more analytical and objective review of the period of colonial rule in Indochina to emerge in France in the twenty-first century. Benjamin Stora's work on memory and on Algeria could provide a model for the re-examination of the nation's Indochinese legacy; and his more recent comparative analyses of the French and American wars in Indochina seem to be taking some steps in that direction.[1]

However, the most concrete steps towards a re-evaluation and reassessment of the complex relationship between France and Indochina are beginning to take place and shape in a perhaps unlikely medium. In the early 1990s, Lax and Giroud published a two-volume *bande dessinée* entitled *Les Oubliés d'Annam* in which a Franco-Vietnamese woman, spurred on by an intrepid French reporter, attempts to trace her white French father, and to retrace his *parcours* across a war-torn Indochina of the 1950s.[2] It transpires that her father, Joubert, a French army officer, was so repulsed by the bloody French repression of the Vietnamese during the Franco-Indochinese War that he finally defected to the nationalist cause. An embarrassment to the French Army who relentlessly pursued him, and anxiously covered up the truth of his defection, Joubert was finally seized and killed although not before recruiting further disaffected French *militaires* to his renegade band of troops. Joubert, it is suggested, is an avatar of the destruction or disintegration of the French myth of their colonial war in Indochina. For his story is said to be mirrored in the experience and choices of countless French soldiers. Within this context, the Eurasian *métis* (unlike *Indochine*'s appropriated, contained and gallicised *métis*) functions as the prime motivator and figure in the reworking, reinterpreting and perhaps redressment of French memories of Indochina. The mixed-race child functions not simply as a comforting reminder of former Franco-Indochinese complicity, but as a reminder of the less palatable, and often rigorously concealed aspects of colonial rule, war and decolonisation in Indochina.

In their preface to the first volume of *Les Oubliés d'Annam*, Lax and Giroud write a compelling indictment of France's response to its colonial past in Indochina, an extract of which it seems appropriate to quote here in conclusion to this work:

la France est encore mal guérie de ses blessures coloniales. (. . .) Nous vivons dans un pays où l'on préfère travestir le passé immédiat plutôt que de le regarder en face et de l'analyser objectivement, hors de toute passion politique.

Notes

1. Stora, B., *Imaginaires de guerre: Algérie – Viêt-Nam, en France et aux Etats-Unis* (Paris: La Découverte, 1997).
2. Lax [Christian Lacroix] and Giroud [Franck], *Les Oubliés d'Annam* (2 vols) (Marcinelle: Dupuis, 1990).

Bibliography

Abbatucci, Dr, 'Aperçu sur les stations climatiques des colonies tropicales françaises', in Royer, J., *L'Urbanisme aux colonies*, vol. 2 (Paris: Editions d'Urbanisme, 1935), pp. 12–16.

Abrams, L., and Miller, D., 'Who were the French Colonialists? A Reassessment of the *Parti Colonial* 1890–1914', *Historical Journal*, vol. 19, 1976, pp. 685–719.

Ageron, C-R., *France colonial ou parti colonial ?* (Paris: PUF, 1978).

——, 'La Perception de la puissance française en 1938–1939: le mythe impérial', *Revue française d'Histoire d'outre-mer*, no. 69, 1982, pp. 7–22.

——, 'Les Colonies devant l'opinion publique française 1919–1939', *Revue française histoire d'outre-mer*, no. 77, 1990.

——, 'Les Colonies devant l'opinion publique française (1919–1939)', *Revue française d'Histoire d'outre-mer*, no. 77, 1990, pp. 31–73.

——, 'Vichy, les Français et l'Empire', in Azéma, J-P., and Bédarida, F., *Vichy et les Français* (Paris: Fayard, 1992).

——, *Anticolonialisme en France de 1871 à 1914* (Paris: PUF, 1973).

——, *La Décolonisation française* (Paris: Armand Colin, 1991).

Ajalbert, J., *Raffin Su-su suivi de Sao Van Di* (Paris: Kailash, 1995).

Albertini, R.,von, *European Colonial Rule 1880–1940: The Impact of the West on India, Southeast Asia and Africa* (Translated by J. Williamson), (Oxford: Clio Press, 1982).

Aldrich, R., *Greater France: A History of French Overseas Expansion* (Basingstoke: Macmillan, 1996).

AlSayyad, N., *Forms of Dominance: On the Architecture and Urbanism of the Colonial Enterprise* (Aldershot: Avebury, 1992).

Altbach, P., and Kelly, G., (eds) *Education and Colonialism* (London: Longman, 1978).

Altbach, P., and Kelly, G., (eds) *Education and the Colonial Experience* (2nd revised edition), (London: Transaction Books, 1984).

Ancel, R., and Maurel, G., *Premières notions d'histoire de France* (Cours élémentaire, 1ère année), (Liguré: Saint-Martin, 1896).

Anderson, B., *Imagined Communities: Reflections on the Origin and Spread of Nationalism* (London: Verso, 1991).

Andreu, A., 'Cinéma français: la reconquête de l'Indochine', *L'Evénement du jeudi*, 16–22 April, 1992, pp. 112–113.

——, 'Pierre Schoendoerffer: "Oui, cette bataille a été une histoire d'amour!"', *L'Evénement du jeudi*, 27 February – 4 March 1992, pp. 91–92.

Andrew, C., 'The French Colonialist Movement during the Third Republic: the unofficial mind of imperialism', *Transactions of the Royal Historical Society*, Fifth Series, vol. 26, 1976.

Ang, I., 'Hegemony in Trouble: Nostalgia and the Ideology of the Impossible in European Cinema', in Petrie, P., (ed) *Screening Europe* (London: BFI, 1992), pp. 21–31.

'Angkor et dix siècles d'art khmer', *Le Petit journal des grandes expositions*, no. 284, February/May 1997.

'Angkor: l'art khmer au Cambodge et en Thailande', *Dossiers Histoire et Archéologie*, no. 125, March 1988.

Annaud, J-J., dir. *L'Amant*, (France, 1992).

August, T., *The Selling of Empire: British and French Imperialist Propaganda 1890–1940* (London: Greenwood, 1985).

Austin, G., *Contemporary French Cinema: An Introduction* (Manchester: MUP, 1996).

Babut, E., *Un Livre de diffamation indochinoise: Les Civilisés* (Hanoi: [n.p.], 1907).

Barnett, A., 'Cambodia will never disappear', *New Left Review*, no. 180, 1990, pp. 101–125.

Barthélemy, P., (Gouvernement général de l'Indochine, Direction de l'Instruction publique), *L'Enseignement du français à l'école franco-indigène* (suivi de l'arrêté du 7 juillet 1927 comportant les nouveaux programmes), (Hanoi: Imprimerie de l'Extrême-Orient, 1927).

Barthes, R., *Mythologies* (Paris: Seuil, 1957).

Beautheac, N., and Bouchart, F-X., *L'Europe exotique* (Paris: Société Nationale des Editions du Chêne, 1985).

Bénard, C., *Au service de l'Indochine: l'oeuvre de Maurice Long 1919–1923* (Paris: Larose, 1931).

Benjamin, W., *Illuminations* (London: Cape, 1970).

——, *Reflections* (New York: Schocken, 1986).

Benot, Y., *Massacres coloniaux 1944–1950: la IVe république et la mise au pas des colonies françaises* (Paris: La Découverte, 1994).

Betts, R., *Assimilation and Association in French Colonial Theory 1890–1914* (London: Columbia University Press, 1961).

——, *Tricouleur: the French Overseas Empire* (London: Gordon and Cremonesi, 1978).

——, *France and Decolonisation 1900–1960* (London: Macmillan, 1991).

Bhabha, H., 'Difference, Discrimination and the Discourse of Colonialism', in Barker, F., et al, *The Politics of Theory* (Colchester: Essex Conference of the Sociology of Literature, 1982), pp. 194–211.

Bhabha, H. (ed.), *Nation and Narration* (London: Routledge, 1990).

——, *The Location of Culture* (London: Routledge, 1994).

Bibliothèque d'Orientation professionnelle (Guide des carrières), *Les Carrières dans le corps des administrateurs coloniaux* (Paris: Carus, 1931).

Biondi, J-P., and Morin, G., *Les Anti-colonialistes 1881–1962* (Paris: Laffont, 1992).

Boisanger, C. de, *On Pouvait éviter la guerre d'Indochine* (Paris: Maisonneuve, 1977).

Boissière, P., *Fumeurs d'Opium* (Paris: Flammarion, 1895), (repr. Paris: Kailash, 1993).

——, *Les Propos d'un intoxiqué* (Paris: Michaud, 1911).

Bonnetain, P., *L'Opium* (Paris: Charpentier, 1886).

Boudot-Lamotte, E., 'Le Musée des colonies', *L'Architecture*, 46, (7), July 1931, p. 239.

Boulanger, P., 'Des danseuses cambodgiennes aux cavaliers algériens: visions d'empire – les affiches des expositions coloniales de Marseille 1906–1922', in Blanchard et al, *L'Autre et nous: scènes et types* (Paris: ACHAC, 1995).

Bourotte, B., *La Pénétration scolaire en Annam* (Gouvernement général de l'Indochine – Direction générale de l'Instruction publique), (Hanoi: Imprimerie de l'Extrême-Orient, 1930).

Boyarin, J. (ed.), *Remapping Memory: The Politics of Timespace* (Minneapolis: University of Minnesota Press, 1994).

Brébion, J., 'La Naissance et les premières années de Saigon, ville française', *Bulletin de la Société des Etudes indochinoises*, vol. 2, no. 2, 1927, pp. 63–138.

Breton, A., 'Ne Visitez pas l'Exposition coloniale', *Tracts surréalistes et déclarations collectives 1922–39* (Paris: Le Terrain Vague, 1980), pp. 194–5.

Brocheux, P., and Hémery, D., *Indochine: la colonisation ambiguë* (Paris: Editions la Découverte, 1995).

Bruno, G., *Le Tour du monde par deux enfants* (Cours moyen), (Paris: Belin, [n.d.]).

Brunschwig, H., *Mythes et réalités de l'impérialisme colonial français 1871–1914* (Paris: Armand Colin, 1960).

Cable, J., *The Geneva Conference of 1954 on Indochina* (London: Macmillan, 1986).

Carr, S., Francis, M., Rivlin, L., and Stone, A., *Public Space* (Cambridge: Cambridge University Press, 1992).

Cartier, H., *Comment la France "civilise" ses colonies* (Paris: Bureau d'Editions, 1932).

Casseville, H., *Sao, Lamoureuse tranquille* (Paris: G. Cres, 1928).

Ce que tout candidat colonial doit savoir avant de s'expatrier (Marseille: Société anonyme du 'Sémaphore de Marseille', 1932).

Césaire, A., *Discours sur le colonialisme* (Paris: Editions Présence africaine, 1955).

Challaye, F., *Souvenirs sur la colonisation* (Paris: Picart, 1935).

Chansons exotiques et coloniales (Paris: EPM, 1995).

Cheam, F., 'L'Insertion en France des communautés asiatiques: fidélité au pays d'origine et inclusion des diasporas dans le monde', in *Migrations Etudes*, no. 80, avril–mai 1998.

Citron, S., *Le Mythe national: l'histoire de la France en question* (Paris: Etudes et Documentation internationales, 1987).

Clancy-Smith J., and Gouda, F., *Domesticating the Empire; Race, Gender and Family Life in French and Dutch Colonialism* (Charlottesville: University Press of Virginia, 1998).

Claudel, P., *Oeuvres complètes de Paul Claudel: Tome 4, Extrême-Orient* (Paris: Gallimard, 1952).

Clifford, J., *The Predicament of Culture: Twentieth-Century Ethnography, Literature, Art* (London: Harvard University Press, 1988).

Cointet, M., *Histoire Culturelle de la France 1818–1959* (Paris: SEDES, 1989).

Conférences publiques sur l'Indo-Chine faites à l'Ecole Coloniale pendant l'année scolaire 1907–1908 (Paris: Imprimerie de la Dépêche Coloniale, [n.d.]).

Conklin, A., 'Redefining "Frenchness": Citizenship, Race Regeneration and Imperial Motherhood in France and West Africa, 1914–40' in Clancy-Smith and Gouda, *Domesticating the Empire*, pp. 65–83.

Conley, T., and Ungar, S. (eds), *Identity Papers: Contested Nationhood in Twentieth Century France* (Minneapolis: University of Minnesota Press, 1996).

Cooper, N., 'Urban Planning and Architecture in Colonial Indochina', *French Cultural Studies*, vol. 11, part 1, no. 31, February 2000, pp. 75–99.

Copin, H., *L'Indochine dans la littérature française des années vingt à 1954: exotisme et altérité* (Paris: L'Harmattan, 1996).

Costa-Lascoux, J., and Yu-Sion, L., *Paris XIIIème; Lumières d'Asie* (Paris: Autrement, 1995).

Courneau, A., dir. *Fort Saganne*, (France, 1984).

Crouzet, P., *L'Enseignement dans les colonies françaises depuis la guerre* (Paris: Armand Colin, 1924).

Crozier, B., *South-East Asia in Turmoil* (London: Penguin, 1965).

Cultru, P., *Leçon d'ouverture du cours d'histoire coloniale* (fondé par les gouvernements généraux de l'Indo-Chine et de Madagascar, 23 janvier 1906, Université de Paris, Faculté des Lettres), (Besançon: Jacquin, 1906).

Dagens, B., *Angkor: la forêt de pierre* (Paris: Gallimard, 1989).

Daguerches, H., *Consolata, fille du soleil* (Paris: Calmann Levy, 1906).

——, *Le Kilomètre 83* (Paris: Calmann-Lévy, 1913), (repr. Paris, Kailash, 1993).

——, *Monde, vaste monde* (Paris: Calmann Levy, 1909).

Dalloz, J., *La Guerre d'Indochine 1945–1954* (Paris: Seuil, 1987).

——, *Dien Bien Phu* (Paris: La Documentation française, 1991).

Daniel, V., *La Francophonie au Vietnam* (Paris: L'Harmattan, 1992).

Dao Van Minh, *Premier livre de lecture française* (Conformément aux programmes officiels et à l'arrêté du 7 juillet 1927, cours préparatoire et cours élémentaire, ouvrage adapté par la Commission des manuels scolaires pour les écoles franco-indigènes de l'Indochine), (Haiphong: Thuy-Ky, 1929).

de Beauplan, R., 'Les Palais de l'Indochine', *L'Illustration*, no. 4612, juillet 1931.

de Certeau, M., *L'Invention du quotidien 1: arts de faire* (Paris: Gallimard/folio essais, 1990).

——, Giard, L., and Mayol, P., *L'Invention du quotidien 2: habiter, cuisiner* (Paris: Gallimard/folio essais, 1994).

de Gantès, G., 'Du Rôle des "grands hommes" aux colonies: l'exemple d'Henri de Montpezat en Indochine', *Revue française d'histoire d'outre-mer*, vol. 80, no. 301 (4), 1993.

de Gaulle, C., *Discours et messages pendant la guerre: juin 1940 – janvier 1946* (Paris: Plon, 1970).

de la Gorge, P-M., *The French Army: a military-political history* (London: Weidenfeld and Nicolson, 1963), translated by K. Douglas.

de Pouvourville, A., *Le Cinquième bonheur* (Paris: Michaud, 1911).

Decoux, *A la barre de l'Indochine: histoire de mon Gouvernement général* (Paris: Plon, 1949).

Deferre, G. (ed.), *L'Orient des Provençaux: Les Expositions coloniales 1906–1922* (Vieille Charité, CBR, Nov 1982–Fév 1983).

Delpey, R., *Dien Bien Phu: l'Affaire* (Paris: Editions de la pensée moderne, 1974).

Demaison, A., *L'Exposition coloniale internationale 1931 Guide officiel*, (Paris: Mayeux, 1931).

Descours-Gatin, C., and Villiers, H., *Guide de recherches sur le Vietnam: biblio-graphies, archives et bibliothèques de France* (Paris: L'Harmattan, 1983).

Dirks, N. (ed.), *Colonialism and Culture* (Ann Arbor: University of Michigan Press, 1992).

Dorgelès, R., *Sur la route mandarine* (Paris: Albin Michel, 1925), (repr. Paris: Kailash, 1994).

Dorsenne, J., *Loin des blancs* (Paris: 1933).

Duras, M., *Un Barrage contre le Pacifique*, (Paris: Gallimard, 1950).

——, *L'Eden cinéma* (Paris: Mercure de France, 1977).

——, *L'Amant* (Paris: Minuit, 1984).

Durtain, L., *Dieux blancs, hommes jaunes* (Paris: Gallimard, 1930).

Ennis, T., *French Policy and Developments in Indochina* (Chicago: University of Chicago Press, 1936).

'Ernest Hébrard en Indochine', *Urbanisme*, no. 12, 1933, pp. 169–72.

Exposition Coloniale internationale Paris 1931, Indochine française, Section des services d'intérêt social, Direction générale de l'Instruction publique, *Les Manuels scolaires et les publications pédagogiques de la Direction générale de l'Instruction publique* (Hanoi: Imprimerie de l'Extrême-Orient, 1931).

Fanon, F., *Peau noire: masques blancs* (Paris: Seuil, 1952).

Farrère, C., *Les Civilisés* (Paris: Flammarion, 1905), (repr. Paris: Kailash, 1993).

——, *Fumée d'opium* (Paris: Ollendorff, 1911).

——, *La Bataille* (Paris: Ollendorff, 1911).

——, *Une Jeune fille voyagea* (Paris: Flammarion, 1925).

Faucier, N., *Pacifisme et antimilitarisme dans l'entre-deux-guerres 1919–1939* (Paris: Spartacus, 1983).

Ferrand, L-H., *Géographie de la France et de se colonies* (Cours moyen, préparation au certificat d'études), (Paris: Cornély, 1904).

Ferrandi, J., *Les Officiers français face au Viet Minh 1945–1954* (Paris: Fayard, 1966).

Folin, J., de *Indochine 1940–1955* (Paris: Perrin, 1993).

Foucart, G., and Grigaut, M., *La Géographie au brevet élémentaire: La France et ses colonies* (Paris: Delagrave, 1909).

Foucault, M., *Surveiller et punir* (Paris: Gallimard /Collection tel, 1975).

Fougères, M., 'Les Ruines khmères dans la littérature française', *Présence francophone*, no. 1, Autumn 1970, pp. 71–89.

Franchini, P. (ed.), *Saigon 1925–45: de la 'Belle Colonie' à l'éclosion révolutionnaire ou la fin des dieux blancs* (Paris: Les Editions Autrement/série mémoires, no. 17, 1992).

Franchini, P., *Les Guerres d'Indochine* (Paris: Pygmalion, 1988).

Gaffarel, P., *Lectures géographiques et historiques sur l'Algérie et les colonies françaises* (Paris: Garnier, 1888).

Gallouédec, L., and Maurette, F., *La France et ses colonies* (3ème année, conforme aux programmes de 1920), (Paris: Hachette, 1922).

Garnier, F., *Voyage d'exploration en Indochine* (Paris: Hachette, 1873).

Gettleman, M. (ed.), *Vietnam: History, Documents and Opinions on a Major World Crisis* (Middlesex: Penguin, 1965).

Gide, A., *Voyage au Congo, retour du Tchad* (Paris: Gallimard, 1927).

Gidley, M., *Representing Others: White Views of Indigenous Peoples* (Exeter: University of Exeter Press, 1992).

Girardet, R., 'Les Trois couleurs', in Nora, P., *Les Lieux de mémoire 1: La République* (Paris: Gallimard, 1984).

——, *L'Idée coloniale en France* (Paris: La Table Ronde, 1972).

——, *Le Nationalisme français: anthologie 1871–1914* (Paris: Seuil/Points histoire, 1983).

Gouvernement général de l'Indochine, Direction de l'Instruction publique, *Enseignement primaire et élémentaire franco-indigène et certificat d'études primaires franco-indigènes* (Arrêtés du 17 juin 1927), (Hanoi: Imprimerie de l'Extrême-Orient, 1933).

Gouvernement général de l'Indochine, Direction générale de l'Instruction publique, *La Cochinchine scolaire: l'enseignement dans le pays le plus évolué de l'Union indochinoise* (Hanoi: Imprimerie de l'Extrême-Orient, 1931).

Gouvernement général de l'Indochine, Direction de l'Instruction publique, *Plan d'études et programmes de l'enseignement primaire supérieure franco-indigène: réglementation du diplôme d'études primaires supérieures franco-indigènes* (Arrêtés des 26 décembre 1924, 16 janvier 1925, 13 mars 1926, 1 juin 1926, 23 novembre 1926), (Hanoi: Imprimerie de l'Extrême-Orient, 1928).

Grimal, H., *La Décolonisation 1919–1963* (Paris: Armand Colin, 1965).

Groslier, G., *A L'Ombre d'Angkor* (Paris: Emile Paul, 1916).

——, *La Route du plus fort* (Paris: Emile Paul, 1925), (repr. Paris: Kailash, 1997).

——, *Le Retour à l'argile* (Paris: Emile Paul, 1928), (repr. Paris: Kailash, 1994).

Guiot, J., and Mane, F., *Histoire de France depuis les origines jusqu'à nos jours* (Cours élémentaire des écoles primaires; troisième édition), (Paris: Delaplane, 1912).

Hall, D., *History of South-East Asia* (London: Macmillan, 1960).

Hammer, E., *The Struggle for Indochina* (Stanford: Stanford University Press, 1954).

Hardy, G., *Géographie de la France extérieure* (Les Manuels coloniaux, collection dirigée par M. Georges Hardy, directeur de l'ecole Coloniale), (Paris: Larose, 1928).

Hargreaves, A., *The Colonial Experience in French Fiction: a Study of Pierre Loti, Ernest Psichari and Pierre Mille* (London: Macmillan, 1981).

——, *Immigration, 'Race' and Ethnicity in Contemporary France* (London: Routledge, 1995).

Harmand, J., *L'Homme du Mékong: un voyageur solitaire à travers l'Indochine inconnue* (Paris: Phébus, 1994).

Harvey, D., *Social Justice and the City*,(London: Edward Arnold, 1973).

——, *The Condition of Postmodernity: an Enquiry into the Origins of Cultural Change* (Oxford: Blackwell, 1989).

Hazareesingh, S., *Political Traditions in Modern France* (Oxford: OUP, 1994).

Hébrard, E., 'L'Urbanisme en Indochine', in Royer, J., *L'Urbanisme aux colonies et dans les pays tropicaux*, vol. 1, (La Charité-sur-Loire: Delayance, 1932), pp. 278–89.

——, 'L'Architecture locale et les questions d'esthétique en Indochine', in Royer, J., *L'Urbanisme aux colonies*, vol 2 (Paris: Editions d'Urbanisme, 1935), pp. 32–4.

——, 'L'Habitation en Indochine', in Royer, J., *L'Urbanisme aux colonies*, vol. 2, 1935, pp. 58–62.

——, 'La Conservation des Monuments anciens et des vieilles villes indigènes de l'Indochine', in Royer, J., *L'Urbanisme aux colonies*, vol. 2 (Paris: Editions d'Urbanisme, 1935), pp. 25–6.

Hémery, D., *Ho Chi Minh: de L'Indochine au Vietnam* (Paris: Découverte Gallimard/Histoire, 1990).

Histoire, special issue: 'Les Temps des colonies', no. 69, 1984.

Hobsbawm, E. (ed.), *The Invention of Tradition* (Cambridge: CUP, 1983).

Hodeir, C., 'L'Epopée de la décolonisation à travers les expositions universelles du 20ème siècle', in *Le Livre des expositions universelles 1881–1989* (Paris: Editions des Arts décoratifs-Herscher, 1983).

——, 'Etre "indigène" aux expositions', in Blanchard et al, *L'Autre et nous: scènes et types* (Paris: ACHAC, 1995).

——, and Pierre, M., *L'Exposition coloniale* (Brussels: Editions complexe, 1991).

Horne, J., 'In Pursuit of Greater France: Visions of Empire among Musée social Reformers', in Clancy-Smith J., and Gouda, F., *Domesticating the Empire: Race, Gender and Family Life in French and Dutch Colonialism* (Charlottesville: University Press of Virginia, 1998).

Hue, B. (ed.), *Indochine: reflets littéraires*, Pluriel 3, (Rennes: Presses universitaires de Rennes, Centre d'étude des littératures et civilisations francophones, 1992).

Indochine, *Le Péril Jaune* (Paris: Clémence Melody, 1983).

Isoart, P. (ed.), *L'Indochine française 1940–45* (Paris: PUF, 1982).

Jacnal, J., *Rêves d'Annam* (Paris: 1913).

Jacobs, J., *Edge of Empire: Postcolonialism and the City* (London: Routledge, 1996).

Jenkins, B., *Nationalism in France: Class and Nation since 1789* (London: Routledge, 1990).

Josset, E., *A Travers nos colonies: livre de lectures sur l'histoire, la géographie, les sciences et la morale* (Cours moyen et supérieur), (Paris: Armand Colin, 1901).

Jourda, P., *L'Exotisme dans la littérature française depuis Chateaubriand, Tome II Du Romantisme à 1939* (Montpellier: PUF, 1956).

Kaplan, A., *Looking for the Other: Feminism, Film and the Imperial Gaze* (London: Routledge, 1997).

Karp, I., and Levine, S. (eds), *Exhibiting Cultures: The Poetics and Politics of Museum Display* (London: Smithsonian Institution Press, 1991).

Kelly, D., and Holman, V., *France at War in the Twentieth Century: Myth, Metaphor, and Propaganda* (Oxford: Berghahn, 2000).

King, A., *Urbanism, Colonialism and the World Economy: Cultural and Spatial Foundations of the World Urban System* (London: Routledge, 1990).

Knibiehler, Y., and Goutalier, R., *La Femme au temps des colonies* (Paris: Stock, 1985).

Knight, M., 'French Colonial Policy: The Decline of Association', *Journal of Modern History*, vol. 5, 1933, pp. 208–24.

Kolko, G., *Vietnam: Anatomy of a War 1940–75* (London: Allen and Unwin, 1986).

Krop, P., 'Dien Bien Phu: les vraies raisons du désastre', *L'Evénement du jeudi*, 27 February – 4 March 1992, pp. 88–91.

L'Illustration, Album hors série sur l'Exposition coloniale, no. 4603, 23 mai 1931.

La France au Temps des Colonies, (Collection Alain Decaux), (TF1 Entreprises, 1994).

La Guerre d'Indochine 1945–54 (Paris: Cassettes Radio France, 1991).

Lacouture, J., *André Malraux: une vie dans le siècle* (Paris: Seuil, 1973).

——, *Ho Chi Minh* (Paris: Seuil, 1977).

Lafont, P. (ed.), *Péninsule indochinoise: études urbaines* (Paris: L'Harmattan, 1991).

Lancaster, D., *The Emancipation of French Indochina* (Oxford: OUP, 1961).

Landry, D., and Maclean, G., *The Spivak Reader* (London: Routledge, 1996).

Langlois, W., *André Malraux: l'Aventure indochinoise* (translated from the English by Jean-René Major), (Paris: Mercure de France, 1967).

Laude, P., *Exotisme indochinois et poésie* (Paris: Sudestasie, 1990).

Lavisse, E., *Histoire de France* (Cours moyen, préparation au certificat d'études primaires), (Paris: Armand Colin, 1912).

Lax [Christian Lacroix], and Giroud [Franck], *Les Oubliés d'Annam*, Tome I (Marcinelle: Dupuis, 1990).

—— and ——, *Les Oubliés d'Annam*, Tome II (Marcinelle: Dupuis, 1991).

Le Huu Khoa, *L'Immigration asiatique: espaces économiques communautaires et stratégies d'ascension professionnelle* (Paris: Direction de la Population et des Migrations, 1994).

——, *Les Vietnamiens en France: Insertion et identité* (Paris: L'Harmattan, 1985).

Le Monde dossiers et documents, 'Les Guerres du Vietnam', no. 179, July–August 1990.

Le rôle et la situation de la famille française aux colonies (Paris: Editions du journal des coloniaux et de l'Armée coloniale réunis, 1927).

Le Roman colonial: itinéraires et contacts de cultures, vol. 7 (Paris: L'Harmattan/ Publication du Centre d'études francophones de l'Université de Paris XIII, 1987).

Le Roman colonial: itinéraires et contacts de culture, vol. 12 (suite) (Paris: L'Harmattan/Publication du Centre d'études francophones de l'Université de Paris XIII, 1990).

Le Roux., P., 'Avec ou sans trait d'union, note sur le terme "l'Indo-Chine"', *Cahiers des Sciences humaines*, vol. 32, 3, 1996.

Lê, N-D., *Les Missions étrangères et la pénétration française au Viêt-Nam* (Paris: Mouton, 1975).

Lebel, R., *Histoire de la littérature coloniale en France* (Paris: Larose, 1931).

Lebovics, H., *True France: the Wars over Cultural Identity 1990–45* (London: Cornell University Press, 1992).

Lefèvre, K., 'Eves jaunes et colons blancs', in Franchini, P. (ed.), *Saigon 1925– 45: de la 'Belle Colonie' à l'éclosion révolutionnaire ou la fin des dieux blancs* (Paris: Les Editions Autrement/série mémoires, no. 17, 1992), pp. 111–19.

Léger, M., 'L'Habitation coloniale du point de vue médical', in Royer, J., *L'Urbanisme aux colonies*, vol. 2 (Paris: Editions d'Urbanisme, 1935), pp. 39– 46.

Leprun, S., *Le Théâtre des colonies: scénographie, acteures et discours de l'imaginaire dans les expositions 1855–1937* (Paris: L'Harmattan, 1986).

Leroy, G., and Roche, A., *Les Ecrivains et le Front Populaire* (Paris: Presses de la Fondation Nationale des Sciences Politiques, 1986).

Lethève, J., *La Caricature et la presse sous la Troisième République* (Paris: Armand Colin, 1961).

Leuba, J., *L'Aile du feu* (Paris, 1926).

Lewis, R., *Gendering Orientalism: Race, Feminity and Representation* (London: Routledge, 1996).

Loti, P., *Propos d'exil* (Paris: Calmann-Lévy, 1887).

——, *Pêcheur d'Islande* (Paris: Calmann Levy, 1893), (repr. Paris: Bookking International/Classiques français, 1994).

——, *Un Pèlerin d'Angkor* (Paris: Calmann-Lévy, 1912), (repr. Paris: Kailash, 1994).

Loubet, *L'Enseignement en Indochine en 1929* (Hanoi: Imprimerie de l'Extrême-Orient, 1929).

Loutfi, M., *Littérature et colonialisme: l'expansion coloniale vue à travers la littérature romanesque française 1871–1914* (La Haye: Mouton, 1971).

Lowe, L., *Critical Terrains: French and British Orientalisms* (Ithaca: Cornell University Press, 1991).

'L'Urbanisme en Indochine', *L'Architecture*, vol. 36, no. 7, 1923, p. 97.

Lyautey, *Lettres du Tonkin et de Madagascar 1894–1899* (Paris: Armand Colin, 1933).

Mackenzie, J. (ed.), *Imperialism and Popular Culture* (Manchester: Manchester University Press, 1986).

Malleret, L., *L'Exotisme indochinois dans la littérature française depuis 1860* (Paris: Larose, 1934).

Malraux, A., *La Voie royale* (Paris: Grasset, 1930).

Manceron, G., 'Images et idéologies: l'Europe, l'Afrique et le monde arabe dans les manuels scolaires d'hier et d'aujourd'hui', in Blanchard, P. et al, *L'Autre et nous: scènes et types* (Paris: ACHAC, 1995).

Mane, F., *Géographie élémentaire de la France et de ses colonies* (Classe de 7ème, enseignement classique, certificat d'études primaires), (Marseille: Laffitte, 1905).

Manuel élémentaire à l'usage des officiers et sous-officiers appelés à commander des indigènes coloniaux dans la métropole: Fascicule no. 1: Indochinois (Paris: Charles-Lavauzelle, 1926).

Mariol, H., *Abrégé de législation coloniale: préparation aux grands concours de l'Administration coloniale* (Paris: Larose, 1927).

Marr, D., *Vietnamese Tradition on Trial 1920–45* (Berkeley: University of California Press, 1981).

Marrast, J., 'Dans quelle mesure faut-il faire appel aux arts indigènes dans la construction des édifices?', in Royer, J., *L'Urbanisme aux colonies*, vol. 2 (Paris: Editions d'Urbanisme, 1935), p. 24.

——, 'L'Habitation coloniale', in Royer, J., *L'Urbanisme aux* colonies, vol. 2 (Paris: Editions d'Urbanisme, 1935), p. 38.

Marseille, J., *Empire colonial et capitalisme français: histoire d'un divorce* (Paris: Albin Michel, 1984).

——, *L'Age d'or de la France coloniale* (Paris: Albin Michel, 1986).

Mathé, R., *L'Exotisme* (Paris: Bordas, 1985).

McClintock, A., *Imperial Leather: Race, Gender and Sexuality in the Colonial Contest* (London: Routledge, 1995).

Méthode de langage français et annamite destinée aux écoles de l'Indochine (Cours élémentaire), (Quinhon: Imprimerie de Quinhon, 1923).

Meyer, C., *Les Français en Indochine* (Paris: Hachette, 1985).

Meyer, J., Tarrade, J., Rey-Goldzeigeur, A., Thobie, J., *Histoire de la France coloniale dès origines à 1914* (Paris: Armand Colin, 1991).

Michel, M., 'De Lattre et les débuts de l'Américanisation de la guerre d'Indochine', in *Revue française d'Histoire d'outre-mer*, no. 72, 1985, pp. 321–34.

Monet, P., *Les Jauniers: histoire vraie* (Paris: Gallimard, 1930).

Monsarrat, G., 'L'Organisation administrative et la législation urbaine et rurale aux colonies', in Royer, J., *L'Urbanisme aux colonies*, vol. 2 (Paris: Editions d'Urbanisme, 1935), pp. 98–102.

Mouhot, H., *Voyages dans les royaumes de Siam de Cambodge et de Laos* (Paris: Hachette, 1868), (repr. Geneva: Olizane, 1989).

Moulin, J-P., *Enquête sur la France multiraciale* (Paris: Calmann-Lévy, 1985).

Moura, J-M., *Lire l'exotisme* (Paris: Dunod, 1992).

Murphey, R., 'Traditionalism and Colonialism: Changing Urban Roles in Asia', *Journal of Asian Studies*, vol. 29, no. 1, November 1969, pp. 67–84.

Nguyen Duc Bao, *Pour nos jeunes écoliers: lecture courante et expliquée* (cours élémentaire et cours moyen, 1ère année des écoles franco-annamites), (Hanoi: Tan Dan Thu Quan, 1925).

Nguyen, P., *Le Roman de Mademoiselle Lys* (Hanoi: L'Imprimerie tonkinoise, 1921).

Nora, P., 'Lavisse, instituteur national: Le Petit Lavisse, évangile de la République', in *Les Lieux de mémoire I: La République* (Paris: Gallimard, 1984).

Norindr, P., 'L'Indochinois dans l'imaginaire colonial français', in Blanchard, et al, *L'Autre et nous:scènes et types* (Paris: ACHAC, 1995).

——, 'Representing Indochina: the French colonial fantasmatic and the Exposition Coloniale de Paris', in *French Cultural Studies*, vi, February 1995, pp. 35–60.

——, *Phantasmatic Indochina: French Colonial Ideology in Architecture, Film, and Literature* (Durham: Duke University Press, 1996).

Noury, J., *L'Indochine en cartes postales: avant l'ouragan 1900–1920* (Paris: Publifusion, 1992).

O'Ballance, E., *The Indo-China War 1945–1954* (London: Faber, 1964).

Parenteau, R., and Champagne, L. (eds), *La Conservation des quartiers historiques en Indochine* (Paris: Editions Karthala, 1997).

Pasquel-Rageau, C., 'Indochine: de la gravure à la photographie', in Blanchard et al, *L'Autre et nous: scènes et types* (Paris: ACHAC, 1995).

Pavie, A., *A la Conquête des coeurs* (Paris: PUF/Collection Colonies et Empires, 1947).

Pavrel, G., *Hygiène colonial: comment on doit vivre aux colonies* (Paris: 'Colonia', 1912).

Pederson, J., 'Special Customs: Paternity Suits and Citizenship in France and the Colonies 1870–1912', in Clancy-Smith J., and Gouda, F., *Domesticating the Empire: Race, Gender and Family Life in French and Dutch Colonialism* (Charlottesville: University Press of Virginia, 1998).

Pervillé, G., *De l'empire français à la décolonisation* (Paris: Hachette, 1993).

Pham-Dinh-Dien, and Vu-Nhu-Lâm, *Manuel d'histoire d'Annam* (Conforme au programme d'études de 1930, à l'usage des élèves des cours moyens et supérieurs et des candidats au certificat d'études primaires franco-indigènes), (Nam-Dinh: Imprimerie My Thang, 1931).

Philastre, P., *Le Code annamite* (2 vols) (Taipei: Ch'eng-Wn, 1967).

Phillips, R., *Mapping Men and Empire: A Geography of Adventure* (London: Routledge, 1997).

Pineau, L-G., 'Le Plan d'aménagement et d'extension de Dalat', *La Vie Urbaine*, no. 49, 1939, pp. 29–49.

Pluvier, J., *South-East Asia from Colonialism to Independence* (London: OUP, 1974).

Pourtier, J., *Mékong* (Paris: Grasset, 1931), (repr. Paris: Kailash, 1993) .

Pouyanne, A., (Inspection générale des Travaux publics), *Les Travaux publics de l'Indochine* (Hanoi: Imprimerie de l'Extrême-Orient, 1926).

Pratt, M-L., *Imperial Eyes: Travel Writing and Transculturation* (London: Routledge, 1992).

Priestley, H., *France Overseas: A Study of Modern Imperialism* (London: Cass & Co., 1966).

Prost, A., 'Verdun', in Nora, P., *Les Lieux de mémoire: La Nation III* (Paris: Gallimard, 1986).

Pujarniscle, E., *Le Bonze et le pirate* (Paris: G. Crès & Cie., 1929), (repr. Paris: Kailash, 1994).

Quella-Villéger, A. (ed.), *Indochine: un rêve d'Asie* (receuil), (Paris: Omnibus, 1995).

Rabant, J., *L'Anti-militarisme en France 1810–1975: faits et documents* (Paris: Hachette, 1975).

Ramirez, F., and Rolot, C., 'D'une Indochine à l'autre', *Cinémathèque*, 2, November 1992, pp. 40–55.

Rapport général (présenté par le Gouverneur général Olivier), 9 vols, (Paris: Imprimerie nationale, 1932–5).

Raymond, G., 'French Culture and the Politics of Self-esteem: the Vietnam Experience', in Melling, P., and Roper, J., *America, France and Vietnam: Cultural History and Ideas of Conflict* (London: Avebury, 1991).

Reynaud, P., *L'Empire français*, (discours prononcé à l'inauguration de l'Exposition coloniale), (Paris: Guillemot et Lamothe, (s.d)).

Riesz, J., 'L'Ethnologie coloniale ou le refus de l'assimilation: les "races" dans le roman colonial entre les deux guerres', in Blanchard, P. et al, *L'Autre et nous: scènes et types* (Paris: ACHAC, 1995).

Robertson, G., Mash, M., Tickner, L., Bird, J., Curtis, B., and Putnam, T. (eds), *Traveller's Tales: Narratives of Home and Displacement* (London: Routledge, 1994).

Robiquet, P., *Discours et opinions de Jules Ferry, tome 5: Discours sur la politique extérieure et coloniale* (Paris: Armand Colin, 1897).

Rocolle, P., *Pourquoi Dien Bien Phu?* (Paris: Flammarion, 1968).

Rogeaux, C., Lanier, L., and Laborde, A., *Cours de géographie méthodique: La France et ses colonies, notions générales, les cinq parties du monde* (Cours élémentaire et cours moyen, 1ère année, 212ème édition, complètement refondue conformément au programme de 1923), (Paris: Belin, 1926).

Rosaldo, R., 'Imperialist Nostalgia', *Representations*, 26, Spring 1989, pp. 107–22.

Ross, R., and Telkamp, G. (eds), *Colonial Cities: Essays on Urbanism in a Colonial Context* (Dordrecht: Martinus Nijhoff, 1985).

Roubaud, L., *Vietnam: la tragédie indochinoise* (Paris: Valois, 1931).

Ruane, K., *War and Revolution in Vietnam 1930–75* (London: University College Press, 1998).

Ruscio, A., 'Dien Bien Phu: du coup de génie à l'aberration, ou comment les contemporains ont vécu l'ultime bataille de la guerre française d'Indochine', in *Revue française d'Histoire d'outre-mer*, no. 72, 1985, pp. 335–47.

——, *Dien Bien Phu: la fin d'une illusion* (Paris: L'Harmattan, 1986).

——, 'French Public Opinion and the War in Indochina 1945–1954', in Scriven, M., and Wagstaff, P. (eds), *War and Society in Twentieth-Century France* (London: Berg, 1991).

——, *La Guerre française d'Indochine 1945–54* (Bruxelles: Editions complexe, 1992).

Said, E., *Orientalism* (London: Routledge, 1978).

——, *The World, the Text, and the Critic* (London: Vintage, 1991).

——, *Culture and Imperialism* (London: Chatto and Windus, 1993).

SarDesai, D., *South East Asia: Past and Present* (Basingstoke: Macmillan, 1989).

Sarraut, A., *Grandeur et servitude coloniales* (Paris: Sagittaire, 1931).

——, *La Mise en valeur des colonies françaises*, (Paris: Payot, 1923).

Schneider, W., *An Empire for the Masses: the French Popular Image of Africa 1870–1900* (Westport: Greenwood Press, 1982).

Schoendoerffer, P., dir. *Dien Bien Phu*, (France, 1992).

——, dir. *La 317ème section* (France, 1965).

——, dir. *Le Crabe-tambour* (France, 1977).

Schwab, R., *La Renaissance orientale* (Paris: Payot, 1950).

Schwartz, W., *The Far-East in Modern French Literature 1800–1925* (Paris: Bibliothèque de la Revue de la Littérature comparée, 1927).

Scultz, Y., *Les Sampaniers de la Baie d'Along* (Paris: Plon, 1932).

Segalen, V., *Essai sur l'exotisme: une esthétique du divers (notes)* (Paris: Fata Morgana, 1978).

Semaines sociales en France, *Le Problème social aux colonies: XXIIe session 1930* (Lyon: Chronique sociale de la France, 1930).

Semidei, M., 'De l'Empire à la décolonisation à travers les manuels scolaires français', *Revue française de science politique*, vol. 16, 1966, pp. 56–86.

Sherzer, D. (ed.), *Cinema, Colonialism, Postcolonialism: Perspectives from the French and Francophone World* (Austin: University of Texas Press, 1996).

Shipway, M., *The Road to war: France and Vietnam 1944–1947* (Oxford: Berghahn, 1996).

Simon, P., 'Portraits coloniaux des Vietnamiens (1858–1914)', in Guiral, P., and Temime, E. (eds), *L'Idée de race dans la pensée politique française contemporaine* (Paris: Editions du CNRS, 1977).

Simon-Barouh, I., *Rapatriés d'Indochine: Deuxième génération – les enfants d'origine indochinoise à Noyant-d'Allier* (Paris: L'Harmattan, 1981).

Sorlin, P., 'The Fanciful Empire: French Feature Films and the Colonies in the 1930s', *French Cultural Studies*, ii, June 1991, pp. 135–51.

Sorum, P., *Intellectuals and Decolonization in France* (Chapel Hill: University of North Carolina Press, 1977).

Spurr, D., *The Rhetoric of Empire: Colonial Discourse in Journalism, Travel Writing and Imperial Administration* (Durham: Duke University Press, 1994).

Stora, B., *Imaginaires de guerre: Algérie – Viêt-Nam, en France et aux Etats-Unis* (Paris: La Découverte, 1997).

Taboulet, G., *La Geste française en Indochine: Histoire par les textes de la France en Indochine des origines à 1914: Tome I* (Paris: Maisonneuve, 1955).

——, *La Geste française en Indochine: Histoire par les textes de la France en Indochine des origines à 1914: Tome II* (Paris: Maisonneuve, 1956).

Tarr, C., 'The Lover's Guide to Indochina', *Contemporary French Civilisation*, vol. 19, no. 1, Winter–Spring 1995, pp. 85–98.

Thobie, J., Meynier, G., Coquery-Vidrovitch, C., and Ageron, C.-R., *Histoire de la France coloniale 1914–1990* (Paris: Armand Colin, 1990).

Thomas, N., *Colonialism's Culture: Anthropology, Travel and Government* (Oxford: Polity Press, 1994).

Thornton, K., 'Selected Memories of the French War of Decolonisation in Indochina', in Aldrich, R., and Merle, I., *France Abroad: Indochina, New Caledonia, Wallis and Futuna, Mayotte* (Sydney: University of Sydney Press, 1996), pp. 1–17.

Tiet, Tran-Minh, *Problèmes de défense du sud-est asiatique* (Paris: Nouvelles Editions Latines, 1967).

Todorov, T., *Nous et les autres: la reflexion française sur la diversité humaine* (Paris: Seuil/Points essais, 1989).

Trevey, X., 'L'Ecole coloniale', *Revue politique et parlementaire*, no. 17, 1898, pp. 577–91.

Truong Dinh Tri, and de Teneuille, Albert, *Ba-Dam* (Paris: Fasquelle, 1930).

Tuck, J., *French Catholic Missionarioes and the Politics of Imperialism in Vietnam 1857–1914* (Liverpool: Liverpool University Press, 1987).

Vaillat, L., 'L'Esthétique aux colonies', in Royer, J., *L'Urbanisme aux colonies*, vol. 2 (Paris: Editions d'Urbanisme, 1935), pp. 21–3.

Van, N., *Viet-nam 1920–1945: révolution et contre-révolution sous la domination coloniale* (Paris: L'Insomniaque, 1995).

Vella, W. (ed.), *Aspects of Vietnamese History* (Hawaii: University Press of Hawaii, 1973).

Vigné d'Octon, P., *Au Pays des fétiches* (Paris: [n.p.], 1891).

Viollis, A., *SOS Indochine* (Paris: Gallimard, 1935).

Vivier de Streel, M., 'Urbanisme et colonisation', in Royer, J., *L'Urbanisme aux colonies*, vol. 2 (Paris: Editions d'Urbanisme, 1935), pp. 2–4.

Ware, V., *Beyond the Pale: White Women, Racism and History* (London: Verso, 1992).

Wargnier, R., dir. *Indochine*, (France, 1991).

Wollen, T., 'Over our Shoulders: Nostalgic Screen Fictions for the 1980s', in Corner, J., and Harvey, S., *Enterprise and Heritage: Cross-currents of National Culture* (London: Routledge, 1991), pp. 178–93.

Woodside, A., 'The Development of Social Organizations in Vietnamese Cities in the Late Colonial Period', *Pacific Affairs*, no. 44, 1971, pp. 39–64.

Woodside, A., *Community and Revolution in Modern Vietnam* (Boston: Houghton Mifflin, 1976).

Woolf, S., 'French Civilisation and Ethnicity in the Napoleonic Empire', *Past and Present*, no. 124, 1989, pp. 96–120.

Wright, G., 'Tradition in the Service of Modernity: Architecture and Urbanism in French Colonial Policy', *Journal of Modern History*, no. 59, 1987, pp. 291–316.

——, and Rabinow, P., 'Savoir et pouvoir dans l'urbanisme moderne colonial d'Ernest Hébrard', *Cahiers de la recherche architecturale* (villes nouvelles, cités, satellites, colonies: de l'art urbain à l'urbanisme), no. 9, 1981, pp. 27–43.

Wright, G., *The Politics and Design of French Colonial Urbanism* (London: University of Chicago Press, 1991).

Yacono, X., *Les Etapes de la décolonisation* (Paris: PUF/Que sais-je? 1982).

Yeager, J., *The Vietnamese Novel in French: A Literary Response to Colonialism* (Hanover: University of New Hampshire Press, 1987).

Young, R., *White Mythologies: Writing, History and the West* (London: Routledge, 1990).

Index

Index

Index

Lightning Source UK Ltd.
Milton Keynes UK
UKOW06f0218031215

263951UK00005B/80/P